숭실대학교 한국기독교박물관 소장

베어드 선교사 부부의 한국어 학습서

이 자료총서는 2018년 대한민국 교육부와 한국연구재단의 지원을 받아 수행된 연구임(NRF-2018S1A6A3A01042723)

메타모포시스 자료총서 08

숭실대학교 한국기독교박물관 소장

베어드 선교사 부부의 한국어 학습서

• English-Korean & Korean English Dictionary of Parliamentary, Ecclesiastical and Some Other Terms
• Fifty Helps for the Beginner in the Use of the Korean Language

초판 1쇄 발행   2020년 12월 30일

저 자 | 윌리엄 마틴 베어드(William Martyn Baird)
          애니 베어드(Annie L.A. Baird)
번역·해제| 윤영실
펴낸이 | 윤관백
펴낸곳 | 도서출판 선인

등 록 | 제5-77호(1998.11.4)
주 소 | 서울시 마포구 마포대로 4다길 4(마포동 324-1) 곳마루 B/D 1층
전 화 | 02) 718-6252 / 6257
팩 스 | 02) 718-6253
E-mail | sunin72@chol.com

정가 30,000원
ISBN 979-11-6068-378-3 93710

· 잘못된 책은 바꿔 드립니다.

메타모포시스 자료총서
08

숭실대학교 한국기독교박물관 소장

베어드 선교사 부부의 한국어 학습서

·English-Korean & Korean English Dictionary of Parliamentary,
Ecclesiastical and Some Other Terms
·Fifty Helps for the Beginner in the Use of the Korean Language

윌리엄 마틴 베어드(William Martyn Baird) · 애니 베어드(Annie L.A.Baird) 지음
윤영실 번역 및 해제

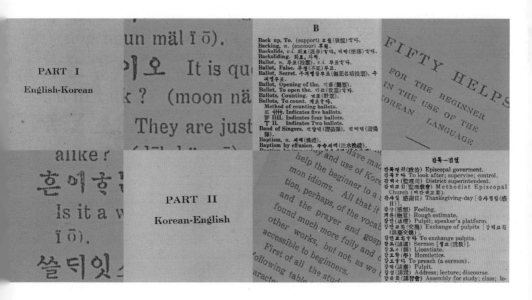

도서출판 선인

▎ 간행사 ▎

숭실대학교 한국기독교문화연구원은 1967년 설립된 한국기독교문화연구소를 모태로 하고 1986년 설립된 〈기독교사회연구소〉와 통합하여 확대 개편함으로써 명실공히 숭실대학교를 대표하는 인문학 연구원으로 발전하여 오늘에 이르렀다. 반세기가 넘는 역사 동안 다양한 학술행사 개최, 학술지 『기독문화연구』와 '불휘총서' 발간, 한국기독교박물관 소장 자료의 연구에 주력하면서, 인문학 연구원으로서의 내실을 다져왔다. 2018년 한국연구재단의 인문한국플러스(HK+) 사업 수행기관으로 선정되며 또 다른 도약의 발판을 마련하였다.

본 HK+사업단은 "근대전환공간의 인문학 – 문화의 메타모포시스"라는 아젠다로 문·사·철을 아우르는 다양한 연구자들이 학제간 연구를 진행하고 있다. 개항 이래 식민화와 분단이라는 역사적 격변 속에서 한국의 근대(성)가 형성되어온 과정을 문화의 층위에서 살펴보는 것이 본 사업단의 목표다. '문화의 메타모포시스'란 한국의 근대(성)가 외래문화의 일방적 수용으로도, 순수한 고유문화의 내재적 발현으로도 환원되지 않는, 이문화들의 접촉과 충돌, 융합과 절합, 굴절과 변용의 역동적 상호작용을 통해 형성되었음을 강조하려는 연구 시각이다.

본 HK+사업단은 아젠다 연구 성과를 집적하고 대외적 확산과 소통을 도모하기 위해 총 네 분야의 기획 총서를 발간하고 있다. 〈메타모포시스 인문학총서〉는 아젠다와 관련된 연구 성과를 종합한 저서나 단독 저서로 이뤄진다.

〈메타모포시스 번역총서〉는 아젠다와 관련하여 자료적 가치를 지닌 외국어 문헌이나 이론서들을 번역하여 소개한다. 〈메타모포시스 자료총서〉는 숭실대 한국기독교박물관에 소장된 한국 근대 관련 귀중 자료들을 영인하고, 해제나 현대어 번역을 덧붙여 출간한다. 〈메타모포시스 대중총서〉는 아젠다 연구 성과의 대중적 확산을 위해 기획한 것으로 대중 독자들을 위한 인문학 교양서이다.

동양과 서양, 전통과 근대, 아카데미즘 안팎의 장벽을 횡단하는 다채로운 자료와 연구 성과들을 집약한 메타모포시스 총서가 인문학의 지평을 넓히고 사유의 폭을 확장하는 데 기여할 수 있기를 바란다.

2020년 11월

숭실대학교 한국기독교문화연구원 HK+사업단장

장경남

▌ 목 차 ▐

『베어드 선교사 부부의 한국어 학습서』 해제

윤영실*

『베어드 선교사 부부의 한국어 학습서』는 숭실대 한국기독교문화연구원 인문한국(HK+) 사업단의 자료총서로 윌리엄 베어드(W.M. Baird)의 『회의, 교회 및 기타 용어들에 관한 영한, 한영사전』과 애니 베어드(Annie L.A. Baird)의 『한국어 사용 초보자를 위한 50가지 도움말』의 영인 및 번역문을 함께 수록했다. 숭실대 한국기독교박물관에 소장되어 있는 두 자료는 해방 이전 시기 서양 선교사들이 선교 사역과 교회 운영을 위해 낯선 언어인 한국어를 익히려고 고투했던 모습을 생생하게 보여준다. 외국인을 위한 한국어 교재와 학습법은 물론이요, 한국어 자체의 표기법이나 문법 체계도 제대로 갖춰지지 않은 상황에서, 서양 선교사들은 그들 나름의 지식을 동원하여 한국어의 문법 체계를 세우고, 영어에 대한 번역어를 정비하고, 선교에 필요한 표현들을 속성으로 익히기 위한 학습법을 개발했다. 이들의 '언어횡단적'(trans-linguistic) 실천은 현대 어학의 관점에서 보면 여러 한계를 갖는 '낡은' 지식에 불과할 수도 있으나, 이(異)문화들이 처음으로 접촉하고 충돌하는 과정에서 빚어지는 기이한 굴절과 변용의 장면들을 담고 있다는 점에서는 여전히 흥미롭다. 눈 밝은 독자들이 언젠가 이 옛 텍스트의 갈피에서 새로운 앎을 길어 올리기를 기대하며, 약간의 해제를 덧붙인다.

* 숭실대학교 한국기독교문화연구원 HK교수

1. 윌리엄 베어드, 『회의, 교회 및 기타 용어들에 관한 영한, 한영사전』 (English-Korean & Korean-Enlish Dictionary of Parliamentary, Ecclesiastical and Some Other Terms, 1928)

사전의 편찬자인 윌리엄 베어드(William Martyne Baird, 1862~1931)는 미국 장로교 선교사로 1862년 미국 인디애나 주에서 출생했고, 하노버 대학(Hanover College)과 맥코믹 신학교(McCormick Theological Seminary)에서 수학했다. 1891년 부인 애니 베어드와 한국에 건너와 부산에서 선교 사역을 시작했고, 대구 계성학당, 서울 경신학당 등에서 교육을 담당했다. 1897년부터 평양에 숭실학교를 건립하고 1906년에는 한국 최초의 고등교육기관인 숭실대학으로 발전시켰다. 1916년 숭실대학장을 사임한 후에는 교재 발간 등 문서선교에 힘쓰다가 1931년 장티푸스로 별세했다. 한국 이름은 배위량(裵偉良)이며 현재 숭실대학에는 그를 기념하는 베어드 홀이 건립되어 있다.[1]

윌리엄 베어드가 편찬한『회의, 교회 및 기타 용어들에 관한 영한, 한영사전』(English-Korean & Korean-Enlish Dictionary of Parliamentary, Ecclesiastical and Some Other Terms)은 제목 그대로 교회 모임과 회의에 필요한 용어들을 주로 선별해놓은 특수 목적의 소사전이다. 조선예수교서회에서 1928년 9월 29일 발행되었다. 저자는 미국인 배위량(裵偉良)으로, 발행자는 영국인 반우거(班禹巨)로 표기되어 있다. 반우거의 본명은 제럴드 본위크(Gerald Bonwick, 1872~1954)로 1908년 10월1일 구세군 개척사단의 일원으로 내한했다가, 1910년 10월부터 조선예수회 총무를 맡아 여러 기독교 서적 출간에 관여했다.

베어드의 이 소사전은 개화기에서 식민지기에 걸쳐 발간된 다른 이중어사

---

[1] 윌리엄 베어드의 생애에 대한 자세한 기록으로는 Richard Baird, 김인수 옮김, 『배위량 박사의 한국선교』(William M. Baird of Korea), 쿰란, 2004; 한국기독교문화연구소 편, 『베어드와 한국선교』, 숭실대학교출판부, 2008 참조.

전들과 견주어 볼 때 그 의의가 더 명확하게 드러날 것이다. 참고로 황호덕·
이상현이 편찬한 『한국어의 근대와 이중어사전』(박문사, 2012) 총 11권의 목
록을 살펴보면 다음과 같다.

1. Ridel, Felix Clair, 『한불자뎐 韓佛字典』(*Dictionnaire Coreen-Franeais*), Yokohama: C. Levy Imprimeur-Libraire, 1880.

2. Underwood, Horace Grant, 『韓英字典 한영자뎐』(*A Concise Dictionary of the Korean Language*), Yokohama: Kelly & Walsh, 1890.

3. Scott, James, *English-Corean Dictionary: Being a Vocabulary of Corean Colloquial Words in Common Use*, Corea: Church of England Mission Press, 1891.

4. Jones, George Heber, 『英韓字典 영한자뎐』(*An English-Korean Dictionary*), Tokyo: Kyo Bun Kwan, 1914.

5. Gale, James Scarth, 『韓英字典 한영자뎐』(*A Korean-English Dictionary*), Yokohama: Kelly & Walsh, 1897.

6. Gale, James Scarth, 『韓英字典 한영자뎐』(*A Korean-English Dictionary*), Yokohama: The Fukuin Printing CO., L'T., 1911.
   Gale, James Scarth, 『韓英字典 한영자뎐』(*A Korean-English Dictionary*(*The Chinese Character*), Yokohama: The Fukuin Printing CO., L'T., 1914.

7. 朝鮮總督府, 『朝鮮語辭典』, 朝鮮總督府, 1920.

8. Gale, James Scarth, 『三千字典』(*Present day English-Korean: Three Thousand Words*), 京城: 朝鮮耶蘇敎書會, 1924.
   Underwood, Horace Grant & Underwood, Horace Horton, 『英鮮字典』(*An English-Korean Dictionary*), 京城: 朝鮮耶蘇敎書會, 1925.

9. 金東成, 『最新鮮英辭典』(*The new Korean-English Dictionary*), 京城: 博文書館, 1928.

10. Gale, James Scarth, 『韓英大字典』(*The Unabridged Korean-English Dictionary*), 京城: 朝鮮耶蘇敎書會, 1931.

11. 李鍾極, 『鮮和兩引 모던朝鮮外來語辭典』(*The New Dictionary of Foreign Words in Modern Korean*), 京城: 漢城圖書, 1937.

목록에서 확인할 수 있듯 베어드의 사전은 위 영인본에는 포함되지 않았
다. 이중어사전의 전체적 얼개를 살펴보는 글에서는 다른 수십 종의 사전과
함께 베어드의 사전도 목록에 포함되었으나, 소장처 불명으로 기재되어 있
다.[2] 이런 점에서 이번 자료총서에서 베어드 사전의 소개는 기존 연구의 누
락 부분을 적게나마 보완한다는 의의를 갖는다. 지금까지 확인한 바에 따르
면 베어드의 사전을 직접 언급한 연구는 오구라 신페이의 『朝鮮語學史』가 유
일한데 그 내용 또한 매우 소략하다. 오구라는 12종의 서양인 저술 사전을 열
거하면서 게일 등의 사전은 비교적 상세히 설명한 반면, 베어드의 사전에 대
해서는 다음과 같은 짤막한 언급에 그치고 있다.

"책 제목이 보여주듯 주로 법령, 교회 등에 관한 단어를 수집하여 해석을 한 수진
식(袖珍式) 소사전이며, 영선(英鮮) 및 선영(鮮英)의 2부로 되어 있다."[3]

베어드의 사전은 1928년이라는 비교적 늦은 시기에 출간되었고, 분량도 100여
쪽에 불과하여 매우 소략하다. 한영과 영한사전 각각은 50페이지 정도에 불과
해서, 1911년에 출간된 게일의 『한영ᄌᆞ뎐』이 1,100여 쪽에 달하는 것에 비교
할 바가 아니다. 그럼에도 불구하고 베어드의 사전은 회의 및 교회 사무와 관
련된 용어들을 선별하여 싣고 있다는 점에서 독자적인 가치를 갖는다. 베어
드는 서문에서 이 사전의 필요성을 다음과 같이 강조하고 있다.

"나는 공중(公衆)에게 회의와 교회 용어들에 대한 사전을 제공할 필요성에 대해
어떤 변명도 필요 없다고 판단한다. 놀라운 것은 우리가 지금까지 그런 책이 없이
도 교회를 운영해올 수 있었다는 점이다. 교회의 모든 회합들이 그 필요를 증명하

2) 황호덕, 「이중어사전의 얼개와 역사적·자료적 가치」, 『개념과 역사, 근대 한국의 이중어
사전: 외국인들의 사전 편찬 사업으로 본 한국어의 근대 1: 연구편』, 박문사, 2012, 68쪽.
3) 小倉進平, 河野六郎 補註, 『朝鮮語學史』(增訂補注), 東京: 刀江書院, 1964, 40頁.

고 있음에도 말이다."

기독교가 도입된 이래 교회의 예배와 주일학교, 위원회 등 각종 교회 사무는 한국인들에게 낯선, 새로운 문화적 경험이었다. 베어드는 선교 현장에서 교회와 관련된 새로운 용어들이 임시방편으로 만들어지고 서로 다른 용어들이 혼용되고 경합하는 혼란스러운 과정을 몸소 겪으면서, 이러한 용어들에 특화된 사전의 필요성을 절감했다. 베어드의 사전은 교회 사무에 특화된 목적을 띠는 만큼, 소략한 분량에도 불구하고 이전의 이중어사전에는 보이지 않는 용어들을 포함하고 있다. 아래의 몇 가지 사례들은 1911년 게일의 사전은 물론 1920년 조선총독부가 편찬한 『朝鮮語辭典』에도 나오지 않는 용어들이다.

> 동의 動議 to move
> 직청 再請 to second
> 토의 討議 debate
> 공천위원 nominating committee
> 거슈투표 to vote by a show of hands
> 경상비 經常費 current ordinary expenditure

흥미로운 점은 교회 사무와 관련한 베어드의 사전이 민주주의의 근간인 회의와 의결에 관련된 용어들을 다수 포함하고 있다는 점이다. "Parliamentary, Ecclesiastical and Some Other Terms"라는 사전의 제목 역시 이 점을 명시하고 있다. parliamentary는 비록 국정(國政)을 논하는 의회가 아니라 교회 사무에 국한된 각종 회의를 지시하는 것이지만, 특정 사안에 대한 토의와 회의, 의결의 절차와 관련 용어들은 비슷하거나 같았다. 베어드는 이와 관련된 용어들과 절차는 로버트 회의법(Robert's Rules of Order)을 준용했다고 밝힌다. 로버트 회의법은 미국 공병장교였던 헨리 로버트(Henry. M. Robert)가 1876년에 발간한 회의 진행에 대한 지침서다.[4] 원래는 교회의 의사 진행을 좀 더 체계화하기 위해 도입한 것인데, 여러 사람의 의견을 수렴하여 회의 목적을 효율적으로 달성하기 위한 가장 모범적인 규칙으로 오늘날까지도 다양한 공공기관 및 사회단체에서 널리 준용되고 있다. 한국에서는 윤치호의 축약본인 『議會通用規則』(1898)으로 처음 번역되었고, 김병제의 『사회승람』(1908), 『경남일보』(1910), 『演說及式辭法』(1920), 『實地應用演說方法』(1923), 『十分間演說集』(1925) 등에도 부분적으로 재수록되었다.[5]

베어드의 사전은 비록 교회 사무라는 제한적 목적을 위해 편찬되었지만, 여기에 포함된 의회 민주주의의 용어들은 식민지 조선에서 기독교의 문화적 역할에 대해 시사하는 바가 적지 않다. 봉건왕조와 식민지하에서 공적인 정치공간에 참여할 기회가 없었던 조선인들에게 교회의 회의 및 의결 문화는 근대 민주주의의 형식을 학습하고 실천하는 공간이기도 했던 것이다.

2. 애니 베어드, 『한국어 사용 초보자를 위한 50가지 도움말』(Fifty Helps for the Beginner in the Use of the Korean Language)

애니 베어드(Annie L.A. Baird, 1864~1916),[6] 한국 이름으로 안애리(安愛理)는 윌리엄 베어드의 부인으로 숭실학교를 중심으로 선교사, 번역가, 저술가, 교육가로서 활발한 활동을 펼친 인물이다. 그녀는 1864년 미국 인디애나 출생으로 미스 피바디즈 신학교(Miss Peabady's Female Seminary), 하노버 대학

---

4) Henry M. Robert, *Robert's Rules of Order Pocket Manual of Rules of Order for Deliberative Assemblies*, Chicago: S.C.Griggs & Company, 1876.

5) 윤치호의 『의회통용규칙』의 번역 및 재수록 양상에 대해서는 류충희, 「개화기 조선의 민회 활동과 〈의회통용규칙〉 - 「의회통용규칙」의 유통과 번역 양상을 중심으로」, 『동방학지』 167, 연세대 국학연구소, 2014.9 참조.

6) 선행 연구들은 한글 표기로 에니 베어드라고 쓴 경우도 많으나, 이 글에서는 선행 논문의 제목을 제외하고는 모두 애니 베어드로 통일하여 표기하였다.

(Hanover College), 워시번 대학(Washburn University)에서 수학했다. 결혼 전부터 해외 선교의 꿈을 불태우다가 캔자스의 YWCA에서 만난 윌리엄 베어드와 결혼하여 1891년 조선으로 건너왔다.[7]

그녀의 재능은 평양 숭실에서 저술과 교육에 종사하면서 본격적으로 꽃피우기 시작했다. 숭실학당과 대학에서 애니 베어드가 강의한 과목은 식물학, 천문학, 화학, 물리학, 지리학, 수학, 미술, 작문 등 폭넓은 영역에 걸쳐 있다.[8] 『동물학』(1906), 『식물도설』(1908), 『생리학초권』(1908) 등의 교재를 직접 저술하거나 번역하기도 했다.[9] 그녀는 문학적 재능도 뛰어나서 오늘날까지도 애창되는 찬송가 375장 「나는 갈길 모르니」와 387장 「멀리 멀리 갔더니」의 작사가로도 알려져 있다. 선교 목적으로 저술한 『샛별전』(1905), 『고영규전』(1911), *Daybreak in Korea: A Tale of Transformation in the Far East*(1909), *Inside Views of Mission Life*(1913)[10] 등은 문학사와 선교사 양 방면에서 관심을 받아왔다.

여기서 소개하는 『한국어 사용 초보자를 위한 50가지 도움말』(이하 『50가지 도움말』로 약칭. *Fifty Helps for the Beginner in the Use of the Korean*

---

7) 애니 베어드의 삶에 대한 개략적인 고찰로는 박보경, 「에니 베어드의 삶과 선교사역에 대한 고찰」, 『장신논단』 49:4, 장로회신학대학교, 2017.12.

8) 숭실대학교 100년사 편찬위원회, 『숭실대학교 100년사: 평양숭실편 (1)』, 숭실대학교출판부, 1997, 90·150쪽.

9) 애니 베어드가 저술하거나 번역한 교과서들에 대한 연구는 오선실 외, 『한국 기독교 박물관 자료를 통해 본 근대 수용과 변용』, 선인, 2020 참조.

10) 애니 베어드의 영문저서들은 한국어로도 번역, 출간되었다. Annie Baird, 심현녀 옮김, 『어둠을 헤치고: 빛을 찾은 사람들』(*Daybreak in Korea*), 다산글방, 1994; Annie Baird, 성신형·문시영 옮김, 오지석 해제, 『개화기 조선 선교사의 삶』, 2019, 선인. 애니 베어드의 소설과 문서사역에 대한 연구로는 김성연, 「근대 초기 선교사 부인의 저술활동과 번역가로서의 정체성」, 『한국현대문학연구』 55, 한국현대문학회, 2015; 곽승숙, 「에니 베어드의 신소설 연구」, 『한국문학이론과 비평』 63, 한국문학이론과 비평학회, 2014.6; 고예진, 「에니 베어드이 저서에 나타난 한국문화이해 양상 고찰」, 『인문과학 연구논총』 33, 명지대학교 인문과학연구소, 2012.2; 오지석, 「한국교회 초기 혼인관에 대한 연구: 에니 베어드의 「고영규전을 중심으로」, 『기독교사회윤리』 12, 한국기독교사회윤리학회, 2006. 그밖에 애니 베어드의 출간물 목록과 연구사 목록은 『개화기 조선 선교사의 삶』 해제를 참조하라.

Language)은 이제 막 한국에 건너온 선교사들을 위해 간단한 한국어 문법 지식과 용례들을 정리한 한국어 학습서다. 1898년 초판이 발행된 이래 1926년까지 총 6판이 발행되었다. 각 판본의 기본적인 서지사항과 구성은 다음과 같다.[11]

판본	발행처	1. 예비학습	2. 문형	3. 부록·색인	p.
초판 1896	Trilingual Press	① 학습 안내 ② 한국어학습에 유용한 표현	40개	① 종교용어 목록 ② 복음서의 유용한 단문 ③ 기도문 ④ 기피 사항 ⑤ 모음 ⑥ 자음 ⑦ 문화 소개 등의 에필로그	64
2판 1898	미상	① 학습 안내 ② 모음 ③ 자음 ④ 한국어학습에 유용한 표현	42개	① 종교용어 목록 ② 복음서의 유용한 단문 ③ 기도문 ④ 기피사항 ⑤ 문화 소개 등의 에필로그	63
3판 1903	Methodist Publishing House	① 학습 안내 ② 모음, 자음 ③ 한국어학습에 필요한 유용한 표현	42개	① 종교적 어휘 ② 복음서의 단문 ③ 기도문 ④ 한국어 사용 및 학습에서 유의할 점 ⑤ 한국인에 대한 이해	63

---

11) 애니 베어드의 『50가지 도움말』은 서양인의 한국어 학습 초창기를 규명한 일련의 연구들에서 부분적으로 다뤄져 왔다. 고예진, 『19세기 서양인의 한국어 교재 연구』, 부산대학교 박사논문, 2013; 박새암, 『개신교 선교사 한국어교육의 형성과 전개에 대한 사적 연구』, 한성대학교 박사논문, 2018 등. 『50가지 도움말』만을 대상으로 한 본격적인 연구로는 오대환과 이숙의 논문을 들 수 있다. 오대환의 논문은 판본 비교 등 서지적 정보가 상세하고, 이숙의 논문은 내용에 대한 소개가 자세하다. 오대환, 「선교사의 조선어 학습서 Fifty Helps for the Beginner in the Use of the Korean Language에 관한 연구」, 『언어와 문화』 15:1, 한국언어문화교육학회, 2019.2; 이숙, 「애니 베어드의 한국어학습서 Fifty Helps의 내용 연구」, 『어문론총』 80, 한국문학언어학회, 2019.6.

4판 1911	Fukuin	① 모음 ② 자음 ③ 학습에 유용한 표현 ④ 명사의 격변화 ⑤ 대명사 ⑥ 동작 동사 ⑦ 형용사적 동사 ⑧ 부사 ⑨ 후치사	50개	① 종교용어 목록 ② 복음서의 유용한 단문 ③ 기도문 ④ 기피사항	100
5판 1921	Fukuin	상동	50개	상동	100
6판 1926	The Christian Literature Society of Korea (한국기독교 서회)	상동	50개	① 종교용어 목록 ② 복음서의 유용한 단문 ③ 기도문 ④ 추가적인 도움말 (20항목) ⑤ 기피사항 ⑥ 색인(Index)	117

* 이 표는 오대환, 「선교사의 조선어 학습서 Fifty Helps for the Beginner in the Use of the Korean Language에 관한 연구」의 표1(207쪽)과 표2(209~210쪽)를 바탕으로 일부 수정하였다.

30년에 걸쳐서 6판까지 발행된 것에서 알 수 있듯, 애니 베어드의 『50가지 도움말』은 선교 현장에서 한국어를 막 배우기 시작한 외국인들에게 즐겨 사용되는 교재였다. 개신교 선교부의 언어위원회에서 한국어학습 과정을 안내한 기록에 따르면, 『50가지 도움말』은 1891년, 1901년, 1911년에 학습서로 사용되었고, 애니 베어드 사후인 1920년대의 Language School에서도 초급용 학습서로 사용되었다. 1914년 George H. Winn이 저술한 『일본어 사용 초보자를 위한 50가지 도움말』(Fifty Helps for the Beginner in the Use of the Japanese Language)은 애니 베어드의 책을 일본어 학습에 맞게 각색한 것으로서, 서양인들에게 애니 베어드의 책이 효율적인 학습서로 인식되었음을 보여준다.

그렇다면 최종판을 기준으로도 불과 100여 페이지에 불과한 이 책은 과연 어떤 특징을 띠고 있기에 효율적인 한국어 학습서로 통용될 수 있었을까? 우선 이 책은 한국어에 대한 방대하고 체계적인 학습서가 아니라 한국어 초보자들이 선교 현장에서 바로 쓸 수 있게 하겠다는 실용적 목적을 분명히 했다. 복잡한 문법 설명이 아닌, 자주 활용되는 문형 중심의 학습법이 이러한 목적을 뒷받침한다. '50개의 도움말'은 한국어의 동사 활용을 중심으로 자주 사용되는 문형들을 50개로 정리하여 제시하고 있다. 1판에서 3판까지는 예비 학습과 부록에 해당하는 내용까지 포함하여 『50개의 도움말』이라는 제목을 붙였지만, 4판부터는 문형 연습만으로 50개 항목을 구성하고 예비 학습과 부록은 따로 첨가하였다. 최종판인 6판에서는 〈부가적인 도움말〉 20개를 추가하여 문형 연습을 더 확장시켰다. 문형 중심의 학습법은 오늘날에도 회화 위주의 언어 학습에서 그 가치를 인정받는데, 애니 베어드는 1896년이라는 이른 시기에 이를 도입함으로써 한국어 학습의 효율성을 도모했던 것이다.

둘째, 이 책은 외국인에게 한국어를 가르치는 것을 넘어 외국인이 한국인 선생님에게 어떻게 한국어를 가르치도록 할 것인지에 대한 교수법을 제시한다. 이 책이 출간되고 활용되었던 시점이 한국어를 모르는 외국인 학습자와 외국어를 모르는 한국인 교사가 대면하여 한국어를 가르치고 배우는 기이한 상황이었다는 점은 특기할 만하다. 언어와 문화가 상이한 양측이 어떤 과정을 통해 가장 효율적으로 한국어를 학습할 수 있을 것인가. 더욱이 당시의 상황은 한국어 자체의 표기법이나 문법조차 확립되어 있지 않았을 때였다. 따라서 애니 베어드 같은 초기 선교사들은 한국어의 문법과 체계를 영어 등 자신의 모국어인 서양어 문법을 바탕으로 체계화하려고 시도했다. 나아가 이를 바탕으로 한국어 학습자가 문법적 지식이 없는 한국인 선생님에게 어떻게 한국어를 가르치도록 할 것인가를 가르쳐야 했다. 『50가지 도움말』은 바로 이러한 곤혹스러운 상황에 놓인 한국어 학습자에게 최적화된 방식으로 기술되었다. 예비 학습 부분에서 학습자가 한국인 선생님에게 할 수 있는 인사말과

"이것 무엇이오?" 같은 기초적인 질문들을 제시하고, 부록에서는 문화적 차이로 인해 범할 수 있는 무례를 방지하도록 세심한 주의사항까지 덧붙이고 있다. 한편 예비학습으로 한국어의 기본 표기와 발음을 익히고, 현재/과거/미래 같은 시제나 낮은말(낮춤말)/가운데말(예삿말)/높은말(높임말) 등의 기본 문법 용어들을 정리한 후, 각각의 문형에서 이러한 문법적 변이들을 반복 연습할 수 있도록 함으로써, 최소한의 지식으로 최대한의 활용이 가능하도록 안배하였다. 따라서 학습자는 선생님에게 한국어에 대한 체계적인 설명을 요구하지 않고도, 다만 발음과 문형 연습상의 교정만으로 요구하고도 한국어 학습이 무리 없이 이뤄질 수 있었다.

마지막으로 애니 베어드의 『50가지 도움말』은 한국에서 낯선 언어뿐만 아니라 낯선 문화에도 적응해야 했던 초보 선교사들이 한국 문화를 존중하면서도 선교의 목적을 달성할 수 있도록 돕기 위한 세심한 충고를 담고 있다. 1·2판 부록의 〈문화 소개 등의 에필로그〉, 3판 부록의 〈한국인에 대한 이해〉, 4·5·6판 부록의 〈기피사항〉이 이에 해당한다. 애니 베어드는 서양인에 비해 더 섬세한 예절과 에티켓을 중시하는 한국인의 특성을 강조하면서, 선교의 목적을 달성하기 위해서는 무엇보다 체면과 관습을 중시하는 한국 문화에 대한 존중이 필요함을 역설한다. 나아가 서양인의 솔직한 감정 표현이 한국인에게는 무례함으로 비칠 수 있음을 충고하고, 이러한 신중함이 변화의 속도를 따라잡느라 각박해진 서구 문화에서는 부당하게 폄하되고 있음을 지적한다. 애니 베어드의 충고는 서양 선교사들이 조선을 비롯한 비서구 문화에 대해 갖기 쉬운 편견과 우월감에 경종을 울리면서, 기독교 선교가 이문화에 대한 존중을 바탕으로 이뤄져야 함을 역설한다는 점에서 귀감이 될 만하다.

애니 베어드의 『50가지 도움말』은 한국어의 근대적 문법 체계가 성립되기 이전 서양인들이 한국어 학습을 목적으로 서양 문법 체계에 맞춰 구축한 번안문법 시대[12]의 산물인 만큼 오늘날의 한국어 문법과는 다른 점이 많다. 예비 학습 부분에 나온 한국어 문자들과 음운 표기는 윌리엄 베어드의 「한국어 음가의 로마자화」("The Romanization of Korean Sounds", *The Korean Repository*, May, 1895)를 따르고 있고, 발음 구별 기호는 웹스터의 국제어 사전(*Webster's International Dictionary*) 체계를 기초로 했다. 문법은 리델(Félix Clair Ridel, 李福明, 1830~1884)의 『조선어문법』(*Grammaire Coréenne*, 1881) 이래 언더우드의 『한영문법』까지 이어지는 서양문법의 기본 체계를 따른다. 예컨대, 현대 한국어 문법은 명사나 대명사가 격변화를 하지 않는 것으로 간주하지만, 『50개의 도움말』은 서양 문법에 따라 명사의 격변화를 주격, 도구격, 소유격 등 7개로 구분한다. 한국어에서는 동사와 형용사가 모두 독립적으로 서술어가 될 수 있지만, 이 책에서는 동사를 동작동사로, 형용사를 형용사적 동사로 기술한다. 영어에는 없는 조사의 개념은 영어 전치사에 대응시키면서 명사 뒤에 온다는 점에서 후치사로 설명하고 있다. 조선총독부가 1912년에 제정하고 1921년에 개정한 〈보통학교용언문철자법〉은 아래아(·)를 ㅏ로, 뻐, 까를 써, 까로 통일했지만, 『50개의 도움말』은 이를 준용하지 않고 독자적인 표기법을 고수했다.13) 『50개의 도움말』이 30년간 6판에 걸쳐 개정, 증보되는 동안 한국어 표기와 문법을 둘러싸고 한국인, 일본인, 서양선교사들 사이에 어떤 상호작용과 굴절이 이뤄져 왔는지는 향후 면밀한 고찰을 필요로 하는 연구주제다. 이번 자료총서가 그 지난한 연구의 도정에 작은 보탬이라도 되길 바란다.

---

12) 권재선은 한국어 근대 문법 연구사를 다음과 같이 시기적으로 구분한다. ①1880~1905: 외국문법을 통한 번안문법시대, ② 1905~1915: 고전국어학인 동문학의 영향 아래 서양문법에서 벗어나 고전국어학 전통을 바탕으로 새로운 문법체계를 모색하던 신문법시대 ③ 1915~1930: 신문법+일본인의 번안문법을 받아들여 서양 전통으로 방향전환한 전환문법 시대 ④ 1930~1950: 전환문법을 계승해서 일본, 서양 이론을 기초로 선진문법 체계를 세우려 한 종합문법시대. 권재선, 『국어학발전사: 현대국어학』, 대구: 우골탑, 1988 참조. 1896년에 처음 출간된 『50개의 도움말』은 ①, ②, ③의 시대에 걸쳐 6판까지 개정되었으나, 한국어 문법의 기본체계는 여전히 번안문법의 틀에 머물러 있다.

13) 윤여탁 외, 『국어교육100년사』 1, 서울대학교출판부, 2006, 45~51쪽.

회의, 교회 및 기타 용어들에 관한
영한, 한영사전

서문[1]

　나는 공중(公衆)에게 회의와 교회 용어들에 대한 사전을 제공할 필요성에 대해 어떤 변명도 필요 없다고 판단한다. 놀라운 것은 우리가 지금까지 그런 책이 없이도 교회를 운영해올 수 있었다는 점이다. 교회의 모든 회합들이 그 필요를 증명하고 있음에도 말이다.

　이 책이 완벽하다거나 최종적이라고 주장하지는 않겠다. 실수들이 발견된다면, 저자가 다음 판에서는 이런 실수들을 바로잡을 수 있도록 주의를 환기해주시면 감사하겠다.

　기술적 용어들은 변경될 수 있다. 어떤 단어들은 더 이상 사용되지 않고 어떤 용어들은 최근에 생겼기에 좋은 용례로서 최종적인 지위를 얻지 못했다. 그렇기에 정확한 용어법은 아직 기대할 수 없다. 과거에 사용된 단어들, 이제 막 사용되기 시작한 용어들도 다양한 요구들을 충족시키기 위해 이 책의 목록에 포함되었다. 아마도 낡은 단어들 중 일부는 유지되어야 할 수도 있다.

　명백히 잘못되거나 바람직하지 않은 용례의 경우에도 굳이 이를 바꾸려고 시도하지 않았다. 이미 사용되고 있는 단어들은 수정하면 좋을 것처럼 보이더라도 이 책에 포함시켰다. 예를 들면 '회(whoi)', '부(poo)', '위원(wiwun)' 같은 단어들의 사용에는 커다란 혼란이 있다. 현재의 용례에 따르면 '위원'이라는 단어를 사용할 때 화자가 위원회(committee)를 뜻하는지 아니면 위원회의 한 구성원만을 뜻하는지 구별하는 게 불가능하다. 비슷하게 '전도부(chundo poo)'라는 단어들이 사용될 때, 그것이 선교회(a missionary society)를 뜻하는지 해외선교부(Board of Foreign Missions)를 의도한 것인지 구분할 수 없다. 단어들이 사용될 때 완전한 정확성은 불가능하다. 그러한 혼란은 어떤 권위 있

---

[1] 서문은 영한사전 앞과 한영사전 앞에 각기 영어와 국문으로 붙어있는데, 국문 서문은 내용이 좀 더 소략하므로 영문을 기준으로 번역하였다.

는 단체의 결정이나 관행상의 어떤 통일성에 의해서만 해결될 수 있다. 그러한 통일성은 현재로서는 존재하지 않는다. 사전편찬자가 할 수 있는 최선은 현재 사용되는 단어들을 목록화하는 것뿐이다.

회의 및 교회 용어들 이외에도 다른 많은 유용한 단어들, 특히 주일 학교 업무에서 사용되는 여러 새로운 용어들을 포함시켰다. 이들 대부분은 C.A.Clark 박사[2]와 J.G.Holderoft 박사[3]의 힘을 빌렸다.

이 책은 내가 개인적인 용도로 여러 해 동안 의회 및 교회 용어들의 목록을 수집한 결과다. 이외에도 나는 아들 Rev.W.M.Baird,Jr가 만든 비슷한 목록들로부터 귀중한 도움을 받았음을 인정하고 싶다. 이 책의 편집 및 배열에 관해서는 장신국(Chang Shin Kook) 씨의 도움을 받았는데, 그는 이 사전의 초고를 쓸 때 품이 많이 드는 값진 도움을 제공했다.

(10장에서 12장까지) 우선순위에 따라 배치된 다양한 의안들과 원안, 보조안, 부수안, 특권안으로 의안들을 분류한 설명(10장, 11장)이 도움이 되기를 바란다. 이 규칙들은 Robert 회의법(Robert's Rules of Order)을 준용했다. 기억을 환기시키기 위해서, 그리고 의결 기구에서 행해지는 업무의 일반적인 절차에 대해 배우고자 하는 이들에게 작은 도움을 주기 위해서, 로버트 회의법에 대한 짧은 개요를 덧붙였다.

두 부분으로 나눠진 배치는 한국어 사용자와 영어 사용자 모두에게 도움이 되도록 의도한 것이다. 이 책이 두 언어를 배우고자 하는 이들에게만이 아니

---

[2] Charles Allen Clark(1878~1961). 한국 이름 곽안련[郭安蓮]. 북장로회 선교사로 1902년 내한한 이후 일제의 신사참배 강요로 추방(1941.7)되기까지 40년 동안 한국의 선교사역에 종사했다. 1908년부터 평양신학교에서 실천신학 교수로 재직했으며, 51권에 달하는 신학 관련 서적을 저술하는 등 목회와 신학, 성경주석, 건축 등 다양한 분야에서 많은 업적을 남겼다.

[3] Rev.Dr.J.Gordon Holdcroft(1878~1972). 한국 이름은 허대전(許大殿). 미국 시카고 출신으로 프린스턴 신학대학원을 졸업한 후 1909년부터 한국에서 선교사로 사역했다. 한국에서 주일학교를 시작하고 교사를 양성하는 데 크게 공헌했으며, 신사참배 문제로 귀국한 후 ICCC 선교위원장, Faith 신학대학원 부이사장 등을 역임했다.

라 좀 더 수준 높은 학습자들의 기억을 환기시키는 데도 유용하길 바란다. 이 작은 책이 교회 사무를 좀 더 효율적으로 수행하는 데 보탬이 되길 기원한다.

W.M.Baird

1928년 가을

【부록】4)

회무순서

1. 고숙(叩肅, 회석정돈)
2. 전(前) 회록(會錄) 낭독
3. 상비위원의 보고
4. 선정 (혹 임시) 위원의 보고
5. 미진(未盡) 사건
6. 신(新) 사건
7. 폐회

각종 동의(動議)

1. 동의(動議)
2. 재청
3. 개의(改議)
4. 재개의(再改議)
5. 대신(代身) 동의의 동의
6. 보고(報告) 청취하자는 동의
7. 보고 수리(受理) 혹은 채용하자는 동의
8. 위임하자는 동의
9. 유기(有期) 연기하자는 동의
10. 무기(無期) 연기하자는 동의
11. 존안(存案) 동의

---

4) 부록은 영한사전 앞에 영문으로, 한영사전 뒤에 국문으로 붙어 있는데, 여기서는 당대의 표현을 알기 위해 영문을 번역하기보다 국문을 기준으로 현대어로 바꾸었다.

12. 기안(起案) 동의

13. 재론 동의

14. 동의의 취소 동의

15. 토의 제한하자는 동의

16. 토의 제한을 연기하자는 동의

17. 토의 마치자는 동의

18. 의사일정의 동의

19. 의사일정 변경하자는 동의

20. 의사일정에 특별사건을 가입하자는 동의

21. 회의록에서 삭제하자는 동의

22. 회장의 판결에 항의하자는 동의

23. 규칙을 잠시 중지하자는 동의

24. 기립 보고하자는 동의(전회 위원회에만 해당)

25. 특권안의 동의

26. 선결 문제의 동의

27. 어떤 의안을 재론하지 말자는 동의

28. 폐회 동의

29. 폐회시간 동의

네 가지 의안

Ⅰ. 원안 혹 주요안

Ⅱ. 보조안

Ⅲ. 부수안

Ⅳ. 특권안

Ⅰ. 원안은 무슨 문제를 결정하기 위하여 일어나는 의안이니 다른 아무 의안도 회에 일어나지 않을 때에만 진행될 수 있으며 두 원안이 동시에 진행될 수는 없음

Ⅱ. 보조안은 원안에 응용되는 것이니 원안의 선두가 되며 특권안과 부수안에 양보함. 보조안은 다음과 같아 그 순서대로 됨

   1. 존안(存案)

   2. 선결문제

   3. 유기한 연기

   4. 위임 혹 재임

   5. 개정(改正)

   6. 무기한 연기

Ⅲ. 부수안은 원안과 보조안에서 일어나 그 선두가 되며 특권안에 양보하니 다음과 같음

   1. 회장 판결에 항의

   2. 재론하지 말자는 동의

   3. 서류 낭독을 청(請)함

   4. 동의 취소의 인가를 청함

   5. 규칙을 일시정지(暫止)하자는 동의

Ⅳ. 특권안은 원안과 보조안과 부수안의 선두가 되니 회나 회원의 권리와 특권에 관계되는 것 외에는 토의하지 못함.(아래 예3) 특권안을 사용하되 결코 회무에 장애가 되거나 지체하게 말 것이니 특권안은 다음과 같아 그 순서대로 됨

   1. 폐회시간의 결정

   2. 폐회

   3. 권리와 특권에 관계되는 문제

4. 의사일정 청(請)

아래 의안은 토의하지 못하나 그 나머지 의안은 토의할 수 있음

1. 폐회시간의 결정 (이 의안은 다른 의안이 회에 있는 때에는 토의하지 못하고 아무 의안도 회에 없는 때에는 다른 원안과 마찬가지로 토의할 수 있음)
2. 폐회
3. 의사 일정의 동의
4. 회무 선후에 관계되는 문제
5. 항의 (어떤 다른 의안이 미결로 있을 때에 함)
6. 의안을 숙고하지 말자는 동의
7. 존안(存案) 동의
8. 기안(起案) 동의
9. 선결문제
10. 토의 못할 의안의 재론

아래 동의는 개의할 수 없음

1. 개의
2. 의사 일정의 동의
3. 부수안 (이상 네 가지 의안 제 3을 보라)
4. 존안
5. 선결문제
6. 재개의
7. 무기연기
8. 재론

아래 의안이 결정되기까지는 원안을 토의할 수 있음

1. 위임
2. 무기연기
3. 회록 삭제
4. 토의할 수 있는 의안의 재론

의안 중에 투표 과반수로 결정되는 것이 많으나 하기 의안은 3분의 2를 요구함

1. 규칙 개정
2. 규칙 잠지(暫止)
3. 특별순서 제정
4. 모의안의 순서 변경
5. 의안을 숙고하지 말자는 동의
6. 토의 제한의 연장
7. 토의의 제한 혹은 종결
8. 선결문제

한국어 사용 초보자를 위한
50가지 도움말

한국어 사용 초보자를 위한 50가지 도움말

애니 베어드
개정판, 6쇄

한국기독교서회 1926

"너를 언어가 다르거나 말이 어려운 백성에게... 언어가 다르거나 말이 어려워 네가 그들의 말을 알아 듣지 못할 나라들에게... 보내는 것이라"

에스겔 3장 5~6절.

"그 백성은 방언이 어려워 네가 알아듣지 못하며 말이 이상하여 네가 깨닫지 못하는 자니라"

이사야 33장 19절

한국어 사용 초보자를 위한 50가지 도움말

이 소책자는 한국어 공부와 사용이 상당히 진전된 이들을 위해 기획된 것이 아니라, 단지 초심자가 몇몇 관용어구들을 빨리 사용할 수 있도록 돕기 위해 고안되었다. 이 책이 포함한 모든 단어들은 종교 용어들이나 기도 및 선교 현장에서 사용되는 문장들을 제외하고는, 대개 다른 책들에서 더 완전하고 주의 깊게 다루고 있을 것이다. 그러나 다른 책들은 이런 용어들을 초심자가 접근할 수 있는 형태로 다루고 있지는 않은 것 같다.

학습자는 먼저 아래 표에 나오는 문자를 식별할 수 있도록 학습함으로써 게일(Gale)의 한영사전이나 다른 출간 서적들을 사용할 준비를 갖추게 된다.

한국어 문자들과 영어 발음표*1)

모음

이 ï 혹은 ĭ,

아 ä,

어 ŭ 혹은 û,

으 eu,

오 ō 혹은 ô,

우 o͞o or o͝o

ᄋᆞ ä 혹은 거의 무음,

애 ă,

에 ā 혹은 ĕ,

외 wā와 비슷하지만 약간의 w 소리가 첨가,

ᄋᆡ ă.

각각의 모음에 연결된 문자 ㅇ은 이 모음 앞에 자음이 올 경우에는 생략된다.

---

1) (원주) 다음 논문에서 가져옴. Rev. W. M. Baird, 「한국어 음가의 로마자화」("The Romanization of Korean Sounds"), *The Korean Repository*, May, 1895. 발음 구별 기호는 웹스터의 국제어 사전(*Webster's International Dictionary*) 체계를 기초로 함.

1. 이 = ï in machine, 〈예〉 비, pï (rain); 깁다 kïpta, (to mend).

   = ĭ in pin, 〈예〉 집, chip, (house); 깁다, kĭpta, (to be deep).

2. 아 = ä in father, 〈예〉 갓 kät, (hat).

3. 어 = ŭ in tub, 〈예〉 법 pŭp, (custom).

   = û in purr, 〈예〉 벗 pût (friend); 머오, mûō (to be far); 건너가오, kûn nŭ[2] käō, (to cross over)에서는 두 소리가 다 나온다.

4. 으 = 프랑스어의 eu, 〈예〉 그 keu, (that).

5. 오 = ō in note, 〈예〉 솜 sōm, (cotton); 동ᄂᆡ, tōng-nă, (a neighborhood).

   = ô in for, 〈예〉 동산, tông săn, (a garden).

6. 우 = o͞o in moon, 〈예〉 문, mo͞on, (a door).

   = o͝o in wo͝ol 〈예〉 풀, p'o͝ol, (grass).

7. ᄋᆞ = ä in father, 〈예〉 ᄆᆞᆯ, mäl, (a horse).

   = 사ᄅᆞᆷ, säram, (person)의 두 번째 음절처럼 강세가 없는 폐음절 (closed syllabel)[3]에서는 거의 무음에 가깝다.

8. 애 = ă in hat, 〈예〉 개, kă, (a dog).

9. 에 = ā in fate, 〈예〉 제가, chā ga, (he or she or I).

   = ĕ in met, 〈예〉 가겟소, kägĕsso, (I will go).

10. 외 = 이 문자는 영어에서 정확히 상응하는 발음이 없다. 그것은 wā와 비슷하지만 w음이 더 약하게 발음된다. 〈예〉 죄, chwā, (fault or sin).

11. ᄋᆡ = ă in hat, 〈예〉 ᄎᆡᆨ, ch'ăk, (a book).

2) 원문에는 n 뒤에 ŭ가 누락되었다.

3) 폐음절(closed syllabel)이란 뒤에 자음이 오는 모음을 뜻한다.

이중모음들(Diphthongs)

진정한 이중모음은 하나밖에 없다.

12. 의 = 프랑스어 eui. ï앞에 매우 약한 w음이 앞에 오는 소리와 비슷하다.
〈예〉 의원, euï wŭn, (a physician).

모음으로서의 W는 10번과 12번에서 언급된 것을 제외하고는 언어적 표상을 갖지 않는다. Y는 어디에서도 모음으로 쓰이지 않는다. 그들은 자음으로서 다음과 같이 다른 문자들과 결합된다.

Y와 결합된 모음들

13. 야 = father에서의 ä에 y음이 선행, 〈예〉 양 yäng, (a sheep).
14. 여 = tub에서의 ŭ에 y음이 선행, 〈예〉 병, pyŭng, (a bottle).
    = purr의 û에 y음이 선행, 〈예〉 면ㅎ다, myûn häda, (to escape, avoid).
15. 요 = note의 ō 앞에 y음이 옴, 〈예〉 욕, yōk, (abuse).
    = for의 ô 앞에 y음이 옴, 〈예〉 쌰쪽ㅎ다의 첫 음절, byô chōk hädä (to be sharp, pointed).
16. 유 = moon의 o͞o 앞에 y음이 옴, 〈예〉 유식하다, yo͞o sik häda, (to be learned).
    = wool의 o͝o 앞에 y음이 옴, 〈예〉 흉년, hyo͝ong nyŭn, (famine year).
17. 예 = fate의 ā 앞에 y음이 옴, 〈예〉 예순, yāsoon, (sixty).
    = met의 ĕ 앞에 y음이 옴, 〈예〉 예, yĕ, (yes).

W와 결합된 모음들

18. 와 = father의 ä 앞에 w음이 옴, 〈예〉 실과, sil gwä, (fruit).

19. 왜 = hat의 ǎ 앞에 w음이 옴, 〈예〉 왜인, wǎ ïn, (a Japanese).

20. 워 = tub의 ǔ 앞에 w음이 옴, 〈예〉 원, wǔn, (an official).

= purr의 û 앞에 w음이 옴, 〈예〉 원ㅎ다, wûn häda, (to wish, to desire).

21. 위 = machine의 ï 앞에 w음이 옴, 〈예〉 위ㅎ다, wï häda, (to worship). ㅁ(m)이나 ㅂ(p) 뒤에서는 w음이 사라진다. 〈예〉 뮈워ㅎ다, mï wǔ häda, (to hate,); 뷔다, pïda, (to be empty).

22. 웨 = fate의 ā 앞에 w음이 옴, 〈예〉 웬 wān, (what sort of? what manner of?)

23. 위 = machine의 ï 앞에 w보다 조금 약한 음이 옴. 〈예〉 춰ㅎ다, ch'wï häda, (to be drunk). 이 조합은 ㅊ(ch'), ㅈ (ch), ㅌ (t') 뒤를 제외하면 거의 일어나지 않음.

모음에 관한 주의점

'외'라고 불리는 기호 'ㅣ'는 마치 그것이 독립된 문자인 것처럼 종종 혼자 쓰인다. 그러나 그 자체로는 음가가 없고 다만 앞에 나오는 모음의 소리를 변형시키는 효과만 있다.

한국어에서는 한 모음이, 바로 뒤나 혹은 자음 뒤에 나오는 다른 모음의 영향을 받아, 움라우트(umlaut)[4] 내지 음운굴절(deflection)을 일으키는 현상을

---

[4] a, o, u 등의 모음이 후속음절의 영향으로 소리가 변하는 현상을 일컫는다.

발견할 수 있다.

밥(päp, food)의 주격에서처럼 ä 뒤에 ï가 오면 밥이(păpï)와 같이 ä가 ă에 가까워진다.

썩(dŭk, bread)의 주격에서처럼 ŭ 뒤에 ï가 오면 썩이(dāgï)와 같이 ŭ가 ā에 가까워진다.

약(yäk, medicine)의 주격에서처럼 yä 뒤에 ï가 오면 약이(yăgï)와 같이 ä가 ă에 가까워진다.

병(pyŭng, bottle)의 주격에서처럼 yŭ 뒤에 ï가 오면 병이(pyĭngï)와 같이 ŭ가 ĭ에 가까워진다.

선생님과 함께 ㅁ음이(밉이), 형편(헹편), 경영ㅎ다(계영ㅎ다)와 같은 단어들을 연습해보라.

자음
단순자음

ㄱ k, ㅁ m, ㄴ n, ㄹ l or r, ㅂ p, ㅅ s or sh, ㄷ t, ㅈ ch, ㅇ ng.

격음들(Aspirated Consonants)

이 문자들은 그 이름이 가리키는 것처럼 숨을 격하게 내뱉는 방식으로 발음된다. 이 소리들을 음사(音寫)할 때 임의로 붙인 ᾿라는 기호는 격음을 표시하는데, 첫 번째 문자의 경우는 원래 격음(a natural aspirate)이기에 ᾿를 붙이지 않는다.[5]

---

5) 아래 나오는 사례들 중 k, p, t, ch와 달리 h는 원래 영어에서도 격음(aspirate)으로 발음되기 때문에 따로 ᾿를 붙이지 않는다는 의미이다.

ㅎ = h, 〈예〉 흙, heulk, (earth).

ㅋ = k', 〈예〉 코, k'ô, (nose).

ㅍ = p', 〈예〉 피, p'i, (blood).

ㅌ = t', 〈예〉 툿, t'at, (fault).

ㅊ = ch' 〈예〉 촌, ch'on, (village).

중복 자음들(Duplicated Consonants) 혹은 된시옷(ㅅ)과 결합된 자음들

ㄲ 혹은 ㅅㄱ = g, 〈예〉 꽃, gôt, (flower).

ㅃ 혹은 ㅅㅂ = b, 〈예〉 뼈, byŭ, (bone).

ㅆ = s 혹은 거의 z, 〈예〉 썩다, sûkta, (to rot, or decay).

ㄸ 혹은 ㅅㄷ = d, 〈예〉 따리다, därida, (to strike, beat).

ㅉ 혹은 ㅅㅈ = j, 〈예〉 쫓다, jôtta, (to drive away).

단순자음의 발음은 단어 안에서의 위치에 따라 달라진다. 자음이 첫 소리로 올 때나 한 단어의 중간에서 다른 자음과 중복해서 나올 때, 다음과 같이 발음된다.

첫 소리에 오는 자음들 혹은 중간에 중복해서 나오는 자음들

ㄱ = k, 〈예〉 갑시, käpsi, (price); 각각 käk-käk, (each).

ㅁ = m, 〈예〉 맛, mät (taste); 암만 ämmän, (in whatever way).

ㄴ = n, l 혹은 y, 〈예〉 내가, nägä, (I); 손님, sôn nim (guest).

　　ㄴ이 단어 중간에서 ㄹ과 중복해서 나올 경우 둘 다 l이 된다.

　　〈예〉 본릭, pôllă, (originally)

ㄴ은 때로 y가 되거나 거의 묵음이 된다. 〈예〉 니, yi, (tooth).

ㄹ = l, n, 혹은 무음, 〈예〉 릭일, năil, (tomorrow).

    ㄹ이 단어 중간에서 ㄴ과 중복해서 나올 경우 1로 발음된다.

    〈예〉 위에 나온 본릭, pôllă, (originally)

    ㄹ은 y와 결합된 자음들 앞에서는 거의 묵음이 된다.

    〈예〉 as 룡, yông, (dragon).

ㅂ = p, 〈예〉 발, päl, (the foot); 입병, ïp pyûng, (disease of the mouth).

ㅅ = s, 때로는 거의 sh에 가까운 소리 〈예〉 신 sĭn, (shoe); 잇소, ïsso, (to be).

ㄷ = t, 〈예〉 돈, ton, (money); 맛당ᄒ다, mättanghada, (to be necessary).

ㅈ = ch, 〈예〉 자다, chädä, (to sleep).

ㅇ = 묵음으로서 모음들의 조성을 도움. '으힝'이라고 불린다.

단순자음들이 단어 중간에서 [다른 자음과 중복되지 않고] 혼자 쓰일 때 다음과 같이 발음된다.

중간에 단독으로 나오는 자음들

ㄱ = g, 〈예〉 먹엇다, mŭgŭttä (ate).

    혹은 ㅁ이나 ㄴ 소리 앞에서 ng가 된다.

    〈예〉 칙망ᄒ다, chăng mäng häda, (to reprove); 넉넉ᄒ오, nŭng nŭk
        häo (enough).

ㅁ = m, 〈예〉 아마, ämä, (perhaps).

    혹은 ㄱ 소리 앞에서 ng가 된다. 〈예〉 님금, inggeum, (king).

ㄴ = n, 〈예〉 안히 änhă, (wife).

    혹은 ㄱ 소리 앞에서 ng가 된다. 〈예〉 반갑다, pänggäptä (to be glad).

ㄹ = l, 〈예〉 울다, ōolta, (to cry).

혹은 두 모음 사이에서 r이 된다. 〈예〉 우리, ōorï, (our).

ㅂ = p, 〈예〉 합ㅎ다, häp hädä, (to agree, to suit).

혹은 두 모음 사이에서 b가 된다 〈예〉 보비, pōbă, (treasure).

ㄴ 앞에서는 m 소리를 취한다. 〈예〉 읍니, eumnă, (the official town of a district).

ㅅ = s, 〈예〉 다시, täsï, (again).

혹은 ㄴ과 ㅁ 앞에서 n이 된다.

〈예〉 믿는, minnan, (believing); 갓모, känmo, (hat-cover).

ㅂ 앞에서는 ㅂ이 된다. 〈예〉 깃부다, kippuda, (happy).

ㄱ 앞에서는 ㄱ이 된다. 〈예〉 갓갑다, kakkapta, (near).

ㄷ = t, 〈예〉 업다, ûpta, (to be gone, not to be).

혹은 두 모음 사이에서 d가 된다.

〈예〉 신둙, gädälk, (reason, cause); ㅎ다, hädä, (to do).

ㅈ = j, 〈예〉 미쟝이 mïjăngï, (a plasterer).

ㅇ = ng, 〈예〉 링수, nängsōo, (fresh water).

자음이 단어 끝에 올 때는 다음과 같이 발음된다.

단어 끝에 오는 자음들

ㄱ = k, 〈예〉 벽, pyŭk, (a wall).

ㅁ = m, 〈예〉 몸, môm, (body).

ㄴ = n, 〈예〉 산, sän, (a mountain).

ㄹ = l, 〈예〉 일, ïl, (work).

ㅂ = p, 〈예〉 손톱 sôn t'ŏp, (finger-nail).

ㅅ = t, 〈예〉 밧, pät, (a field).

ㅇ = ng, 〈예〉 상, säng, (a table).

자음에 관한 주의점

ㄷ과 ㅌ은 뒤에 y가 오거나 y로 시작하는 복합음이 오면 ch와 ch'가 된다. 처음에 오는 자음들은 음운의 중복으로 겹자음(reduplication)이 된다.

한국인들은 k와 g, l과 r, p와 b, t와 d, ch, j, ng을 영어에서처럼 분명히 구별하여 발음하지 않는다. 한국인이 ㄱ을 발음하면 우리에게는 종종 k와 g의 중간음처럼 들린다. 단어 중간에 오는 ㄹ은 흔히 r과 비슷하다. ㅂ은 p로도 b로도 들린다. ㄷ은 t와 d에, ㅈ은 ch와 j에 걸쳐있다. 그리고 어떤 단어들에서 ㅇ의 ng음은 거의 들리지 않는다.

한국어 음운 중에서 선생님과 함께 가장 꾸준히 연습해야 하며 외국인이 가장 습득하기 어려운 것은 모음 4, 10, 12번째,[6] 그리고 격음과 중복자음들이다.

제일 먼저 거쳐야 할 단계는 이 발음표를 꼼꼼하게 공부해서 발음상의 중대한 실수를 하지 않도록 주의하는 것이다. 가령 죠션(Cho sŭn, Korea)의 두 번째 음절을 amen의 두 번째 음절처럼 '조슨'이라고 발음한다든지, 약방(yäk päng, medicine room)을 작상(Jack sang)이라고 발음하는 것처럼 말이다.

다음

다음은 선생님과 함께 학습을 해나가는 데 도움이 될 만한 몇 가지 점들이

---

[6] 앞 절의 내용에 따르면 이들은 각기 ㅡ, ㅚ, ㅢ에 해당한다.

다. 우선 선생님을 'you'라고 부르거나 선생님에 대해서 '그'라고 말하지 말고 그의 이름으로 불러야 한다. 혹은 선생님이 당신과 별로 나이 차이가 나지 않는다면 김셔방(Kǐm sŭbäng), 고셔방(Kō sŭbäng), 뎡셔방(Chǔng sŭbäng) 같은 식으로 불러도 좋다. 선생님이 당신보다 훨씬 나이가 많다면 '선생'으로 부르거나 호칭해야 하는데, 이 단어는 문자 그대로 '먼저 태어난'이라는 뜻을 갖지만 영어의 'teacher'라는 단어에 상응하는 용법을 지닌다. 만약 그에게 직위가 있다면 홍장로(Hong Chang No) 혹은 셔초시(Sǔ Ch'ō Si)처럼 그 직위로 부르는 게 좋다.

선생님이 아침에 온다면 "평안히 줌으셨소?"("Have you slept peacefully?")라고 여쭤보며 인사하는 것이 정중하다.

선생님께 의자를 내밀며, "안지시오."("Please be seated.")라고 권한다.

선생님이 집을 떠날 때 "평안히 가시오."("Go in peace.")라고 인사한다. 선생님은 분명 당신에게 답례로 "평안히 계시오."("Remain in peace.")라고 인사할 것이다.

다음의 짧은 단어와 구절 목록은 당신이 처음 [한국어를 배울 때] 쓸 수 있는 것들이다.

이, this, (ï)　　　　　　　　이것, this thing, (ï gǔt).
그, that, (keu)　　　　　　　그것, that thing, (keu gǔt).
이러케, this way, (ï rǔ k'ě).　　그러케, that way, (keu rǔ k'ě).

이것 무엇이오, What is this thing? (ï gǔn moo ǔ sī ō).
이말 무엇이오, What is this word? (ï mäl moo ǔ sī ō).

지금말[7]이오, It is present talk, or tense. (chǐ keǔm mäl ï ō). 이것과 다음

구절들은 단지 문장 끝을 올려서 발음하면 의문문으로 바뀔 수 있다.

전말이오 It is past talk; or, Is it past talk? (chŭn mäl ï ō).

후말이오 It is future talk; or, Is it future talk? (hoo mäl ï ō).

시제들은 또한 다음과 같이 표현된다.

현지, Present,

과거, Past,

미래, Future.

노즌말이오 It is low talk ; or, Is it .low talk? (nä chan mäl ï ō).

가온듸말이오 It is middle talk; or, Is it middle talk? (kä ōn dǎ mäl ï ō).

놉흔말8)이오 It is high talk; or, Is it high talk? (nōp heun mäl ï ō).

뭇는말이오 It is question talk ; or, Is it question talk? (moon nän mäl ï ō).

쏙ᄀᆺ소 They are just alike ; or, Are they just alike? (dok käs sō).

흔히ᄒᆞᄂᆫ말이오 It is a word often used; or, Is it a word often used? (heun ï hä nän mäl ï ō).

쓸듸잇소 It is useful; or, Is it useful? (seul tǎ ïs sō).

쓸듸업소 It is useless; or, Is it useless? (seul tǎ ûp sō).

ᄀᆺ흔말무엇이오 What is a similar word? (kät heun mäl moo ŭ sï ō).

모로겟소 I don't know, (mō ro ges so).

알수업소 I don't know, (äl soo ûp so).

---

7) 지금말, 전말, 후말은 각기 현재, 과거, 미래 시제를 뜻하며, 이후의 설명에서는 현재, 과거, 미래로 통일하여 번역하였다.

8) 노즌말, 가온듸말, 놉흔말은 오늘날 낮춤말, 예삿말, 높임말에 해당하며, 이후의 설명에서는 각기 낮은말, 가운데말, 높은말로 통일하여 표기하였다.

예 or 네 Yes, (yě).

아니오 No, (ä nï ō).

국문 The native written character, (k$\overline{oo}$ng m$\overline{oo}$n).

한문 The Chinese written character, (hän m$\overline{oo}$n).

그만흡세다 Let us stop, (keu män häp sě dä).

이 구절들 중 시제 구분이나 가운데말 같은 몇 가지는 원래 한국어에는 없는 것을 외국인이 만들어낸 것이다. 그래서 경험 많은 선생님을 만나는 행운을 누리지 않는 한, 학생이 해야 할 첫 번째 임무는 선생님에게 어떻게 가르칠지를 가르치는 것이다.

명사의 격변화

어근(Root)	사름	person.
주격(Nominative)	사름이	the person.
도구격(Instrumental)	사름으로	by the person.
소유격(Genitive)	사름의	of the person.
여격(Dative)	사름에게	to the person.
목적격(Accusative)	사름을	the person.
호격(Vocative)	사름아	O person.
처소격(Locative)	사름에	to or in the person.

(그러나 처소격은 생물인 명사에는 사용되지 않는다.)

탈격(Ablative)	사름에셔 혹은 사람의게셔	from the person.
동격(Appositive)	사름은	as for the person.

위의 내용을 암기한 후 격변화의 끝부분을(endings)[9])을 다른 명사들, 예컨
대 물(horse), 갓 (hat), 밧(field), 나라(kingdom), 새(bird) 등에 적용해보도록 하
라. 이 과정에서 당신은 어근이 어떤 문자로 끝나느냐에 따라 끝부분의 형태
가 약간씩 변화함을 알게 될 것이다. 여격 '-의게'는 생물 명사를 제외하고는
흔히 쓰이지 않는다. 무생물의 경우 처소격이 더 선호되며, 탈격으로는 '-의게
셔'가 아닌 '-에셔'가 사용된다.

일상적 사물들의 명사 목록을 만들어서 외우도록 하라.

대명사

여기서는 대명사 나(I), 우리(we), 너(you), 누가(who), 제가(self or myself),
뎌가(he, she, or it)를 취해서 격변화를 시켜보자.

나(I)는 다음과 같이 격변화가 이뤄진다.

어근	나	
주격	내, 내가	I.
도구격	날노..........................	by me
소유격	내..........................	my.
여격	내게 혹은 내의게.........	to me.
목적격	날, 나를....................	me.
동격	나는..........................	as for me.

이 틀에 맞춰서 다른 명사들도 격변화를 시켜보고 당신이 한 것에 대해 항
상 선생님께 수정을 받도록 하라. 영어의 관계대명사 표현 방식에 대해서는

[9]) 이 문장에서 endings은 오늘날 한국어 문법에서 조사를 일컫는다.

도움말 43번을 보라. 인칭대명사에 대한 학습은 49번을 보라. 한국어는 대명사가 풍부하지 않으며, 어떤 생각을 표현하기 위해 반드시 필요한 경우가 아니면 가급적 대명사를 사용하지 않고 특히 1인칭을 잘 사용하지 않는다는 점에 주목하라.

동사
동사의 활용

가장 먼저 위대한 동사 'ᄒ다'에 대해 배울 터인데, 그것은 한국어 구조에서 매우 중요한 역할을 한다. 그 다음으로 두 번째와 세 번째로 중요한 '잇다'와 '업다'를 살펴본다.

계사(the copula) '일다'[10]도 매우 중요하다.

먼저 낮은말이라고 알려진, 아이들에게 사용되는 동사 형태를 살펴보자.

낮은말 (Low Form)[11]

ᄒ다, I Make, I Do.
직설법(Indicative)

현재......... ᄒ다.......... I, you, he, we, they, do or make.

과거......... ᄒ엿다....... I, you, etc. did or made.

미래......... ᄒ겟다....... I, you, etc. will do or make.

---

[10] 오늘날의 서술격 조사 '-이다'를 일컫는다.

[11] 오늘날에는 낮춤말, 예삿말, 높임말이라고 부르지만, 이 책의 표현에 따라 각기 낮은말, 가운데말, 높은말로 옮겼다.

명령법(Imperative)

ᄒᆞ여라....... make or do.

ᄒᆞ자......... let us make or do.

관계적 분사(Relative Participles)12)

현재......... ᄒᆞᄂᆞᆫ......... making, doing.

과거.......... ᄒᆞᆫ............ made, done.

미래.......... ᄒᆞᆯ........... to be made or done, about to be made or done.

미완......... ᄒᆞ던.......... made or was making, done or was doing.

완료......... ᄒᆞ엿던....... made, done.

동사적 분사(Verbal Participles)

ᄒᆞ여/ᄒᆞ야/ᄒᆞ여셔..... making, doing or having made or done.

동사적 명사(Verbal Nouns)

ᄒᆞ기.......... doing, making.

ᄒᆞᆷ.......... deed, action.

잇다 I am, HAVE. (도움말 45를 보라)

직설법

현재......... 잇다......... I, you, he, etc. am or have.

과거......... 잇섯다....... I, you, he, etc. was or had.

---

12) 이하의 한국어 문법 설명은 영어 문법의 체계에 따른 것이기에 현대 한국어 문법과 다른 부분이 많다. 예컨대, 여기서 관계적 분사와 동사적 분사로 직역한 용어들은 영어에서 분사구문의 한정적 용법과 서술적 용법에 해당하며, 현대 한국어 문법에서는 동사의 어미변화의 형태들로 설명된다.

미래......... 잇겟다....... I, you, he, etc. shall be or shall have.

명령법

잇서라/잇거라..... be or have.

잇자......... let us be or have.

관계적 분사

현재......... 잇는......... being or having.

과거......... 잇슨....... been or had.

미래........ 잇슬 .... about to be or have.

미완........ 잇던 .... been or had.

완료........ 잇섯던....... been or had.

동사적 분사

잇서/잇서셔..... having been or being.

동사적 명사

잇기.......... being.

잇슴.......... the being.

업다, I AM NOT, I HAVE NOT.

직설법

현재 ....업다.......... I, you, he, etc., have I not or am not.

과거 ....업섯다........ I, you, etc. had not or I was not.

미래 ....업겟다........ I, you, etc. shall not have or be.

명령법 .... 사용하지 않음

관계적 분사

현재.......... 업느.......... not having or being.

과거.......... 업슨.......... not had or been.

미래.......... 업슬.......... about not to have or be.

미완.......... 업던.......... not had or been.

완료.......... 업섯던....... not have or been.

동사적 분사

업서/업서셔..... not having, not being,

or not having had, or not having been.

동사적 명사

업기......... not being or having.

업슴......... the absence.

가운데말

다음으로 동년배들 사이에서나 더 낮은 지위의 성인에게 사용하는 형태가 있는데, 이들은 예삿말(friend talk) 혹은 가운데말(middle form)이라고 한다.

호다

직설법

현재.......... 호오.......... I, he, etc. make or do.

과거.......... ᄒᆞᆼ엿소........ I, you, he, etc, made or did.

미래.......... ᄒᆞᆼ겟소........ I, you, he, etc. shall make or do.

명령법

ᄒᆞ오.......... do or make.

잇소

직설법

현재.......... 잇소.......... I, you, etc. am or have.

과거.......... 잇섯소........ I, you, etc. was or had.

미래.......... 잇겟소........ I, you, etc. shall or will be have.

명령법

잇소.......... be.

업소

직설법

현재.......... 업소.......... I, you, etc. am not or have not.

과거.......... 업섯소....... I, you, etc. was not or have not.

미래.......... 업겟소........ I, you, etc. or shall not be or shall not have.

명령법 .... 사용하지 않음

높은말

다음은 연장자에 대해서나 동년배 사이에서 상당한 존경을 표시할 때 사용하는 형식이다.

하다

직설법

현재.......... 함닉다.......... I, you, etc. make or do.

과거.......... ᄒ엿습닉다.... I, you, etc. made or did.

미래.......... ᄒ겟습닉다.... I, you, etc. shall make or do

명령법

ᄒ시오.......... please do or make.

ᄒᆸ셰다.......... Let us do or make.

잇소

직설법

현재.......... 잇습닉다.......... I, you, etc. am or have.

과거.......... 잇섯습닉다....... I, you, etc. was or bad.

미래.......... 잇겟습닉다....... I, you, etc. shall be or have.

명령법

잇습셰다.......... Let us be.

업소

직설법

　현재......... 업슴니다......... I, you, etc. am not or have not.

　과거......... 업섯슴니다....... I, you, etc. was not or had not.

　미래......... 업겟슴니다....... I, you, etc. or shall not be or shall not have.

명령법 .... 사용되지 않음

아래는 이 세 가지 동사들의 낮은말, 가운데말, 높은말 형태의 의문형이다.

의문형

낮은말

　현재......... ᄒᆞᄂᆞ냐......... do I, you, etc. make or do?

　과거......... ᄒᆞ엿ᄂᆞ냐....... did or have I, you, etc. made or done?

　미래......... ᄒᆞ겟ᄂᆞ냐....... will I, you, etc. make or do?

가운데말의 의문문은 가운데말의 평서문과 형태가 같지만 문장 끝을 올려서 발음한다. 22쪽을 보라.[13]

높은말

　현재......... 홈ᄂᆞᆯ가......... do I, you, etc. do or make ?

　과거......... ᄒᆞ엿슴ᄂᆞᆯ가.... did or have I, you, etc. made or done.

　미래......... ᄒᆞ겟슴ᄂᆞᆯ가.... will I, you, etc. make or do ?

13) 원문 영인본의 쪽수를 의미한다. 이 책의 50-51쪽에 해당한다. (현재)ᄒᆞ오, (과거)ᄒᆞ엿소, (미래)ᄒᆞ겟소의 직설법 형태에 문장 끝의 억양만 올려서 의문문을 만든다는 뜻이다.

낮은말

    현재.......... 잇느냐.......... have I or am I ? you, etc

    과거.......... 잇섯느냐....... did I or was I, you, etc.

    미래.......... 잇겟느냐...... will be or have ?

높은말

    현재.......... 잇슴늬가

    과거.......... 잇섯슴늬가

    미래.......... 잇겟슴늬가

낮은말

    현재.......... 업느냐.......... have or am I not? etc.

    과거.......... 업섯느냐....... have, I , you, etc. not had or been?

    미래.......... 업겟느냐....... will I, you, etc. not have or be?

높은말

    현재.......... 업슴늬가

    과거.......... 업섯슴늬가

    미래.......... 업겟슴늬가

일다 I am. (도움말 45번을 보시오.)

직설법

낮은말

    현재.......... 이다 혹은 일다, I, you, he, etc. am.

    과거.......... 이엿다

미래.......... 이겟다

가운데말
현재.......... 이오
과거.......... 이엿소
미래.......... 이겟소

높은말
현재.......... 임늬다 혹은 이올세다
과거.......... 이엿슴늬다
미래.......... 이겟슴늬다

관계적 분사
현재.......... 인.......... being.
미래.......... 일.......... about to be.

동사적 분사
　　　　이라......... being.

동사적 명사
　　　　이기.......... being.
　　　　임 .... the being.

의문문
낮은말.......... 이냐.......... Am I, you, he, etc.?

가운데말........ 이오

높은말.......... 임ᄂᆡ가 혹은 이오니가

직설법 부정

낮은말.......... 아니다 혹은 아닐다 I. you, he, etc. am not.

가운데말....... 아니오

높은말.......... 아님ᄂᆡ다

의문문 부정

낮은말.......... 아니냐 Am I, you, he, etc. not ?

가운데말....... 아니오

높은말.......... 아님ᄂᆡ가 혹은 아니오니가

일다(이오)는 서술형 명사와 함께 사용되는 계사(copula)다. 명령법을 포함한 몇 가지 문장 형식으로는 쓰이지 않으며 현존하는 문장 형식들 중 일부도 거의 사용되지 않는다.

동작동사들 (Active Verbs)

한국어의 동사들은 동작동사와 형용사적 동사라는 두 부류로 나뉜다. 첫번째 부류는 영어에서 계사인 be를 제외한 동사 단어들 전체에 해당된다. 다음의 동작동사들 목록을 암기하도록 하라. 이들은 암기하는 데 도움이 되는 집합들로 배열되어 있으며, 대개 위에 제시한 모델들에 따라 활용된다.

형용사적 동사들에 대해서는 33쪽에 나온다.[14]

14) 원문 영인본의 쪽수를 의미한다. 이 책의 62쪽에 해당한다.

동작동사 목록

Make, do............... 항다

Go........................ 가다

Come..................... 오다

Walk..................... 거러가다

Run...................... 다라나다

Stand.................... 서다

Crawl.................... 긔여가다

Fly....................... 늘아가다

Swim.................... 헤염치다

Mount, or Ride........ 투다

Sleep.................... 자다

Dream.................. 숨쉬다

Wake................... 씌다

Rise..................... 니러나다

Sit...................... 안다

See...................... 보다

Hear.................... 듯다

Taste................... 맛보다

Smell................... 맛하보다

Touch..................... 문져보다

Talk...................... 말ㅎ다

Eat....................... 먹다

Drink..................... 마시다

Tell...................... 고ㅎ다

Think..................... 싱각ㅎ다

Wonder at................. 이상히녁이다

Laugh..................... 웃다

Cry....................... 울다

Shout..................... 소리지르다

Whisper................... 숙은숙은ㅎ다

Warn...................... 경계ㅎ다

Exhort.................... 권면ㅎ다

Chase..................... 쫏차내다

Drive .... 몰아가다

Lead...................... 인도ㅎ다

Follow.................... 쓰라가다

Push...................... 밀다

Pull...................... 잡아다리다

To be damaged......... 샹ᄒ다

Kill...................... 죽이다

To be born............ 낫다

To live.................. 사다

Marry................... 혼인ᄒ다

Die....................... 죽다

Bury..................... 장ᄉᄒ다

Come out............... 나오다

Come in................ 드러오다

Go out.................. 나가다

Go in.................... 드러가다

Go up................... 올나가다

Godown................ ᄂ려가다

Buy...................... 사다

Sell...................... 팔다

Sew...................... 바ᄂ질ᄒ다

Wash.................... 쌜ᄂᄒ다

Iron .... 다림질ᄒ다

Inquire.................. 무러보다

Answer..................... 딕답ᄒ다

Get......................... 엇다

Ask for.................... 구ᄒ다

Borrow................... 빌다

Steal....................... 도적질ᄒ다

Earn....................... 벌다

Give....................... 주다

Receive................... 밧다

Try.......................... ᄒ여보다

Fail.......................... 못ᄒ다

To feel with the hand.. 어르ᄆ지다

Strike....................... 싸리다

Forget...................... 니져ᄇ리다

Remember................ 긔억ᄒ다

Throw away............... 내여ᄇ리다

Lose......................... 일허ᄇ리다

Find or seek for.......... 찻다

Conquer................... 이긔다

Be beaten................. 지다

To be dry................. 므르다

To rot..................... 썩다

To shut................... 닷다

To open.................. 열다

Grow...................... 자라다

Bloom..................... 픠다

Fade or wither.......... 스러지다

Ripen...................... 닉다

Know...................... 안다(알다)

Not know................. 모르다

Perceive.................. 씨닷다

Guess..................... 짐쟉ᄒ다

Bring...................... 가져오다

Take...................... 가져가다

Send...................... 보내다

Await..................... 기드리다

Prepare for............. 예비ᄒ다

Welcome................. 딕졉ᄒ다

형용사적 동사들

형용사적 동사는 영어에서 서술적 형용사들과 계사 is로 표현하는 것에 해당된다. 이들은 형태상 동사와 닮았지만 그것이 표현하는 관념은 형용사적이다. 예를 들어 '됴타'는 "It is good"을 의미하며 다음과 같이 활용된다.

직설법

현재.......... 됴타.......... I, he, she, etc. am good.

과거.......... 됴핫다....... I, you, he, etc. was good.

미래.......... 됴켓다....... I, you, he, etc. shall be good.

동사적 분사

됴하......... good.

관계적 분사

현재/과거.... 됴흔.......... good.

미래.......... 됴흘.......... good.

형용사적 동사의 또 다른 예는 '넉넉ᄒ다'인데, "It is enough."라는 뜻이다. 형용사적 동사에 쓰이는 'ᄒ다'는 "to make, or do"를 뜻하는 동사와는 달리 "is"를 뜻하는 계사다. 그 활용은 여러 문장형식에서 'ᄒ다'와 다르다. 다음의 평서문 현재형을 19, 23, 24, 25쪽[15]과 비교해보라.

---

15) 원문 영인본의 쪽수를 의미한다. 이 책의 47, 51, 52, 53쪽에 걸쳐 나오는 동사 '하다'의 활용 부분에 해당한다.

직설법

    낮은말.......... 넉넉ㅎ다.......... It is enough.

    가운데말....... 넉넉ㅎ오

    높은말.......... 넉넉ㅎ닏다 혹은 ㅎ올세다 혹은 ㅎ외다.

의문문

    낮은말.......... 넉넉ㅎ냐.......... Is it enough?

    가운데말....... 넉넉ㅎ오

    높은말.......... 넉넉ㅎ닏가 혹은 ㅎ오니가

명령법.................... 사용하지 않음

관계적 분사

    현재/과거..... 넉넉흔.......... Sufficient.

    미래.......... 넉넉흘.......... Sufficient.

형용사적 동사들은 낮은말, 가운데말, 높은말, 의문문 등 모든 형태로 활용된다. 아래에 제시된 목록에서 몇 가지를 선택해서 활용하는 연습을 해보는 것이 좋을 것이다. 이 때 선생님께 꼭 수정을 받아라. 또 동작 동사와 형용사적 동사에서 어미 형태의 미묘하지만 중요한 차이들을 주의 깊게 눈여겨보라.

자주 사용되는 형용사적 동사

Little............... 작다

Big.................. 크다

Flat................ 납작ᄒ다

Round............ 둥그럽다

Thin................ 얇다

Thick............. 두겁다

Long............... 길다

Broad.............. 넓다

Narrow............. 좁다

Tall.................. 키크다

Short .... 잛다

Pretty .... 묘ᄒ다

Ugly................. 흉ᄒ다

Sweet............... 들다

Sour................. 싀다

Bitter............... 쓰다

Sharp............... 밉다

Hot................... 덥다

Cold................. 차다

Lukewarm.......... 미지근ᄒ다

Sick.................... 압흐다
Well.................... 셩흐다

Dull, (as a knife) 무지다
Sharp................. 날카롭다

Blunt.................. 둔흐다
Pointed.............. 섇족흐다

Full.................... ᄀ득흐다
Empty................ 뷔다

Bright................ 빗최다
Dark.................. 어둡다

Black.................. 검다
White.................. 희다

Old..................... 늙다
Young................. 졂다

Old..................... 묵다
New.................... 새롭다

Beautiful............. 아름답다
Hateful.............. 밉다

False................... 거짓되다
True.................... 춤되다

Fierce................. 사오납다
Gentle................. 슌ᄒ다

Right.................. 올타
Wrong................. 그르다

Good.................. 착ᄒ다
Bad.................... 악ᄒ다

Ignorant.............. 무식ᄒ다
Learned.............. 유식ᄒ다

Wise.................. 지혜롭다
Foolish.............. 어리셕다

Early................. 일다
Late.................. 늣다

Near................. 갓갑다
Far.................. 멀다

High................. 놉다

Low...................... 늦다

Sorry.................... 섭섭ᄒ다
Glad...................... 반갑다
Grateful................ 감샤ᄒ다

Cheap................... 헐ᄒ다
Dear..................... 빗사다

Few...................... 적다
Many.................... 만타

Easy..................... 쉽다
Difficult................ 어렵다
Peaceful.............. 평안ᄒ다
Agitated............... 답답ᄒ다

Clean................... 졍ᄒ다
Dirty.................... 더럽다

Weak................... 약ᄒ다
Strong................. 강ᄒ다

Deep.................... 깁다
Shallow............... 엿다

Useful................. 유익ᄒ다
Useless............... 무익ᄒ다

busy.................. 분주ᄒ다
Idle..................... 한가ᄒ다

Slow.................... 쓰다
Fast..................... 날내다

Heavy................. 무겁다
Light.................... 가ᄇ얍다

Soft..................... 부드럽다
Hard.................... 든든ᄒ다

Deficient.............. 부죡ᄒ다
Enough................ 넉넉ᄒ다

부사들
형용사적 동사들로 만든 부사들

이 부사들은 대개의 경우 [형용사적] 동사의 어근에 '-게'라는 음절을 붙여서 형성될 수 있다.

작게......... Little.

크게.......... Greatly.

묘흐게........ Prettily 등.

많은 형용사적 동사들은 '-히'라는 부사적 형태를 취할 수 있다.

슌히.......... Gently.

온젼히....... Entirely.

갓가히....... Near 등.

그밖의 부사 목록

자주 사용되는 몇 가지 부사들은 다음과 같다.

엇지/엇지흐여/엇더케... How.

이러케.......... Thus, this way.

그러케.......... That way.

얼는/어셔/속이/밧비... Quickly, at once.

몃/얼마....... How much? How many.

얼마나.......... About how much?

여러.............. Several.

더러.............. Some.

미우/대단히... Much, very

그만............. Enough.

만/샨.......... Only.

잘............. Well.

다/모도....... All.

너무......... Too much, too.

더............ More.

덜............ Less.

쏘흔/쏘..... And, again, still more.

도.......... Also, too.

더욱....... So much the more.

조곰....... A little.

아마....... Perhaps.

혹.......... Possibly.

웨.......... Why.

어듸........ Where.

언제........ When.

우연이..... Unexpectedly.

홈씌/흔가지로/한썹에.. Together, all at once.

처럼.......... Like.

곳치.......... Like, the same as.

별노/거반... Almost altogether, nearly.

부러/일부러/짐짓.. On purpose, purposely.

블가불........ Of necessity.

미상불........ Probably.

스스로/ᄌ연이/절노.. Naturally, of itself.

ᄎᄎ......... Little by little.

아까......... Just now, a moment ago.

아직......... As yet.

어느째....... When? What time?

임의/발셔... Already.

일싱/홍샹/늘.. Always.

이째......... This time.

그째/뎌째... That time.

잇다가....... Presently, in a moment.

오래......... Long.

요ᄉ이....... These days.

각금/자조... Often.

즉시/곳...... Immediately.

뭇춤내/ᄆ지막... Finally.

미리......... In advance.

몬져......... At first.

나종에....... At last.

시방/지금... Now.

쉬이......... Soon.

다시......... Again, once more.

도로......... Back.

잠깐.......... For a moment.

다음에....... After.

이리/여긔... Here.

거긔/뎌긔... There, yonder.

후치사들(postpositions)[16]

다음은 후치사들의 목록이다. 이들은 영어에서처럼 명사 앞에 오는 게 아니라 명사 뒤에 오기 때문에 후치사라고 불린다.

밋헤.......... Under.

우헤.......... Over, or on top of.

뒤헤.......... Behind.

압헤.......... In front of.

녑헤.......... At the side of.

아래에....... Below.

신지.......... To, until.

부터.......... From, beginning with.

즁에/가온듸... In the middle of, between.

---

16) 오늘날 영어의 postposition은 한국어의 조사에 해당한다. 영어에는 조사가 없으므로 영어의 전치사에 대비하여 명사 뒤에 오는 조사를 후치사(postposition)라고 쓴 것이다. 그러나 여기서 언급되는 후치사는 영어 전치사의 한국어 번역 어휘들로, 현대 한국어 문법에서는 명사+조사(밑에, 위에 등)나 조사(-까지, -부터 등)로 설명되는 표현들이 뒤섞여 있다.

안으로....... Into.

안혜/속에.... Inside.

업시.......... Without.

인ᄒ여....... On account of.

위ᄒ여....... For the sake of.

외에/밧긔... Outside.

끼리.......... Between. 〈예〉 우리끼리 (between us).

건너.......... Across.

딕신.......... Instead of.

후에.......... After. 〈예〉 이후에 (after this).

젼에.......... Before. 〈예〉 이젼에 (before this).

동안에........ During.

만에.......... After.

대로.......... According to. 〈예〉 ᄆᆞᆷ대로 (just as you please).

ᄃᆞ려/더러.... To, as to speak to a person.

이 단어들을 완벽하게 외워야 한다.

이 예비단계를 거쳐 이제 문장 만들기를 시작해보자.

1. 홀수잇소[할 수 있소][17]

이 문장은 '흐다'의 미래시제 관계적 분사 '홀'이 '수단'(means)을 의미하는

[17) 여기서부터 이 책의 제목이 가리키는 50가지 도움말(Fifty Helps)이 시작된다. 원문에 띄어 쓰기가 없어 가독성이 떨어지기에, 도움말 50개의 표제어와 긴 예문들의 경우 [ ] 안에 현 대어 표기를 병기하였다.

명사인 '수'를 수식하고, 동사 '잇다'와 결합하여 구성되었다. 19쪽과 20쪽[18]을 보라. 이는 문자 그대로는 "Doing means are"을 뜻하며 영어 표현으로는 "It can be done"에 상응한다. 부정문의 형태는 다음과 같다.

홀수업소 It cannot be done.

이 두 가지 형태를 취하여 현재, 과거, 미래와 낮은말, 가운데말, 높은말(15쪽을 보라[19]), 그리고 의문문의 모든 변형을 연습해 보라. 선생님이 올바른 형태와 발음을 알려줄 것이다.

그 변형들은 다음과 같을 것이다.

낮은말
　현재..... 홀수잇다
　　　　　홀수업다
　과거..... 홀수잇섯다
　　　　　홀수업섯다
　미래..... 홀수잇겟다
　　　　　홀수업겟다

가운데말
　현재..... 홀수잇소
　　　　　홀수업소
　과거..... 홀수잇섯소

---

18) 원문 영인본의 쪽수를 의미한다. 이 책의 47, 48쪽에 해당한다.
19) 원문 영인본의 쪽수를 의미한다. 이 책의 44쪽에 나오는 높은말, 가운데말, 낮은말에 대한 설명에 해당한다.

　　　　　홀수업섯소
미래..... 홀수잇겟소
　　　　　홀수업겟소

높은말
　현재..... 홀수잇습니다
　　　　　 홀수업습니다
　과거..... 홀수잇섯습니다
　　　　　 홀수업섯습니다
　미래..... 홀수잇겟습니다
　　　　　 홀수업겟습니다

의문문의 낮은말, 가운데말, 높은말, 과거, 현재, 미래는 다음과 같다.

낮은말
　현재..... 홀수잇느냐
　　　　　 홀수업느냐
　과거..... 홀수잇섯느냐
　　　　　 홀수업섯느냐
　미래..... 홀수잇겟느냐
　　　　　 홀수업겟느냐

가운데말
　현재..... 홀수잇소
　　　　　 홀수업소

과거..... 홀수잇섯소
　　　　홀수업섯소
미래..... 홀수잇겟소
　　　　홀수업겟소

높은말
현재..... 홀수잇습늬가
　　　　홀수업습늬가
과거..... 홀수잇섯습늬가
　　　　홀수업섯습늬가
미래..... 홀수잇겟습늬가
　　　　홀수업겟습늬가

이 과정을 가다, 보다, 먹다와 같은 다른 동작 동사들로도 계속 연습해보라.

갈수잇소, I can go.
볼수업소, I can not see.
먹을수업소, I can not eat. 등등

[이런 연습을 통해] 학습자는 자신이 단지 두 가지 형태들[홀수잇소, 홀수업소]만이 아니라 자신이 알고 있는 모든 동작동사들의 수만큼 많은 형태들을 습득했으며, 이런 과정이 이 책에 제시된 모든 연습에서도 마찬가지임을 알게 될 것이다.

한국어에서 대명사들은 드물게 사용되며, 복수형도 의미상 반드시 필요한 경우에만 사용되기에, 이 구문들은 인칭과 성별, 수에 상관없이 모두 통용된다. 예컨대 '갈수업소'는 내가, 너가, 그가, 그녀가, 그들이, 우리가, 그것이 갈 수 없다는 뜻을 포함하며, '올수잇소'도 내가, 너가, 그가, 그녀가, 그들이, 우리가, 그것이 올 수 있다는 의미를 나타낸다. 한국인들은 보통 [대명사를 사용하지 않고] 발화의 맥락에 의지하여 의미를 한정하는데, 우리가 언뜻 생각하는 것과는 달리, 결과적으로 뜻이 모호해지는 경우는 별로 없다.

한국어 문장에서 불변하는 구조에 주목해보라. 우선 주어가 나올 경우 수식어는 그 앞에 붙는다. 그리고 목적어가 있는 경우에는 주어 뒤에 목적어가 나오고 수식어는 그 앞에 붙는다. 마지막으로 동사가 나온다. 예를 들어,

이젼에보지못흔사름이나를잘되졉ㅎ엿소.
[전에 보지 못한 사람이 나를 잘 대접하였소.]

"A person whom I never saw before welcomed me well."
문자 그대로는
"This before not seen person me well has welcomed."

선생님과 사전, 다른 교과서나 그 밖의 이용가능한 정보원들, 예컨대 당신의 하인이나 방문객, 친구들의 도움을 받아, 다음과 같은 표현들을 포함한 짧은 문장 10개를 만들어 보라.

칙볼수업소 [책을 볼 수 없소.]
I can not see, or read the book.

죠션밥먹을수없소 [조선 밥을 먹을 수 없소.]
He cannot eat Korean food.

릭일갈수없는냐 [내일 갈 수 없느냐?]

Can you not go tomorrow? 등등.

천천히 말하면서 당신이 배운 바를 즉각적으로 사용해보도록 하라. 교과서를 가지고 씨름하는 시간보다 많은, 훨씬 많은 시간을 이런 연습에 사용하라.

2. 홀수밧긔업소[할 수밖에 없소]

문자 그대로는 "Doing means beside are not"이며, 영어의 관용표현으로는 "Nothing else can be done."에 해당한다.

이 표현에서 '홀' 대신에 '갈'을 사용하면 '갈수밧긔업소'[갈 수밖에 없소]가 된다.

주어에 따라 내가, 너가, 그가, 그녀가, 그들이, 그것이 '갈 수 밖에 없다'를 뜻한다.

[어근을] '볼'로 대체하면 '볼수밧긔업소'[볼 수밖에 없소]가 된다. 내가, 너가, 그가... 등이 '볼 수밖에 없다'는 뜻이다. 당신이 알고 있는 다른 동사들의 미래시제 분사를 사용하여 현재, 과거, 미래 시제, 낮은말, 가운데말, 높은말, 의문문을 연습해 보라.

이 표현을 표함하는 10개의 짧은 문장을 만들어 보라. 예컨대,

집에갈수밧긔업소 [집에 갈 수밖에 없소.]

I, he, she, etc., cannot but go to the house.

날이더울수밧긔업소 [날이 더울 수밖에 없소.]

The day cannot but be warm. 등등.

3. ᄒᆞ여라

ᄒᆞ여라
Make, or do.

보아라
Look, or see.

가거라
Go.

이는 아이나 하인들이게 사용하는 낮은말 형태의 명령문이다. 당신 자신을 포함하여 말하고자 할 때는 형태가 이렇게 변한다.

ᄒᆞ자
Let us do, or make.

보자
Let us see.

가자
Let us go. 등등.

하인에게 지시를 내릴 때 좀더 높여 말하려면 '-ᄒᆞ게', 혹은 좀더 높여서 'ᄒᆞ오'라고 말한다. 예를 들어,

아기잘보게[아기 잘 보게.]
Watch the baby well.

돈가져오[돈 가져 오시오.]
Bring the money.

당신이 봉사하는 모임의 기독교인들과 대화할 때는 가운데말, 혹은 종종 예삿말이라고 불리는 형태를 사용하는 게 훨씬 더 좋다.

선생님이나 혹은 동급의 사람들에게 지시할 때는 'ᄒ시오'[하시오]라고 말하라. 예컨대,

그러케ᄒ시오[그렇게 하시오.]
Please do so.

사름보내시오[사람 보내시오.]
Please send a man.

일즉오시오[일찍 오시오.]
Please come early.

당신 자신을 포함할 때는 다음과 같이 말한다.

그러캐ᄒᆸ세다[그렇게 합시다.]
Let us do so.

사름보냅세대[사람 보냅시다.]

Let us send a man.

공부홉세대[공부 합시다.]

Let us study.

앞에서와 같이 문장들을 만들어 보라.

4. 흥지마라[하지 마라]

흥지마라

Do not do.

'-지마라'를 취하여 '가오'라는 동사의 어근에 결합하면, 다음과 같다.

가지마라

Do not go.

이번에는 '보다'라는 동사의 어근에 결합하면

보지마라

Do not look.

선생님의 도움을 받아 가운데말과 높은말 형태로도 연습해 보고, 다음과 같이 다른 문장들도 만들어 보라.

오래잇지마오[오래 있지 마오.]
Do not stay long.

거즛말밋지마시오[거짓말 믿지 마시오.]
Do not believe false talk.

5. ᄒ지못ᄒ오

ᄒ지못ᄒ오[하지 못하오.]
I, he, she or it, cannot do or make.

ᄒ지아니ᄒ오[하지 아니하오.]
I, he, she or it, do (does) not do or make.

전자는 할 수 없음을 표현할 때 쓴다. 후자는 단순한 부정이나 할 의지가 없음을 표현한다.

'-지못ᄒ오'와 '-지아니ᄒ오'는 도움말 4번에서처럼 어떤 동사의 어근에도 덧붙일 수 있다.

먹지못ᄒ오[먹지 못하오.]
I, you, he, it, cannot eat.

먹지아니ᄒ오[먹지 아니하오.]
I, you, he, it, do (does) not eat.

됴치못ᄒ오/됴치아니ᄒ오[좋지 못하오/좋지 아니하오.]
It is not good.

'-지안소'는 '-지아니ᄒ오'의 흔히 사용하는 축약어이고, '-치안소'는 '-치아니
ᄒ오'의 축약어다.

멀지안소[멀지 않소.]
It is not far.

깁지안소[깊지 않소.]
It is not deep.

됴치안소[좋지 않소.]
It is not good. 등등.

학습자는 문자보다는 소리에 익숙해지는 것이 더 유리하다. 그렇기 때문에
처음에는 쓰는 연습을 너무 많이 하지 않는 것이 좋다. 문장들을 암기하고 가
능한 빠른 속도로 암송하는 것이 훨씬 더 낫다.

복습을 자주 하고, 여기에 제시된 학습 방법을 당신에게 유용한 어떤 방식
으로든 변형해보라. 이것들은 단지 학습을 위한 제안에 불과함을 기억하라.
그러나 [여기 제시된 것처럼] 기본 문장들을 모든 형태로 변화시켜보는 연습
을 빠트리지 말라. 이것보다 더 좋은 연습 방법은 없다. 92쪽[20]에 나오는 종
교 용어들의 짧은 어휘 목록과 이 책에 제시된 다른 단어들이 이런 목적을
위해 도움이 될 것이다. 당신이 매일매일 배운 단어들과 용어들을 사용하라.

[20] 원문 영인본의 쪽수를 의미한다. 이 책의 121쪽부터 나온다.

6. 홀ᄆ음잇소[할 마음 있소]

홀ᄆ음잇소
Doing mind is.

홀ᄆ음업소
Doing mind is not.

위 문장들은 영어에서 "I have a mind to do (thus or so)"와 "I have no mind to do (thus or so)."라는 관용어구에 해당한다.
이 유용한 형태는 쉽게 적용될 수 있다.

졀에올나갈ᄆ음잇소[절에 올라갈 마음이 있소.]
I have a mind to go up to the (Buddhist) temple.

ᄒ여볼ᄆ음업소[해볼 마음이 없소.]
I have no mind to try.

동싱도아줄ᄆ음업ᄂ냐[동생을 도와줄 마음이 없느냐?]
Have you no mind to help your younger brother?

7. ᄒ고시브오[하고 싶으오]

ᄒ고시브오[하고 싶으오.]
I, you, we, etc., wish to do.

ㅎ기실소[하기 싫소.]
I, you, we, etc., do not wish to do.

적용들.

집구경ㅎ고시브오[집구경 하고 싶으오.]
We wish to see your house.

머리싹기슬태[머리 깎기 싫다.]
He does not want to cut his hair.

쟝에가고시브냐[장에 가고 싶으냐?]
Do you want to go to the fair ?

8. ㅎ기쉽소[하기 쉽소]

ㅎ기쉽소[하기 쉽소.]
Doing is easy.

ㅎ기어렵소[하기 어렵소.]
Doing is hard.

관용 표현으로 "It is easy to do"와 "It is hard to do."에 해당한다.

잘못ᄒ기쉽대[잘못 하기 쉽다.]
Wrong doing is easy.

약먹기어렵소[약을 먹기 어렵소.]
Eating medicine is difficult, or as we would say, "It is hard to take medicine."

선생님께 다음과 같이 비슷한 형태들을 제시해 주도록 부탁하라.

보기됴소[보기 좋소.]
It is good to look at.

보기뮙소[보기 싫소.]
It is hideous to look at.

듯기됴소[듣기 좋소.]
It is good to hear. 등등.

이 문장들을 부정문의 여러 가지 시제들로 연습해 보라.

ᄒ기쉽지안소[하기 쉽지 않소.]......... It is not easy to do.
ᄒ기어렵지안소[하기 어렵지 않소.].... It is not hard to do.
보기됴치안소[보기 좋지 않소.].......... It is not good to see.
보기뮙지안소[보기 싫지 않소.].......... It is not hideous to see.
듯기됴치안소[듣기 좋지 않소.].......... It is not good to hear.

9. ᄒᆞ면됴켓소[하면 좋겠소]

ᄒᆞ면됴켓소
If you do (thus or so), it will be good.

이 문장은 바람을 표현할 때나 지시를 내릴 때 사용하면 편리하며, 명령문 대신 사용할 수 있다. 영어의 조건문 if에 상응하여 다양하게 표현될 수 있다.

오면됴켓소[오면 좋겠소.]
If he comes, it will be well.

교군부르면곳가겟소[교군을 부르면 곧 가겠소.]
If you will call the chair coolies, I will go at once.

일ᄒᆞ면삭주겟소[일을 하면 삯을 주겠소.]
If he does the work I will give him the wages.

부모끠효도ᄒᆞ면안됴켓소[부모께 효도하면 좋지 않겠소?]
If he reverences his parents, is it not well?

10. ᄒᆞ거든[하거든]

ᄒᆞ거든
If or when.

이 형태를 'ㅎ면' 바로 다음에 제시하는 것은 둘 다 영어의 if에 해당하는 관념을 전달하기 때문이다. 그러나 두 형태의 사용에는 매우 중대한 차이가 있다. 'ㅎ면'은 더 넓은 쓰임새를 가지며, 전술된 조건의 결과, 행위자의 행동에 대한 선택이나 명령을 나타내는 절이 뒤따른다. 반면 'ㅎ거든' 뒤에는 결코 결과를 나타내는 절이 나오지 않고, 항상 행위자의 선택이나 명령이 뒤따른다.

칩거든문닷겟소[춥거든 문 닫겠소.]
If it is cold, I will shut the door. (화자가 그렇게 하기로 선택한다.)

방덥거든불긋치오[방이 덥거든, 불을 그만 때시오.]
If the room is warm, cease making a fire.

'-면'과 '-거든'의 용법상 차이를 식별하는 게 외국인들에게는 쉽지 않지만, 선생님께 다음과 같은 문장을 말해보면 두 형태 사이에 진짜 차이가 있음을 쉽게 알 수 있을 것이다.

칩거든못견듸겟소[춥거든 못견디겠소.]
방덥거든파리드러오겟소[방이 덥거든 파리 들어오겠소.]

이밖에도 '-거든' 뒤에 결과가 뒤따르는 어떤 문장이든 선생님께 말해보라. [그러면 선생님은 그 문장의 어색함을 쉽게 알아챌 수 있을 터인데], 왜냐하면 '거든' 뒤에는 [결과가 아니라] 반드시 행위자의 선택이나 명령을 나타내는 말이 와야 하기 때문이다.

11. 흐여야쓰겟소[하여야 쓰겠소]

흐여야쓰겟소

If only you will do (thus or so), it will do ; or, very often, You must do (thus or so).

이 표현도 바람이나 필요를 나타내거나 명령을 내리는 유쾌한 방식 중 하나다.

먹을것잇서야먹겟소[먹을 것이 있어야 먹겠소.]

If only there is something to eat, I will eat it.

귀신만위흐여집이편안흐겟소[귀신만 위하여 집이 편안하겠소.]

If you will but worship the spirits, the house will be peaceful.

돈잇서야흐겟다[돈이 있어야 하겠다.]

I must have the money to do it.

12. 흐게흐오[하게 하오]

흐게흐오[하게 하오.]

To make to do, or, to let to do.

바느질흐게흐오[바느질을 하게 하오.]

Have her do the sewing.

어적긔다ᄒ게ᄒ엿습ᄂᆡ다[어제 다 하게 하였습니다.]
I had it all done yesterday.

목수드러오게ᄒ오[목수 들어오게 하오.]
Let the carpenter come in.

13. ᄒ랴고ᄒ오[하려고 하오]

ᄒ랴고ᄒ오[하려고 하오.]

혹은 종종 다음과 같이 쓰기도 한다.

ᄒ려고ᄒ오
To intend to do (thus or so).

편지쓰랴고ᄒ오[편지를 쓰려고 하오.]
I am intending to write a letter.

싀골언제가랴고ᄒᄂᆡ가[시골 언제 가려고 합니까?]
When do you intend going to the country?

비슷한 표현으로는 'ᄒ고져ᄒ오', 혹은 'ᄒ고쟈ᄒ오'로도 쓴다.

14. ㅎ러가오[하러 가오]

ㅎ러가오[하러 가오.]
To go to do (thus or so).

ㅎ러오오[하러 오오.]
To come to do (thus or so).

용식이제집셰간이사ㅎ러갓소[용식이는 제집 세간 이사하러 갔소.]
Yong Siki has gone to move his household goods.

마부물보러왓소[마부가 말을 보러 왔소.]
The hostler has come to see the horse.

둙사러갓소[닭 사러 갔소.]
He has gone to buy a chicken.

이 '-러'라는 형태는 목적을 표현하기 위해 동작 동사들과 함께 사용된다.

15. ㅎ오마는[하오만]

ㅎ오마는[하오만]
I do or make, but,—

나는공부ㅎ오마는빅호기어렵소[나는 공부를 하오만 배우기 어렵소.]
As for myself I do study, but learning is difficult.

괴롭소마ᄂᆞᆫᆼ수좀주시오[괴롭겠소마는, 냉수 좀 주시오.]
It is troublesome, but please give me a drink.

'마ᄂᆞᆫ'은 다른 시제와도 결합될 수 있다.

ᄒᆞ엿소마ᄂᆞᆫ[했소만]
It did, but,—

가겟다마ᄂᆞᆫ[가겠다만]
I will go, but,—

이 표현과 영어식 표현이 비슷하기에 학습자는 항상 이 표현을 쓰려고 하는 경향이 있으나, 이는 한국어답지 않다. 우리가 종종 "so and so but…"이라고 말하는 경우에, 한국인들은 다음과 같은 표현들을 더 즐겨 사용할 것이다.

16. ᄒᆞ여도[해도]

ᄒᆞ여도[해도]
Although, I, he or she, etc., do (thus or so).

나ᄂᆞᆫ공부부ᄌᆞ런히ᄒᆞ여도비호기어렵소[나는 공부를 부지런히 해도 배우기 어렵소.]
As for myself, although I do study diligently, learning is difficult.

약만히써도안낫소[약을 많이 써도 안 낫소.]
Although I take much medicine, I am no better.

가도관계치안소[가도 관계치 않소.]

Although you go, it is no matter, that is, Go if you like.

과거시제

ㅎ엿서도 or ㅎ엿슬지라도[하였어도/했을지라도] Although I did.

갓서도 or 갓슬지라도[갔어도/갔을지라도] Although I went.

먹엇서도 or 먹엇슬지라도[먹었어도/먹었을지라도] Although I ate. 등등.

미래시제

홀지라도....... Although I will do.

갈지라도....... Although I will go.

먹을지라도.... Although I will eat. 등등.

이 형태들은 "사실에 따라서"든 "사실에 반해서"든 구별 없이 사용된다.

오날갈지라도오래잇지안켓소[오늘 갈지라도 오래 있지 않겠소.]

Although I am going today, I shall not be long.

오날갈지라도맛날수업소[오늘 갈지라도, 만날 수 없소.]

Even if I should go today, I couldn't meet him.

이와 비슷하지만 살짝 다른 표현들인 ㅎ되, ㅎ나, ㅎ거니와, ㅎ려니와 등을 익혀두라.

이쯤 되면 학습자는 이미 배운 형태들을 결합하여 상당히 긴 문장을 만들 수 있게 될 것이다. 이 표현을 사용하여 25문장 정도 만들어보아라. 스스로 문장을 만들고 선생님께 제출하여 수정을 받도록 하라.

답장ᄒ랴고ᄒ엿소도니져ᄇ렷쇠[답장하려고 했어도 잊어버렸소.]
Although I intended to answer (the letter), I forgot it.

풍년되엿소마ᄂ서풍이이처름불면곡식이샹ᄒ기쉽겟소
[풍년이 되었소만, 서풍이 이처럼 불면 곡식이 상하기 쉽겠소.]
An abundant year has become, but if the west wind blows like this, spoiling
of the crops will be easy. 등등.

17. ᄒ니/ᄒ니ᄶ[하니/하니까]

이 두 형태는 매우 흔하게 쓰이며, as, since, because와 같은 뜻을 전달한다.
전자가 둘 중에서 좀더 약한 표현으로서 때로는 단지 and와 같은 의미 정도로
쓰인다.

셩경보니춤말이오[성경을 보니 참말이오.]
I read the Bible and it is true.

도적질ᄒ니ᄶ옥에가도겟대[도적질을 하니까 옥에 가두겠다.]
Because he steals, they will put him in jail.

과거와 미래 시제 형태는 [시제 변형 규칙에 따라] 예상할 수 있는 그대로다.

ᄒ엿스니   ᄒ겟스니

ㅎ엿스니까   ㅎ겟스니까

무당발셔왓스니굿ㅎㄴ소릭곳시작ㅎ겟소[무당이 벌써 왔으니, 굿 하는 소리 곧 시작하겠소.]

Since the exorcist has already come, the noise of the devil worship will begin directly.

릭일은더헐ㅎ겟스니까오늘안삿쇠[내일은 값이 더 싸질테니까 오늘 안 샀소.]
Since they will be cheaper tomorrow, I did not buy today.

선생님이 ㅎ니깐드로, 흔고로, ㅎㄴ고로, 흔쎠문에, ㅎㄴ쎠문에 같은 비슷한 형태들을 알려줄 것인데, 이들은 [인과관계의] 의미가 좀 더 강하다.

18. 홀듯ㅎ오[할 듯하오]

홀듯ㅎ외[할 듯하오]
I, you, etc. will probably do (thus or so).

집힝이가저올듯ㅎ대[지팡이 가져올 듯하다.]
He will probably bring the cane.

날이치우면못갈듯흠닉대[날이 추우면 못갈 듯합니다.]
If the day is cold, he probably cannot go.

정확히 같은 방식으로 사용되는 형태로는 '홀가보오'가 있다.

비올가보오[비가 올까보오.]
It will probably rain.

과거 시제는 다음과 같이 변한다.
ᄒ엿슬듯ᄒ오[하였을 듯하오.]
ᄒ엿슬가보오[하였을까보오.]

샹급발셔밧엇슬듯ᄒ다[상금을 벌써 받았을 듯하다.]
He has probably already received the reward.

제리웃사름다도아주엇슬가보오[모든 이웃사람들이 다 도와주었을까보오.]
His neighbors all probably helped him.

19. 홀번ᄒ엿소[할 뻔하였소]

홀번ᄒ엿소[할 뻔하였소]
I, he, etc., was on the point of doing.

너머질번ᄒ엿소[넘어질 뻔하였소.]
I was on the point of falling, or, I nearly fell.

죽을번ᄒ엿소[죽을 뻔하였소.]
He was on the pointing of dying.

20. 홀만하오[할 만하다]

홀만하오[할 만하다]

It is worth doing.

칙볼만흡늬가[책이 볼만합니까?]

Is the book worth reading?

구경홀만흡늬다[구경할 만합니다.]

The sight is worth seeing.

비슷한 표현이지만 영어 접미사 '-able'의 뜻에 더 가까운 것으로는

흡즉흐오

오늘둙알삼즉흐오[오늘 달걀은 살 만하오.]

Eggs will be purchasable today.

김치닉으면먹음즉흐겟쇼[김치가 익으면 먹음직스럽겠소.]

The "kimchi" (pickles) when ripe will be edible.

21. 하는톄흐오[하는 체하오]

하는톄흐오[하는 체하오]

I, he, etc., am pretending to do.

그으희우는테흔다[그 아이는 우는 체한다.]

That child is pretending to cry.

과거시제

이녀편네국문모로는테ᄒ엿소[이 여인은 국문을 모르는 체하였소.]

This woman pretended not to know kookmoon.

미래시제

모로는사름들이아는테ᄒ겟소[모르는 사람들이 아는 체하였소.]

Those who don't know will pretend to know.

22. 훌싸념려ᄒ오[할까 염려하오]

종종 줄여서 '훌가ᄒ오'

I fear this or that is happening or will happen.

힘만허비할싸념려ᄒ오[힘만 허비할까 염려하오.]

I fear he will only waste his strength.

아니올싸념려ᄒ오[아니 올까 염려하오.]

I fear he will not come.

반대되는 표현은 이런 저런 일이 일어나기를 바란다는 뜻으로
훌싸브라오

뎌집어룬도라을까보라오[저집 어른이 돌아올까 바라오.]

I hope the man of that house will come back.

이 형태는 자연스럽게 미래의 관념을 표현한다. 과거 시제는 다음과 같이 표현된다.

보리잘되엿슬까보랏소[보리농사가 잘 되었을까 바랐소.]

I hoped that the barley had turned out well.

편지아니왓스니까제남편죽엇는가념려ᄒ겟소[편지가 안와서 제 남편이 죽었을까 염려하겠소.]

Since no letter has come, she will fear that her husband has died.

이 문장들에서 희망과 두려움의 대상이 되는 내용뿐 아니라 희망하거나 두려워하는 시점 역시 모든 시제들로 표현될 수 있다는 점에 주목하라. 비슷한 형태로는 홀까무섭소[할까 무섭소], 홀까걱정잇소[할까 걱정 있소], 홀까기드리오[할까 기다리오] 및 희망과 기대, 두려움을 나타내는 그 밖의 동사들이 있다.

23. ᄒ는지[하는지]

이것은 영어의 whether를 표현할 때 사용하며, 종종 아니ᄒ는지[아니하는지]나 못ᄒ는지[못하는지]와 붙어서 whether or not의 의미를 나타낸다.

잘ᄒ는지잘못ᄒ는지모로겟소[그가 잘 하는지 못하는지 모르겠소.]

Whether he is doing well or badly, I do not know.

가ᄂ지안가ᄂ지알수업소[그가 가는지 안 가는지 알 수 없소.]

I don't know whether he is going or not.

'ᄂ지'는 과거시제 'ㅎ엿'이라는 어근에 붙어서 'ㅎ엿ᄂ지'가 되면 과거형을 이룬다.

혼인ㅎ엿ᄂ지알수업소[그가 혼인하였는지 알 수 없소.]

Whether he is married I do not know.

우리집아바지잘줌으셧ᄂ지가보아래[우리집 아버지 잘 주무셨는지 가보아라.]

Go and see whether our father slept well.

'홀ᄂ지'는 종종 '홀넌지'나 '홀지'로 쓰기도 하며 자연스럽게 미래시제를 형성한다.

난리날넌지안날넌지누가알겟소[난리가 날지 안날지 누가 알겠소?]

Who knows whether or not war will arise ?

잘될지잘못될지보아야알겟소[잘 될지 잘못될지 보아야 알겠소.]

Whether it will turn out well or not we must see to know.

학습자는 이 형태들 뒤에 항상 앎이나 무지를 나타내는 절이 따른다는 점을 알 수 있을 것이다. 이 사실에 유념하면, 이것[ㅎᄂ지]과 단지 형태상으로만 유사한 다음 표현[ㅎ던지]이나 30번의 표현[ㅎ지]과 혼동하지 않을 수 있다.

24. ᄒ던지[하든지]

'ᄒ던지' 또한 영어의 whether에 상응하지만 그 뒤에 당신이 알거나 모른다는 것을 나타내는 절이 나오는 것이 아니라, 항상 (지금 굳이 언급할 필요 없는 한 가지 예외를 제외하고) 어떤 결과가 있거나 없다는 관념이 뒤따른다.

ᄒ던지아니ᄒ던지내게샹관업소[하든지 안하든지 내게 상관없소.]
Whether he does or not, it is no matter to me.

살던지죽던지졔ᄉ아니ᄒ겟소[살든지 죽든지 조상 제사를 아니하겠소.]
Whether I live or die, I will not sacrifice (to ancestors).

25. 홀째[할 때]

홀째[할 때]
While or when doing.

감긔들째에바룸부는듸에가지마라[감기들 때 바람 부는 데에 가지 마라.]
When you have a cold (literally, when a cold enters) do not go where the wind is blowing.

밥먹을째마다긔도홈닉다[밥 먹을 때마다 기도합니다.]
He prays every time he eats.

비슷한 표현들에는 '홀졔'와 '홀젹에'가 있으며, 이들 역시 거의 비슷하게 자주 쓰인다.

26. ᄒᆞ기젼에[하기 전에]

ᄒᆞ기젼에[하기 전에]
Before doing.

시작ᄒᆞ기젼에싱각잘ᄒᆞ오[시작하기 전에 생각 잘 하오.]
Before beginning consider well.

숑ᄉᆞᄒᆞ기젼에죄잇ᄂᆞᆫ지업ᄂᆞᆫ지ᄌᆞ셰히알거시오[송사하기 전에 죄가 있는지 없는지 자세히 알아야 하오.]
Before accusing one must know certainly whether or not there is fault.

27. ᄒᆞᆫ후에[한 후에]

ᄒᆞᆫ후에[한 후에]
After doing.

심부림ᄒᆞᆫ후에쏘오너라[심부름 한 후에 또 오너라.]
After you have done the errand, come again.

말ᄉᆞᆷ알아드른후에쏘무러보지아니ᄒᆞ엿소[말씀 알아들은 후에 또 물어보지 아니하였소.]
After he understood the talk, he made no more inquiries.

28. ᄒᆞᆫᄂᆞᆫ줄아오[하는 줄 아오]

ᄒᆞᆫᄂᆞᆫ줄아오[하는 줄 아오.]

I think or know (thus or so).

ᄒᆞᆫᄂᆞᆫ줄모르오[하는 줄 모르오.]

I do not think or know (thus or so).

부인이손님오ᄂᆞᆫ줄아오[부인이 손님 오는 줄 아오.]

The lady knows that guests are coming.

뎌방에잇ᄂᆞᆫ줄아오[저 방에 있는 줄 아오.]

I think it is in that room.

과거시제

ᄒᆞᆫ줄알앗소[한 줄 알았소.]

ᄒᆞᆫ줄몰낫소[한 줄 몰랐소.]

집쥬인이발셔간줄몰낫소[집주인이 벌써 간 줄 몰랐소.]

I did not know that the master of the house had already gone.

여섯살먹은줄알앗소[여섯 살 먹은 줄 알았소.]

I thought he had eaten six New Year's cakes.

(that is, was six years old.)

미래시제

홀줄아오[할 줄 아오.]

홀줄모로오[할 줄 모르오.]

오늘빅올줄알앗소[오늘 배가 올 줄 알았소.]

I thought a boat would come today.

이처럼오래기드릴줄몰낫소[이처럼 오래 기다릴 줄 몰랐소.]

I did not know that you would wait this long.

미래형은 전혀 다른 의미를 전달할 수도 있다. 이러저러한 것을 어떻게 하는지 안다는 의미이다.

미쟝이담곳칠줄아오[미장이가 담을 고칠 줄 아오.]

The mason knows how to mend the wall.

농ᄉ일홀줄모로겟소[농사일을 할 줄 모르오.]

He does not know how to do farm work.

29. ᄒ도록[하도록]

ᄒ도록[하도록]

until, up to the point or time of, the more.

곤ㅎ도록일ㅎ엿소[그는 피곤하도록 일 하였소.]

He worked until he was tired.

우리어머니죽도록알앗소[우리 어머니는 죽도록 앓았소.]

Mother was sick unto death.

사름만토록됴소[사람은 많을수록 좋소.]

The more persons the better.

울도록작란ㅎ엿대[울도록 장난하였다.]

They played until they cried.

'until'의 관념은 또한 동사적 명사에 'ㅅ지'를 붙여서 표현하기도 한다. 예컨대, '죽도록힘쓰소'[죽도록 힘쓰소]라는 말 대신에 한국인은 단지 '죽기ㅅ지힘쓰소'[죽기까지 힘쓰소]라고 말하기도 한다. 죽을 정도로 일한다는 뜻이다. '홀수록'에 대해서는 부가적 도움말의 5번을 보라.

30. 흔지[한지]

때때로 since[-한 이래의 시간]을 표현하는 데 사용된다.

아기난지아홉둘되엿소[아기가 태어난 지 아홉 달 되었소.]

The baby was born nine months ago.

본지오래오[본 지 오래오.]

It has been long since I saw you.

'흔지오'는 "How strange," "How beautiful"처럼 경탄, 두려움, 존경 등을 표현하는 데 사용된다.

엇지큰지오[어찌 큰지요!]

How big!

맛이엇지됴흔지오[맛이 어찌 좋은지요!]

What a good taste!

한국인이 경탄의 의미를 좀더 명백하게 표현하고 싶을 때는 '-오'를 떼고 다음을 붙이기도 한다.

'말홀수업소'[말할 수 없소]

It is inexpressible.

31. 와/과

이들은 동일한 동사에 둘 혹은 그 이상의 주어나 목적어를 결합시키는 연결사(connectives)로서 사용된다.

셕이와칠승이쟝에가셔감과비와둙사왓소[석이와 칠승이가 장에 가서 감과 배와 닭을 사왔소.]

Sāgi and Chil-seungi, having gone to the fair, came back, having bought persimmons, pears and a chicken.

위에 제시된 문장을 보면 '와'와 '과'의 차이는 단지 발음상의 편의를 위한 것임을 알 수 있다. '와'는 모음으로 끝나는 단어들에 사용되고, '과'는 자음으로 끝나는 단어들 뒤에 사용된다.

32. ᄒ고[하고]

'ᄒ고' 역시 위에 나온 '와/과'와 같은 방식으로 사용되는 매우 흔한 연결사다.

사람ᄒ고즘싱이만히죽엇소[사람하고 짐승이 많이 죽었소.]
Many persons and animals died.

고

위에 나온 'ᄒ고'와 동사의 연결형인 '고'가 'ᄒ다'의 어근과 함께 사용되는 경우를 혼동하면 안된다. 이 연결사 '-고'는 and를 의미하며 어떤 동사와도 함께 사용된다.

ᄒ나흔칙잘보고ᄒ나흔잘못본다[한 명은 책을 잘 보고, 한 명은 잘 못 본다.]
One reads the book well, and one reads it badly.

군ᄉ빅로도가고륙로로도갓소[군사들이 배로도 가고 육로로도 갔소.]
The soldiers went by boat and by land.

33. ᄒᆞ여, ᄒᆞ야, ᄒᆞ여셔[하여, 하여서]

이 형태들은 한 문장에서 동등하지 않은 부분들을 연결할 때 사용된다.

하ᄂᆞ님의ᄯᅳᆺ을순죵ᄒᆞ야십계명을잘직히오[하나님의 뜻을 순종하여 십계명을
잘 지키오.]
Obeying the will of God, he keeps the Ten Commandments well,

집을ᄯᅥ나먼곳에갓소[집을 떠나 먼 곳에 갔소.]
Having left home, he went to a distant place.

이 문장들 각각에서 두 동사들이 동일한 주어를 갖는다는 점에 주목하라.
동작동사로 만든 분사의 경우는 항상 그러한데, 다만 동사가 형태상으로는 동
작동사이지만 의미상으로는 강하게 형용사적인 몇몇 경우들은 예외다. 일반
적으로 말해서 동작동사의 분사 바로 뒤에 오는 절은 분사와 동일한 주어를
가져야 한다.

그러나 형용사적 동사에서 분사가 된 경우에는 다음 절의 주어가 분사의
주어와 같을 수도 있고 같지 않을 수도 있다. 예를 들어,

ᄭᅩᆺ이아름다와ᄯᅡᆯᄆᆞ음난대[꽃이 아름다워서, (내가 꽃을) 딸 마음이 난다.]
The flower being beautiful, I feel like plucking it (literally, plucking mind arises).

ᄭᅩᆺ이아름다와사름의ᄆᆞ음을즐겁게ᄒᆞ오[꽃이 아름다워서 사람의 마음을 즐
겁게 하오.]
The flower being beautiful, it makes the mind of man glad.

34. ᄒᆞᄂᆞᄃᆡ[하는데]

이야기를 말 하거나 쓸 때 자주 사용되는 형태로, 인쇄된 글에서는 마침표 만큼 길지는 않지만 쉼표보다는 긴 휴지(休止)를 가리킨다. 영어의 세미콜론 [;]에 해당한다고 말할 수 있다. 말을 할 때는 and나 but으로 번역될 수도 있고, 단지 잠깐 쉬는 것으로 표현될 수도 있다.

지금잔치ᄒᆞᄂᆞᄃᆡ여러가지됴흔음식을예비ᄒᆞ엿소[지금 잔치를 하는데 여러 가지 좋은 음식을 예비하였소.]
They are having a feast now, and have prepared several kinds of nice food.

셥셥ᄒᆞᆫ일나ᄂᆞᄃᆡ웨웃소[섭섭한 일이 일어났는데 왜 웃소?]
A sorrowful affair has occurred; why do you laugh ?

과거와 미래시제는 예상하는 바대로 다음과 같이 형성된다.

셰례를발셔힝ᄒᆞ엿ᄂᆞᄃᆡ더듸왓소[세례식을 벌써 진행하였는데, 늦게 왔소.]
The baptismal ceremony has already been performed; you have come late.

ᄅᆡ일쓰겟ᄂᆞᄃᆡ아직아니삿소[내일 쓰겠는데 아직 안 샀소.]
I will use it tomorrow, but have not yet bought it.

35. ᄒᆞ더라[하더라]

화자는 사실임을 알고 있으나 청자는 아직 보거나 들어본 적이 없는 것에 대해 말할 때 사용되는 종결형이다.

미국학교에셔는소릭조금도업시공부ᄒ더래미국 학교에서는 소리가 조금도 없이 공부하더라.]

In American schools they study without making the least noise.

같은 표현의 정중한 형태는 '홉데다[21]'이다.

영국ᄆᆞᆯ들이대단히큽데대영국 말들이 대단히 큽디다.]

English horses are very large.

(질문) 목ᄉᆞ어ᄃᆡ계신지알겟소[목사님이 어디 계신지 알겠소?]

　　　Do you know where the pastor is?

(대답) 츌입홉데다[츌입합디다.]

　　　He has gone for a walk.

의문형의 높은말이나 낮은말 역시 화자는 모르지만 다른 사람은 보았거나 알고 있는 일에 대해 물을 때 사용된다. 따라서 아이에게 [다음과 같이 물을 수 있다.]

(질문) 아바지어ᄃᆡ가시더냐[아버지 어디 가시더냐?]

　　　Where has your father gone ?

(대답) 촌에갑데다[촌에 갑디다.]

　　　He has gone to a village.

---

21) '-ㅂ디다'의 평안도 방언이다.

(질문) 회당에잇습데까[회당에 있습디까?]

    Is it in the church ?

(대답) 잇습데대[있습디다.]

    It is.

36. 흐더니[하더니]

과거에 미완된 일을 나타내는 연결사로 35번과 비슷하게, 화자는 보았거나 알고 있지만 청자는 모르는 것에 대한 관념을 전달하기 위해 사용되며, 'and' 로 번역될 수 있다.

양씨만밋고든니더니이제는남편도예수를밋소[양씨만 믿고 교회에 다니더니, 이제는 남편도 예수를 믿소.]

Only Yang Ssi believed and attended (church), and now her husband too trusts in Jesus.

35번과 36번의 형태들은 1인칭 주어에 연결된 형용동사에는 사용되지만 동작동사에는 사용될 수 없음에 주의하라. 예를 들어,

어져게곤흐더니오날관계지안소[어저께는 피곤하더니 오늘은 상관없소.]

37. 흐엿더니[하였더니]

이것은 과거에 완료된 일을 나타내는 연결사로 모든 인칭에 다 사용될 수 있다는 점을 제외하고는 36번과 동일한 효력을 갖는다. 예를 들어,

눈물을흘니고긔도ᄒᆞ엿더니하ᄂᆞ님ᄭᅴ셔드르셧쇼[눈물을 흘리고 기도하였더니 하나님께서 들으셨소.]

I (or he) wept and prayed and God heard.

이것은 화자가 어떤 변화가 일어났다는 관념을 전달하고 싶을 때 흔히 사용되며, 'but'으로 번역될 수 있다.

이젼에일만히ᄒᆞ엿더니지금은늙어셔못ᄒᆞᆸ니다[이전에는 일을 많이 하였더니 지금은 늙어서 못합니다.]

Formerly I worked a great deal, but now, being old, I cannot.

38. ᄒᆞ면서[하면서]

동일한 주어를 갖는 동사들 사이에 사용되는 연결사로서 동시에 일어나는 행동을 나타낸다.

길가면셔칙보앗쇼[길 가면서 책을 보았소.]

As he was going along the road, he read a book.

하ᄂᆞ님을공경ᄒᆞ면셔부모의게도효도ᄒᆞᆯ거시오[하나님을 공경하면서 부모에게도 효도할 것이오.]

While we reverence God, we must also be filial to our parents.

39. ᄒᆞ다가[하다가]

중단된 행동을 나타내는 연결사.

길가다가호랑이맛낫쇼[길을 가다가 호랑이를 만났소.]
As he was going along the road, he met a tiger.

하ᄂᆞ님을밋다가불힝히죄에싸졋소[하나님을 믿다가 불행히 죄에 빠졌소.]
He believed God but, unfortunately, he fell into sin.

과거형은 'ᄒᆞ엿다가'로서 완료된 행동을 지시한다. 'ᄒᆞ다가'와 'ᄒᆞ엿다가'의
차이는 다음 문장들을 통해 예시될 수 있다.

셔울가다가도로왓소[서울에 가다가 도로 왔소.]
I went part of the way to Seoul and came back.

셔울갓다가도로왓소[서울에 갔다가 도로 왔소.]
I went to Seoul and came back.

40. 홀쑨더러/홀쑨만아니오[할 뿐더러/할 뿐만 아니오]

홀쑨더러/홀쑨만아니오[할 뿐더러/할 뿐만 아니오]
Not only that but

고싱홀쑨더러죽기싯지ᄒᆞ엿소[고생할 뿐더러 죽기까지 하였소.]
고싱홀쑨만아니오죽기싯지ᄒᆞ엿소[고생할 뿐만 아니라 죽기까지 하였소.]
He not only suffered but died. (Literally, up to death did).

비만흘쑨더러바름도부럿소[비가 많을 뿐더러 바람도 불었소.]

비만흘쑨만아니라ᄇ람도부럿소[비가 많을 뿐만 아니라 바람도 불었소.]

There was not only much rain, but the wind blew.

41. 책임이나 의무의 관념

영어에서 ought로 표현하는 책임이나 의무의 관념은 미래형 분사의 사용을 통해 표현된다. 예를 들어,

슐먹고노름ᄒᄂ거슨어진사ᄅᆷ이홀일아니오[술 먹고 노름하는 것은 어진 사람이 할 일이 아니오.]

Drinking and gambling are not work that an upright man ought to do.

볼일만아셔못왓소[볼일이 많아서 못 왔소.]

There being much work to see to, I could not come.

'것'은 thing을 뜻하며 분사 뒤에서는 거의 대부분 '일'과 바꿔 쓸 수 있다.

42. 간접화법(Indirect Discourse)

간접화법은 인용된 말의 어근 형태에 '-고 하다'라는 동사의 모든 어법이나 시제를 덧붙여 표현할 수 있다.

ᄒ라고ᄒ여래[하라고 하여라.]

Tell him to do, (thus or so).

말ᄒ라고ᄒ여래[말하라고 하여라.]
Tell him to speak.

나무사라고ᄒ시외[나무를 사라고 하시오.]
Please tell him to buy the wood.

학당에가라고ᄒ겟소[학당에 가라고 하겠소.]
I will tell him to go to the school.

교군왓다고홈ᄂ대[교군이 왔다고 합니다.]
He says the chair coolies have come.

새벽에써나겟다고ᄒ엿소[새벽에 떠나겠다고 하였소.]
They said they would leave at day-break.

이밖에도 문장의 모든 어법과 높임의 정도, 시제에 사용될 수 있다.
다음과 같이 바꿔 쓸 수 있다.

ᄒ단말드럿소[한다는 말 들었소.]
I heard he was doing, (thus and so).

압흐단말드럿소[아프다는 말 들었소.]
I heard he was sick.

쟝가갓단말드럿소[장가갔다는 말 들었소.]

I heard you were married.

43. 관계절(Relative clauses)

관계절은 과거, 현재, 미래 분사를 통해 표현할 수 있다.

일ㅎㄴ사룸이돈달나홈니대[일하는 사람이 돈 달라 합니다.]

The man who is doing the work is asking for money.

새로지은집문허졋소[새로 지은 집이 무너졌소.]

The house which was newly built has tumbled down.

오늘홀일별노업소[오늘 할 일이 별로 없소.]

There is no special work which ought to be done today.

44. 동사

동사는 영어에서 필수불가결 하지만, 한국어에서는 종종 사용되지 않는다. 동사적 관념이 '게'나 '의게'를 동반하거나 동반하지 않은 '잇스'[22]로 표현된다. 따라서 영어의 "I have a book"을 한국인은 단지 '췩잇소'[책 있소]라거나 혹은 좀 더 명시적으로 '내게췩잇소'[내게 책 있소]로 표현한다.

---

[22] '잇다' 혹은 '잇소'의 오식으로 보인다.

45. Is

영어에서는 한 단어 is로 표현할 수 있는 의도가 한국어에서는 두 단어를 요구한다. '잇소'는 단지 존재를 표현하며, '-이오'는 본성이나 조건을 표현한다.

착흔사름잇소[착한 사람이 있소.]
There is (or exists) an upright man.

착흔사름이오[그는 착한 사람이오.]
He is an upright man.

이 두 단어의 모든 가능한 형태들 사이의 용법을 구별하는 것은 한국어 말하기에서 가장 어려운 부분 중 하나다.

46. 비교급

비교급은 더(more)와 덜(less)로 표현된다.

염병더무섭소[염병이 더 무섭소.]
Typhus fever is more dreadful.

이밥덜더럽소[이 밥이 덜 더럽소.]
This rice is less dirty.

최상급은 '데일'이라는 말로 표현할 수 있다.

그산뎨일놉소[그 산이 제일 높소.]

That mountain is highest, or literally, first high;

'-즁에'라는 말을 사용하는 경우도 매우 흔하다.

산즁에놉소[산 중에 높소.]

Among the mountains it is high.

대상들 사이의 비교는 '-보담'이나 '-보다'로 표현된다.

이그릇보담그것크다[이 그릇보다 그것이 크다.]

Compared with this vessel that one is large.

47. 긍정의 대답

한국어에 고유한 방식으로 긍정의 답을 하는 것은 상당한 기술을 요하는데, 왜냐하면 모든 상황에서 사용될 수 있는 영어의 yes와 같은 말이 없기 때문이다. '예'가 yes와 가깝기는 하지만 오직 [지위나 나이가] 동등한 사람들 사이에서나 하급자가 상급자에게 대답할 때만 사용된다. '그럿소'[그렇소], '올소'[옳소] 같은 말들도 쓰임새가 있지만, 한국인들이 더 즐겨 쓰는 방식은 동사를 반복함으로써 긍정을 표시하는 것이다.

(질문) 그사름왓소[그 사람 왔소?]

　　　　Has the man come?

(대답) 왓소[왔소.]

　　　　He has come.

(언급) 곡식잘되엿소[곡식 잘 되었소.]

The crops have turned out well.

(동의) 잘되엿소[잘 되었소.]

They have turned out well.

48. Thank you

우리가 많이 사용하는 thank you는 한국어에 정확히 대응되는 단어가 없다. 어떤 친절을 베푼 것에 대해 감사를 표시할 때, 한국인은 '됴소', '잘ᄒ엿소'라 거나 '고맙소'라고 말한다. '고맙소'라는 말은 쓰임새가 thank you와 유사하지 만, "I am grateful"이라는 의미에 더 가깝다. 예컨대, 한 한국인이 친구에게 "나 는 어제 아팠지만 오늘은 훨씬 나아졌소"라고 말한다면, 그 친구는 "고맙소"라 고 답할 것이다.

다른 이의 호의를 구할 때 please라는 관념은 give나 grant를 뜻하는 '주오'라 는 동사를 사용하여 전달한다.

문여러주시오[문 열어 주시오.]

Please open the door.

아기안아주어라[아기를 안아 주어라.]

Please take the baby.

이 형태는 뒤에서 기도 문장들을 언급할 때 볼 수 있듯이, 기도에서 많이 사용된다.

49. 인칭대명사

인칭대명사는 한국인 사이에서는 거의 사용되지 않지만 그 대체물들이 특히 2인칭의 경우에는 흔히 사용되며 유용하다. 형을 뜻하는 '로형'이 남자들 사이에서나 혹은 여자들 사이에서 손윗사람을 가리키는 데 사용된다. '당신, 딕, 딕늬, 공'과 그밖에 선생님이 제안해주는 단어들은 유용한 오전 공부거리가 될 것이다.

어느 경우에나 안전하고 적절한 호칭법은 단지 상대방의 이름이나 직함을 사용하는 것이다. 자기 이름을 갖고 있지 않은 여성들의 경우에는 누구누구의 후손(descendant)이라거나 누구누구의 부인이나 어머니로 불러야 한다. 따라서 고가의 후손은 '고씨'로, 김씨의 아내는 '김셔방딕'(딕의 문자적 의미는 집을 뜻한다)으로, 달셕이의 어머니는 '달셕이모친'으로 부른다. 뒤의 두 표현들을 좀더 낮춰서 말하는 형태는 '김셔방집'이나 '달셕이어머니'이다. 청중을 부를 때는 '여러분들이'라고 하는 것이 유용하다.

50. 사과하기

한국에서 받아들일 만한 방식의 사과 표현은 외국인이 생각하기 쉬운 "I am sorry"의 문자적 번역으로 이뤄지지 않는다. 한국인이 무언가를 하거나 하지 않은 것에 대해 유감을 표시할 때면, 그는 단지 '잘못ᄒ엿소'(I have not done well)라거나 '용셔히주시오'(Please forgive me)라고 말할 것이다. 좀더 격식 있게 표현하고자 할 때는 '허물마시오'라고 말하는데, 이는 허물(fault)을 탓하지 말거나 눈감아 달라는 뜻이다.

종교 용어들의 목록

Angel, 텬스[천사]

Angry, to be, 노ᄒ오[노하다]

Apostle, 스도[사도]

Baptism, 셰례[세례]

Baptize, 셰례주오[세례주다]

Baptized, to be, 셰례밧소[세례받다]

Believe, to, 밋소[믿다]

Believer, 예수밋는사롬, 교우, 교인, 신쟈, 신도[예수 믿는 사람, 신자]

Bible, 셩경[성경]

Bless, to, 복주오[축복하다]

Blessed, to be, 복밧소[축복받다]

Blessing, 복[축복]

Bow, to, 절ᄒ오[절하다]

Born again, to be, 거듭나오[거듭나다]

Buddha, Image of, 부쳐[부처]

Buddhism, 불도[불교]

Church building, 회당, 례빅당[예배당]

Commit, to, as sin, 범ᄒ오, 짓소[죄를 범하다, 짓다]

Confess, to, 즈복ᄒ오[자백하다]

Confucius, 공즈, 부즈[공자, 부자]

Confucianism, 공밍도, 유도[공맹도, 유도]

Congregation, 교회[교회]

Cross, The, 십즈개[십자가]

Crucify, to, 못박아죽이외[못박아 죽이다]

Crucified, to be, 못박혀도라가셧소[못 박혀 돌아가셨다]

Demon, 귀신[귀신]

Destroy, to, 멸망식히외[멸망시키다]

Destroyed, to be, 멸망ᄒ외[멸망하다]

Destruction, 멸망홈[멸망함]

Devil, 마귀[마귀]

Disciple, 뎨ᄌ, 문도[제자, 문도]

Disobey, (a rule or law), 어긔외[규칙이나 법을 어기다]

Doctrine, 교, 도, 도리[교, 도, 도리]

Escape, to, as destruction, 면ᄒ오, 피ᄒ외[멸망함을 면하다, 피하다]

Eternal, 영원흔[영원한]

Eternal life, 영싱[영생]

Faith, 밋음, 신앙[믿음, 신앙]

Fall into, to, as into hell, 쌔지오[빠지다]

Forgive, to, 샤ᄒ오, 용셔ᄒ오, 면ᄒ외[사하다, 용서하다, 면하다]

God, 하ᄂ님 used by Protestant missionaries. 텬쥬, used by Roman Catholics.
    [개신교 선교회에서는 하나님, 로마 카톨릭교에서는 천주]

Gospel, 복음[복음]

Grace, 은혜[은혜]

Heaven, 하늘, 텬당[하늘, 천당]

Heavenly Father, 하늘에계신아바지[하늘에 계신 아버지]

Hell, 디옥[지옥]

Holy Spirit, 셩신[성신]

Jesus Christ, 예수그리스도[예수 그리스도]

Joy, 즐거워흠[즐거워함]

Judgment, 심판, 재판[심판, 재판]

Kneel, to, 무릅쓸다[무릎 꿇다]

Kneel, to, face to the ground as Koreans do ; 업디오[한국인들이 하듯 바닥을 향하여 엎드리다]

Live forever, to, 영원히사오[영원히 살다]

Lord, 쥬[주]

Lord's Supper, 셩찬[성찬]

Love, to, ᄉ랑ᄒ오[사랑하다]

Magic or sorcery, to practise, 굿ᄒ다[굿하다]

Martyr, 슌교쟈[순교자]

Mencius, 밍ᄌ[맹자]

Obey, 슌죵ᄒ오[순종하다]

Pastor, 목ᄉ[목사]

Persecute, to, 핍박ᄒ오[핍박하다]

Persecuted, to be, 핍박밧소, 해밧소[핍박받다, 해를 당하다]

Pity, to, 불샹히녁이오[불쌍히 여기다]

Pitiable, to be, 불샹ᄒ오[불쌍하다]

Pray, to, 긔도ᄒ오, 비오; to Buddha, 념불ᄒ오[기도하다. 빌다, 부처에게 염불하다]

Prayer, 긔도, 비ᄂ말[기도, 비는 말]

Preach, to, 강도ᄒ오, 젼도ᄒ오[강도하다, 전도하다]

Preacher, 젼도ᄒᄂ사ᄅ[전도하는 사람]

Punish, to, 형벌ᄒ오[벌하다]

Punished, to be, 형벌밧소[벌받다]

Punishment, 형벌[벌]

Religion, 종교[종교]

Repay, to, 갑흐오[갚다]

Repent, to, 회기ᄒ오[회개하다]

Resurrection, 다시살아나신것; 부활[다시 살아나신 것, 부활]

Sabbath, 안식일; 쥬일; 례빅날[안식일, 주일, 예배날]

Sacrifice, to, as to ancestors, 졔ᄉᄒ오[제사하다]

Salvation, 구원홈[구원함]

Satan, 마귀[마귀]

Save, to, 구원ᄒ오[구원하다]

Saviour, 구원ᄒ신쥬[구원하신 주]

Sing, to, 찬미ᄒ오[찬미하다]

Sin, 죄[죄]

Sin, to, 죄범ᄒ오, 죄짓소[죄를 범하다, 죄 짓다]

Sinner, 죄인; 죄잇ᄂ사름[죄인, 죄 있는 사람]

Son of God, 하ᄂ님의아들[하나님의 아들]

Soul, 령혼[영혼]

Spirit, 신[신]

Suffer, 고싱하오; 욕보오[고생하다, 욕보다]

Trust, to, 밋소; 의지ᄒ오[믿다, 의지하다]

Worship, or reverence, to, 공경ᄒ오; 위ᄒ오[공경하다, 위하다]

설교할 때 유용한 짧은 문장들

셰샹사름즁에죄업ᄂ사름어듸잇소[세상사람 중에 죄 없는 사람이 어디 있소?]

Among all mankind where is there one without sin?

하ᄂ님씌셔셰샹사름다죄에ᄲᅡ져죽게된거슬불샹히녁이셧소[하나님께서 세상사람이 다 죄에 빠져 죽게 된 것을 불쌍히 여기셨소.]

God pitied the sin-striken and lost condition of man.

죄만히잇섯스되우리를ᄉ랑ᄒ셧소[죄가 많이 있었으되 우리를 사랑하셨소.]

Although our sins were many He loved us.

예수ᄂᆫ하ᄂ님의외아ᄃᆞᆯ이오[예수는 하나님의 외아들이오.]

As for Jesus, He is God's only son.

하ᄂ님씌셔그외아ᄃᆞᆯ을셰샹에보낫셧소[하나님께서 그 외아들을 세상에 보내셨소.]

God sent His son to earth.

우리죄를속하러오셧소[우리 죄를 대속하러 오셨소.]

He came to atone for our sins.

셰샹사름의게해를밧앗소[세상사람에게 박해를 받았소.]

He suffered at the hands of men.

우리죄를디신ᄒᆞ야그몸에악흔형벌밧앗소[우리를 대신하여 그 몸에 악한 형벌을 받았소.]

On account of our sins He received bitter punishment in His own body.

십ᄌ가에못박혀죽으셧소[십자가에 못 박혀 죽으셨소.]

He died nailed to a cross.

엇지ᄒ여야그은혜를갑겟소[어찌 하여야 그 은혜를 갚겠소?]

How can we repay such kindness ?

예수말ᄉᆞᆷ대로ᄒ여야쓰겟소[예수 말씀대로 하여야 쓰겠소.]

We must do according to the word of Jesus.

우리다죄잇ᄂᆞᆫ줄을ᄭᅵᆺ둣고회기ᄒ야죄를ᄇᆞ려야쓰겟소[우리가 다 죄 있는 줄을 깨닫고 회개하여 죄를 버려야 쓰겠소.]

We must realize our sinfulness, and having repented forsake it.

예수를밋으면텬당에가겟소[예수를 믿으면 천당에 가겠소.]

If we believe in Jesus we will go to Heaven.

밋지아니ᄒ면디옥에ᄲᅡ질수밧긔업소[믿지 아니하면 지옥에 빠질 수밖에 없소.]

If we do not believe in Him there is nothing for us but to fall into hell.

이말은사ᄅᆞᆷ의말이아니오[이 말은 사람의 말이 아니오.]

As for these words, they are not the words of man.

하ᄂᆞ님의말ᄉᆞᆷ이오[하나님의 말씀이오.]

They are the words of God.

이 문장들을 가지고 다음에 나오는 기도문처럼 적절한 연결어들을 사용하여 결합해보면 학습자에게 좋은 연습이 될 것이다.

기도문

하늘에계신우리아바지[하늘에 계신 우리 아버지]
Our Father which art in Heaven,

하ᄂ님압헤범흔죄를샤ᄒ여주옵시고[하나님 앞에 범한 죄를 사하여 주옵시고]
Forgive the sins that we have committed against Thee, and,

죄를지을ᄆ옵다시먹지말게ᄒ여주옵쇼셔[죄를 지을 마음을 다시 먹지 말게 하여 주옵소서.]
grant that we may have no more mind to sin.

저의들이약ᄒ고미련흔줄아오니[저희들이 약하고 미련한 줄 아오니]
We know that we are weak and foolish, and,

도아주시고ᄀᄅ쳐주시기를비옵ᄂ대[도와주시고 가르쳐 주시기를 비옵니다.]
we pray that Thou wilt help and teach us.

잠시라도써나지마옵시고[잠시라도 떠나지 마옵시고]
Leave us not for a moment,

ᄒ늘에갈길노인도ᄒ여주옵시기를비옵ᄂ대[하늘에 갈 길로 인도하여 주옵

시기를 비옵니다.]

but lead us, we pray Thee, along the path to Heaven.

남의죄진거슬용셔ᄒ여주게ᄒ옵시고[남이 죄 지은 것을 용서하여 주게 하옵
시고]

Help us to forgive the sins of others, and,

다름사름을우리몸과ᄀ치ᄉ랑ᄒ게ᄒ여주옵쇼셔[다른 사람을 우리 몸과 같
이 사랑하게 하여 주옵소서.]

grant that we may love others as ourselves.

예수모르고안밋ᄂ사름을불샹히녁이시고[예수를 모르고 안 믿는 사람을 불
쌍히 여기시고]

Have pity upon those who know not and trust not Jesus, and,

셩경말ᄉ듯고ᄭ닷게ᄒ여주옵시기를비옵ᄂ대[성경 말씀 듣고 깨닫게 하여
주옵시기를 비옵니다.]

grant that they may hear and understand the words of the Bible.

제몸에잇ᄂ죄를ᄭᄃ라알고[제 몸에 있는 죄를 깨달아 알고]

Realizing their sinfulness, and,

예수ᄭ와셔ᄌ복ᄒ여[예수께 와서 자백하여]

coming and confessing to Jesus,

죄샤흠을엇게ᄒ여주옵시기를비옵고[죄사함을 얻게 하여 주옵시기를 비옵고]

do Thou grant that they may receive forgiveness for their sins, and,

쏘새사름되게ᄒ여주옵시기를비옵ᄂᆡ다[또 새 사람 되게 하여 주옵시기를 비옵니다.]

also, make them to become new persons, we pray Thee.

죠션관쟝브터빅셩신지예수밋기를비옵고[조선의 관리부터 백성까지 예수 믿기를 비옵고]

From the official class to the common people may Koreans become believers, and

하ᄂ님밧긔아모위홀것업ᄂᆫ줄알게ᄒ여주옵시고[하나님밖에 아무 위할 것 없는 줄 알게 하여 주옵시고]

make them to know that beside Thee there is no God, and,

하ᄂ님만공경ᄒ게ᄒ여주옵시기를비옵ᄂᆡ다[하나님만 공경하게 하여 주옵시기를 비옵니다.]

grant that they may worship only Thee.

예수일홈을의지ᄒ야비옵ᄂᆡ다 아멘[예수 이름을 의지하여 비옵니다. 아멘]

Trusting in Jesus' Name we pray. Amen.

부가적 도움말

1. 으로ᄒ여곰[으로 하여금]

우리로ᄒ여곰범죄치안케ᄒ옵소셔[우리로 하여금 죄를 범하지 않게 하옵소서.]
Cause us not to sin.

바로로ᄒ여곰이스라엘빅셩을노아보내게ᄒ셨쇼[바로로 하여금 이스라엘 백성을 놓아 보내게 하셨소.]
He caused Pharaoh to set free and send away the Israelites.

뎌희들노ᄒ여곰됴흔사람이되게ᄒ소셔[저희들로 하여금 좋은 사람이 되게 하소서.]
Cause us to become good people.

2. 으로말매암아[으로 말미암아]

우리가예수로말미암아구원을엇엇쇼[우리가 예수로 말미암아 구원을 얻었소.]
We have obtained salvation through Jesus.

하ᄂ님쯰셔그의아들노말미암아우리를구속ᄒ셨쇼[하나님께서 그의 아들로 말미암아 우리를 구속하셨소.]
God has saved us through His Son.

3. 으로더브러[과 더불어]

긔도ᄒᆞ는것은하ᄂᆞ님으로더브러교통ᄒᆞ는것이오[기도하는 것은 하나님과 더불어 교통하는 것이오.]
Praying is having fellowship with God.

그사람으로더브러농사ᄒᆞ엿소[그 사람과 더불어 농사하였소.]
He farmed in partnership with that man.

4. 겸ᄒᆞ야[겸하여]

농ᄉᆞ와쟝ᄉᆞ를겸ᄒᆞ여셔홈ᄂᆡ다[농사와 장사를 겸하여서 합니다.]
I am engaged in farming and business both.

쟝날과쥬일이겸ᄒᆞᆯᄯᅢ에조심ᄒᆞ야죄짓지마시오[장날과 주일이 겸할 때에 조심하여 죄짓지 마시오.]
When the Lord's Day and market day come on the same day, be careful not to sin.

문동병과폐병이겸힛습니다[문둥병과 폐병이 겸했습니다.]
He had leprosy and consumption both.

5. ᄒᆞᆯᄉᆞ록[할수록]

싱각ᄒᆞᆯᄉᆞ록우셥소[생각할수록 우습소.]
The more I think of it, the funnier it is.

볼수록자미잇소[볼수록 재미있소.]

It gets more interesting the further I read.

그사람돈줄수록더달나고ᄒᆞ오[그 사람 돈 줄수록 더 달라고 하오.]

The more money I give him, the more he asks.

6. ᄒᆞ자/ᄒᆞ자마자[하자/하자마자]

집을짓자마자팔앗소[집을 짓자마자 팔았소.]

He had no sooner built the house than he sold it.

담을쌋자마자험으러젓소[담을 쌓자마자 허물어졌소.]

He had no sooner built the wall than it fell down.

7. 인ᄒᆞ야/위ᄒᆞ야[인하여/위하여]의 대비

죄로인ᄒᆞ야형벌을밧앗소[죄로 인하여 형벌을 받았소.]

He received punishment on account of sin.

예수ᄭᅥ셔죄인을위ᄒᆞ야죽으셧소[예수께서 죄인을 위하여 죽으셨소.]

Jesus died on behalf of sinners.

8. ᄒᆞ듯ᄒᆞ오[하듯 하오]

사람을파리죽이듯힛소[사람을 파리 죽이듯 했소.]

They killed people off like flies.

열심이불붓듯니러낫소[열심이 불붙듯 일어났소.]

Enthusiasm spread (arose) like fire.

9. 홀ᄯᅳ름[할 따름]

사실을말홀ᄯᅳ름이오[사실을 말할 따름이오.]

All you have to do is to state the facts.

순사는죄인을잡을ᄯᅳ름이오[순사는 죄인을 잡을 따름이오.]

All the policeman does is to arrest criminals, (not try them).

10. 홀것ᄀᆞᆺ소[할 것 같소]

비올것ᄀᆞᆺᄒ셔일ᄒ러안갓소[비가 올 것 같아서 일하러 안 갔소.]

It looked like rain, so I did not go to work.

그사람이일잘홀것ᄀᆞᆺ소[그 사람이 일을 잘 할 것 같소.]

He looks as though he would do the work well.

될것ᄀᆞᆺ지안소[될 것 같지 않소.]

It does not seem as though it would work.

11. ᄒ여지다/ᄒ여가다[해지다/해가다]

그사름이늙어감ᄂᆡ다[그 사람이 늙어갑니다.]

He's getting old.

날이ᄎᄎ치워짐니다[날이 차차 추워집니다.]

The days are gradually getting colder.

12. 홀지언뎡[할지언정]

ᄌᆞ식이업슬지언뎡말듯지안은ᄋᆞ히를두지마시오[자식이 없을지언정 말 듣지 않는 아이를 두지 마시오.]

Have no children at all, rather than disobedient ones.

13. ᄒᆞ기에[하기에]

그고양이는쥐잡기에젹슴니대[그 고양이는 쥐를 잡기에 작습니다.]

That cat is too small for catching rats.

하ᄂᆞ님ᄭᅧ셔보시기에합당치안소[하나님께서 보시기에 합당치 않소.]

In the sight of God it is not right.

가겟다ᄒᆞ기에돈주엇소[가겠다고 하기에 돈을 주었소.]

As he said he was going, I gave him the money.

손님이오겟기에방을예비ᄒᆡ두엇소[손님이 오겠기에 방을 예비해 두었소.]

As a guest is coming, I made ready the room.

14. 디호야[대하여]

그일에디ᄒ여셔메라고말슴ᄒ십데가[그 일에 대하여서 뭐라고 말씀하십디까?]
What did he say concerning that matter?

그것디히셔말홀것업소[그것에 대해서 말할 것이 없소.]
I have nothing to say about it.

15. ᄒ나마나ᄒ오[하나마나 하오]

ᄒ나마나ᄒ외[하나 마나 하오.]
It makes no difference whether it is done or not.

잇스나업스나ᄒ외[있으나 없으나 하오.]
It's all the same with or without it.

16. 말고라도

됴흔것말고라도잇ᄂ디로가져오시외[좋은 것 말고라도 있는 대로 가져오시오.]
Even if there are no good ones, bring whatever there are.

17. 의게잇다/의게달녓다[에게 있다/에게 달렸다]

ᄒ고아니ᄒᄂ것이내게잇다[하고 안하는 것이 내게 달려있다.]
Whether to do it or not is for me to decide.

급뎨ᄒ고락뎨ᄒᄂ것이여러분게잇소[급제하고 낙제하는 것이 여러분에게 달려 있소.]

Whether you pass or fail depends on you.

18. ᄒ여버릇[해 버릇]

일즉니러나버릇힛소[일찍 일어나 버릇했소.]

He had the habit of rising early.

먹어버릇을못ᄒ엿스니가그럿치[먹어 버릇 못하였으니까 그렇지.]

It was because he was not in the habit of (accustomed to) eating it.

19. ᄒ엿다말앗다ᄒᄂ사람이오

ᄒ엿다말앗다ᄒᄂ사람이오[하였다 말았다 하는 사람이오.]

He is the kind that does it for a while and then stops.

열엇다닷앗다함늬대[열었다 닫았다 합니다.]

It opens and shuts.

ᄭ윗다ᄲ옵앗다ᄒᄂ책이오[끼웠다 뽑았다 하는 책이오.]

It's a loose-leaf note-book.

20. ᄒᆞᄂᆞᄃᆡ로[하는 대로]

그사름ᄒᆞᄂᆞᄃᆡ로ᄒᆞ래그 사람 하는 대로 하라.]
Do it the way he is doing it.

되ᄂᆞᄃᆡ로가져오시외되는 대로 가져오시오.]
(1) Bring it the way it is.
(2) Bring it whenever it is done.

좀에이ᄂᆞᄃᆡ로큰길노가시외좀 돌아가더라도 큰길로 가시오.]
Go by the big road even though it is a little round about.

어려오신ᄃᆡ로속히오시외어려우시더라도 속히 오시오.]
(1) Do come soon, though it will be difficult for you.
(2) Do come quickly, though it will be difficult for you.

삼가야 할 몇 가지 점들

처음에는 모든 표현을 완전히 숙달하는 데 너무 많은 시간을 쓰지 않는 것이 좋다. 더 좋은 방법은 의문을 제기하지 말고 어떤 단어들과 표현들을 무조건 배우거나 사용하면서 익히는 것이다. 어원적인 구분은 나중에 찾아볼 수 있다. "마는, 때문이, 항상, 혹, 모양 등"과 같은 단어들을 지나치게 사용하지 말아야 한다. 이들 단어도 쓰임새가 있지만 외국인들이 사용할 정도는 아니다.

가능하다면 '-소'라는 종결어만 배타적으로 사용하지 말아야 한다. 의문문을 제외한 다른 경우에는 '-소' 대신에 '-지요'라는 높임형을 사용하면 듣기에 더 괜찮고 다양한 느낌을 줄 것이다.

때때로 초심자들은 낮은말(low talk)이 영어의 'low'의 의미처럼 듣는 이를 하대하는 것이라고 생각해서 사용하지 않으려는 실수를 저지른다. 그러나 낮은말을 적절한 경우에 쓰는 것은 전적으로 괜찮으니 사용하는 데 주저하지 말아야 한다.

기회 있을 때마다 낮은말이나 높은말 사용 연습을 게을리 하지 말아야 한다. 낮은말은 아이들에게 늘 사용하고 이론상으로는 모든 하인들에게도 사용한다.

그러나 실제로는 남녀 하인들에게 예삿말을 사용한다. 특히 시골 지역에서 그러한데, 시골에서는 서울에서보다 계급 구분이 훨씬 덜 엄격하기 때문이다. 또 주인과 종복보다는 친구관계임을 강조하고 싶은 경우에 하인들에게 예삿말을 사용한다.

당신이 아는 사람들 중에 나이가 지긋한 이들은 극존칭 사용법에 귀중한 사례를 제공할 것이다. 당신이 실제 지위가 그리 높지 않은 사람들에게도 극존칭을 사용하면 한국인들 사이에서 당신의 평판에 결코 나쁘게 작용하지는 않을 것이다.

반말(half-talk)은 적절한 형식으로 사용할 수 있도록 상당한 훈련이 되기 전까지는 쓰지 말아야 한다. 언제, 어디에서, 어떻게 써야 할지 알고 나서야 반말을 사용할 수 있다.

당신이 좀 더 나은 것을 배우는 즉시 처음에 임시변통으로 서툴게 사용하던 것들을 버려라. 가능한 빠른 시일 내에 문장 구성과 발음상의 실수들을 바로잡아라.

당신이 현재 한국인들에게 불완전한 말을 사용할 수밖에 없다고 해도, 당신에게 말을 하는 한국인들에게는 불완전한 말을 습관적으로 사용하지 못하도록 해야 한다. 그들이 천천히 간단하게, 그러나 훌륭하고 자연스러운 한국어로 말하도록 요구해라.

당신의 한국어 선생님에게 영어로 말하는 슬픈 실수를 범하지 않도록 해라. 그리고 당신이 말하는 중에 "Well', 'Oh', 'Ah', 'Yes' 등의 감탄사를 끼워 넣지 말아라.

다른 외국인들의 실수들에 주의를 기울여라. 많은 외국인들이 아직 단어들을 잘못 발음하는 경우가 많은데, 이는 우리가 그 단어들을 토착민의 진짜 발음으로 배우지 않고, 잘못된 음역으로 배웠거나 또 다른 외국인에게 들었기 때문이다. 나이든 선교사들에게 도움을 청하러 가는 것을 주저하지 말아야 한다. 그들은 당신이 생각하는 것 이상으로, 당신이 한국어를 배울 때 더 좋은 시작과 더 나은 기회를 얻기를 열망하고 있다.

되도록 많은 한자를 익히되 '사람 인, 마음 심, 아들 자'처럼 그들의 이름을 익혀라. 이렇게 하면 당신이 한자어를 듣거나 볼 때 그 의미를 깨닫는 데 도움이 될 것이다. 예를 들어 당신이 사람에 해당하는 한자가 '인'이고 마음에 해당하는 한자가 '심'이라는 것을 알면, 지적으로 대단히 명민하지 않더라도, '인심'이 '사람의 마음'이나 '기질'을 뜻한다는 점을 쉽게 파악할 수 있을 것이다.

때때로 완곡한 표현으로 한국어가 '꽤 통하는 지식'이라고 말하는 정도에 만족하지 말아라. 당신이 말하고자 하는 모든 것을 편하게 잘 말할 수 없다면, 그 언어 지식은 '꽤 통하는 지식'이 아니다.

당신이 모든 문학적, 사회적 취향을 만족시키면서 동시에 한국어도 익힐 수 있을 거라고 생각하는 것은 잘못이다. 당신은 아마 한국어를 '비둘기'처럼 사용하는 수준에 도달할 수도 있겠지만, 어떤 희생도 없이 한국인처럼 한국어를 말할 수는 없을 것이다. 누구든 그런 수준을 성취하리라는 기대를 가질 권리가 있지만, 그것은 고통과 기도와 인내, 그리고 적절한 공부법을 필요로 하는 가장 위대한 과업이다. 첫 3년의 고역을 충실히 견뎌내면 그 기간이 끝날 때쯤 아직 먼 곳에 있는 약속의 땅이 시야에 들어올 터인데, 그때부터는 공부가 즐겁고 언어를 습득하는 것이 좀 더 기쁜 일이 될 것이다.

구어로 된 주보를 정기적으로 읽음으로써 사람들이 무엇을 생각하고 행하는지 직접 알 수 있도록 하라.

───────

이 소책자는 한국에 새로 온 이들을 돕기 위한 것이니만큼, 외국인들이 이해하는 데 시간이 걸리는 몇 가지 점들을 언급하는 게 부적절하지는 않을 것이다. 한국인이라는 민족은 우리 서구의 국민들보다 예절의 세세한 부분들에 훨씬 더 주의를 기울인다. 따라서 우리가 그들에게 아주 불쾌한 인상을 주지 않으려면 우리는 그들과 비슷한 수준의 예절바른 매너를 지켜야 한다.

예를 들어, 당신의 선생님께나 혹은 그와 비슷한 지위에 있는 다른 한국인들에게 작별인사를 할 때, 아직 그들이 당신 앞에 있는 상태에서 서둘러 반쯤 돌아선 채 말하지 말고, 그들을 제대로 마주보고 서서 마땅한 신중함을 갖춰 인사를 하라.

아랫사람과 윗사람이 당신에게 행하는 정중하고 격식을 갖춘 인사를 항상 제대로 받아야 한다. 대개 아이들이나 하인들에게는 먼저 인사를 하지 않고 그들이 인사하기를 기다려 응답해야 한다.

한국인들과 회의나 대화를 할 때, 남자건 여자건 그들 중에 연장자에게 특별한 주의를 기울여라. 그들이 들어오거나 떠날 때 자리에서 일어서고, 그들에게 최선의 언어로 말해야 한다.

외국인들과 한국인들이 섞여 있는 모임에 있을 때는 한국인들을 배제하고 외국인에게만 전념하지 말도록 주의하고, 대화의 대부분을 한국어로 진행하도록 노력하라.

우리는 이 민족의 가장 좋은 사회적 관습들을 공격하지 않도록 주의해야 한다. 이유가 무엇이든 외국인들은 자기 고국에 있을 때보다 [한국 같은 이방의 땅에서] 더 큰 행동의 자유를 누리려는 유혹을 받는다는 것은 불행하게도 사실이지만, [외국인들은 이방에서] 오히려 훨씬 더 큰 신중함을 지켜야 한다.

외국인 남녀가 길에서 만났을 때, 품위 있는 조심성을 지켜야 한다. 그리고 한국인들이 지켜보고 있을 때는 언제나, 남녀가 너무 격의 없이 구는 것을 피하도록 조심해야 한다. 비록 그것이 단순히 무해한 친근함의 표현이라 할지라도 말이다.

숙녀들은 그들이 항상 익숙하게 행해왔던 자유가 한국의 상위계층 여성들에게는 없었음을 유념해서 [한국식 예절에] 어느 정도 타협하는 수고를 치러야 한다. 예를 들어, 하인을 제외한 선생님들이나 한국의 남성 지인들과 함께 공공장소에 나갈 때가 그렇다. 선생님이 젊은 남성이라면 [그와 함께 공공장소에 모습을 드러내는 것은] 특히 기피할 만하다. 다른 조건이 동일하다면, 미혼 여성은 선생님으로 젊은 남성보다는 나이든 사람을 고르는 것이 좋다.

여성들은 한국 남성들과 농담을 하거나 사교적인 인사말을 나누는 데 신중해야 한다. 외국인들과 접촉하기 이전 한국 토착 양반의 경험에 비춰보면, 멀쩡한 여성이 아버지나 남매, 남편을 제외한 어떤 남성과 아무런 사심 없이 자유롭게 어울리는 것은 도무지 이해할 수 없는 일이기 때문이다.

한국에서 여성들이 순회설교를 할 수 있다는 것은 풍부한 선례로 증명되었지만, [여성 설교자들은] 가능한 공공장소에 모습을 드러내지 않아야 하며, 오해를 살만한 행동을 주의 깊게 예방해야 한다. 예를 들어, 여성 순회설교자가 난잡한 무뢰배들을 향해 말하거나 노래하면서 복음을 전파하는 것은 무익하다기보다 해롭다. 여성 선교사들이 이교도 청중 앞에서 노래하는 것은 어떤 상황에서든 추천할 만한 일이 아니다.

남성 선교사가 토착 여성들과 상대해야 할 때는, 그들이 선교사의 시선(그

시선이 아무리 친절하고 우호적이라 하더라도)에 너무 가깝게 들어오지 않도록 충분한 거리를 유지해야만 훨씬 더 편안하게 느낀다는 점을 빨리 알아차려야 한다.

한국인들을 상대할 때 이들만큼 자존심을 중시하는 민족이 없다는 점을 잘 유념하면 불필요한 말썽을 상당히 줄일 수 있을 것이다. 한국인에게 어떤 손실(loss)도 타인들 앞에서 '체면을 잃는'(lose face) 것보다 심각한 것은 없다. 만약 [한국인에게] 엄중한 질책을 해야 하는 경우가 있다면 사적인 자리에서 하도록 해라. 이러저러한 행동이 문제가 있다는 암시를 전해야 한다면, 우호적인 제 3자를 매개로 삼거나 다른 우회적인 방법으로 하는 것을 추천한다. 당신이 [한국인들과] 행복[한 관계]를 유지하면서도 목적을 달성하고자 한다면, 앵글로색슨식의 [대놓고 말하는] 무례함을 반드시 피해야 한다.

한국인들을 상대하려면 말이나 태도뿐 아니라 표정에서도 초조함이나 짜증의 모든 흔적들을 가능한 지워내는 법을 일찌감치 배워야 한다. 선교사는 동등한 상대를 대할 때의 사랑에서 우러나오는, 지속적이고 규칙적이면서 부드럽고도 단호한 태도를 취함으로써 합당한 결과를 성취할 수 있을 것이다. 신참 선교사들은 왜 굳이 이런 말들이 필요한지 명확히 알지 못할 수도 있지만, 그가 한국에 오래 머무른다면 틀림없이 깨닫게 될 것이다. 거의 참을 수 없을 만큼 짜증스러운 상황들이 그의 계획과 목표를 방해하고 좌절시키는 일이 종종 있다는 점을 말이다. 그런 경우에 처하여 그가 자연스러운 감정인 분노와 초조를 표출한다면, 자신이 신실함과 기도로 유지해온 노력들을 망치게 될 것이다. 이 점을 잘 유념할 필요가 있는데, 앵글로색슨인에게는 진실함과 정직함이 중요한 것처럼, 한국인에게는 인내와 참을성, 예의바른 태도가 중요하기 때문이다.

한국의 토착 기독교인이 뻔한 거짓말을 하는 것이 우리에게 충격적인 것만큼이나 우리가 화를 드러내는 것이 그들에게는 충격적이다. 이와 관련하여

신구약 성경이 진실과 솔직함의 중요성을 과소평가하지 않았던 것만큼이나 형제애, 온유함, 인내, 자제와 같은 덕들을 강조했다는 점을 상기하면 좋을 듯 하다. 이 후자의 덕들은 오늘날 서구인들에게는 삶의 압박과 스트레스 때문에 그리 인기 있는 덕목이 아니지만 말이다.

더 많은 점들을 세세하게 제시해도 좋겠지만, 사려 깊은 독자라면 한국에서 하거나 하지 말아야 할 것들의 특징에 대해 나름의 결론을 내릴 수 있을 만큼은 충분히 말한 것 같다.

이 작은 책의 내용들은 "이미 이루었다"라고 자부하는 영혼을 지닌 독자들이 아니라, 그 자신[바울]처럼, [예수를] "뒤따르려는" 이들을 향한 것이다.[23]

---

[23] "내가 이미 얻었다 함도 아니요, 온전히 이루었다 함도 아니라. 오직 내가 그리스도 예수께 잡힌 바 된 그것을 잡으려고 달려가노라."(빌립보서 3:12)를 인용하고 있다.

색인

도움말

1. 홀수잇소 Can do

2. 홀수밧긔업소 No way out of it.

3. ᄒ여라 Imperative.

4. ᄒ지마라 Negative imperative.

5. ᄒ지못ᄒ오 Cannot do.

   ᄒ지아니ᄒ오 Does not do.

6. 홀ᄆᆞᆷ잇소 Mind to do.

7. ᄒ고시브오 Wish to do.

   ᄒ기슬소 Do not wish to do.

8. ㅎ기쉽소 Easy to do.

　ㅎ기어렵소 Hard to do.

9. ㅎ면 If

10. ㅎ거든 If, or when.

11. ㅎ여야쓰겟소 Must do

12. ㅎ게ㅎ오 Cause to do.

13. 하랴고ㅎ오 Intend to do.

14. ㅎ러가오 Go to do.

15. ㅎ오마는 Do, but.

16. ㅎ여도 Although.

17. ㅎ니 As, since.

18. 홀듯ㅎ오 Probable.

19. 홀번ㅎ엿소 On the point of doing.

20. 홀만ㅎ오 Worth doing.

21. ㅎ는테ㅎ오 Pretend to do.

22. 홀까념려ㅎ오 To fear lest.

23. ㅎ는지 Whether (knowledge.)

24. ㅎ던지 Whether (consequence.)

25. 홀째 While or when.

26. ㅎ기젼에 Before doing.

27. ㅎ후에 After doing.

28. ㅎ는줄아오Think or know that.

29. ㅎ도록 Until.

30. 흔지 Time since.

31. 와 and 과And.

32. ᄒᆞ고 And.

33. ᄒᆞ여, ᄒᆞ야, ᄒᆞ여셔 Connectives.

34. ᄒᆞᄂᆞᄃᆡ Connective.

35. ᄒᆞ더라 Indirect Verbal Forms.

36. ᄒᆞ더니 Past Imperfect Connective.

37. ᄒᆞ엿더니 Past Perfect Connective.

38. ᄒᆞ면서 Simultaneous action.

39. ᄒᆞ다가 Interrupted action.

40. 홀쑨더러, 홀쑨만아니오 Not only that but.

41. 의무나 책임 Duty or obligation.

42. 고ᄒᆞ다 Indirect Discourse.

43. 관계절 Relative Clauses.

44. Have.

45. Is.

46. 비교 Comparison.

47. 동의 Assent.

48. 감사 Thanks.

49. 인칭대명사 Personal Pronouns.

50. 사과 Apology.

종교 용어들

짧은 설교 문장들

기도문들

부가적 도움말들

삼가야 할 몇 가지 점들

원문

회의, 교회 및 기타 용어들에 관한
영한, 한영사전

(English–Korean & Korean–Enlish Dictionary of
Parliamentary, Ecclesiastical and Some Other Terms)

PREFACE.

I judge that no apology is needed for the presentation to the public of a dictionary of parliamentary and ecclesiastical terms. The wonder is that we have managed so long without such a book. Every meeting of the church assemblies proves this need.

No claim is made that this book is either perfect or final. When mistakes are discovered the author will be thankful to have his attention called to them in writing so that future editions may be corrected.

It is recognized that technical terminology is changing. Some words are passing out of use, and some have recently come, and so have not won a final place in good usage. Exact terminology cannot yet be hoped for. Some words formerly in use, and some words just coming into use, have been included in these lists in order to meet various needs. It may be that some obsolete words have been retained.

No attempt has been made to change usage even though usage is manifestly wrong or unfortunate. Words in use have been inserted even though a correction might seem desirable. For instance there is great confusion in the use of the words "whoi" (회), "poo" (부), "wiwun" (위원), &c. According

(IV)

to present usage it is often impossible to tell whether in using "wiwun" the speaker means a committee or only one member of a committee. Similarly when the words "chundo poo" (젼도부) is used it may be impossible to determine whether a missionary society is meant or whether the "Board of Foreign Missions" is intended. When words are used indefinitely precision becomes impossible. Such confusion can only be remedied by the decision of some authoritative body or by some uniformity in practice. Such uniformity does not exist at present. All that the lexicographer can do is to list the words at present in use.

In addition to parliamentary and ecclesiastical terms many other useful words have been included, particularly a number of the newer terms used in Sunday School work. For most of these we are indebted to Dr. C. A. Clark and Dr. J. G. Holdcroft.

This book is the result of my having collected lists of parliamentary and ecclesiastical terms for many years for personal use. In addition I desire to acknowledge valuable assistance from similar lists made available to me by my son, Rev. W. M. Baird, Jr.

In the compilation and arrangement of this book I am indebted to Mr. Chang Shin Kook who has given laborious and valuable assistance in writing the manuscript copy of this dictionary.

(V)

It is hoped that the arrangement of the various kinds of parliamentary questions in their order of precedence (as found on pages X to XII), and the statement of various classes of questions, such as, principal, subordinate, incidental, and privileged (pages X and XI), may be helpful. For these rules Robert's Rules of Order is credited. This brief outline is included in order to refresh the memory, and as a slight help to those who wish to learn the ordinary order of business as conducted in parliamentary bodies.

The arrangement in two parts is intended as an aid to both Korean and English users. It is hoped that the book may prove useful not only to learners in both languages but as a refreshment to the memory of more advanced students. May this little book prove one more aid to increased efficiency in carrying on the work of the church.

W. M. BAIRD.

September, 1928.

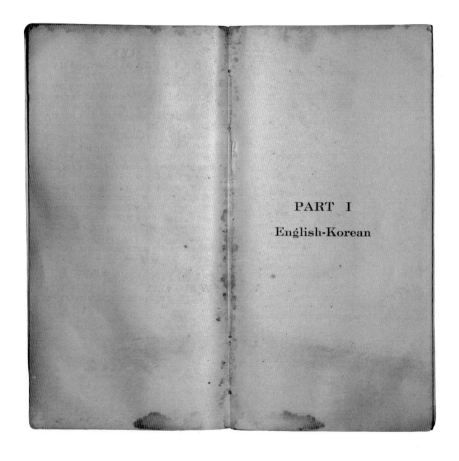

PART I

English-Korean

(IX)

Order of Business.

1. Call to order.
2. Reading of the minutes of the previous meeting.
3. Reports of Standing Committees.
4. Reports of Select(or special) Committees.
5. Unfinished business.
6. New business.
7. Adjournment.

Various Kinds of Motions.

1. To move any motion.
2. To second a motion.
3. To amend a motion.
4. To make an amendment to an amendment.
5. To move a substitute motion.
6. To receive a report.
7. To accept or to adopt a report.
8. To move to commit or refer.
9. To move to postpone to a certain time.
10. To move to postpone indefinitely.
11. To move to lay on the table.
12. To move to take from the table.
13. To move to reconsider a question.
14. To move to withdraw a motion.
15. To move to limit debate.
16. To move to extend the limit of debate.
17. To move to close debate.
18. To move the order of the day.
19. To move that the order of the day be changed.

(X)

20. To move that a subject be made the special order of the day.
21. To move to rescind from the minutes.
22. To move to appeal from the decision of the Chair.
23. To move to suspend the rules.
24. To move to rise and report (Only in Committee of the whole).
25. To move a question of privilege.
26. To move the previous question.
27. To object to the consideration of a question.
28. To move to adjourn.
29. To move to fix the time to which to adjourn.

Four Kinds of Questions.

I. Principal Questions.
II. Subsidiary Questions.
III. Incidental Questions.
IV. Privileged Questions.

I. Principal or Main Questions. Such questions introduce for discussion some particular subject. They may be made only when no other question is before the assembly.

II. A Subsidiary Question is applied to principal questions. It takes precedence of principal questions, and yields to privileged and incidental questions. Subsidiary questions are as follows and in the following order of precedence :—

(XI)

1. To lay on the table.
2. The previous question.
3. To postpone to a certain time.
4. To commit, refer, or re-commit.
5. To amend.
6. To postpone indefinitely.

III. Incidental Questions. These arise out of principal and subsidiary questions and take precedence of them. They yield to privileged questions. They are as follows :—

1. To appeal from the decision of the Chair.
2. Objection to the consideration of a question.
3. Call for the reading of papers.
4. Request for permission to withdraw a motion.
5. Motion to suspend the rules.

IV. Privileged Questions. These take precedence of all principal, subsidiary and incidental questions. They are undebatable except when relating to the rights and privileges of the assembly or its members. They should never be used to interrupt or delay business. They are as follows in the following order of precedence :—

1. To fix the time to which the assembly shall adjourn.
2. To adjourn.
3. Questions relating to the rights and privileges of the assembly or any of its members.

(XII)

4. Call for the orders of the day.

The Following Questions are undebatable.
All others are debatable.

1. To fix the time to which to adjourn. (This question is undebatable if made when another question is before the assembly. If made when no other question is before the assembly it is, like any other main question, debatable).
2. To adjourn.
3. Motions for the orders of the day.
4. Questions relating to priority of business.
5. An appeal (if made when certain other questions are pending).
6. Objection to the consideration of a question.
7. Motion to lay on the table.
8. Motion to take from the table.
9. The previous question.
10. To reconsider an undebatable question.

The Following Motions cannot be amended.

1. To adjourn.
2. Motion for the orders of the day.
3. All incidental questions. (See No. III above).
4. To lay on the table.
5. The previous question.
6. An amendment to an amendment.
7. To postpone indefinitely.

(XIII)

8. To reconsider.

The Following Questions open the main question to debate.

1. To commit or refer.
2. To postpone indefinitely.
3. To rescind.
4. To reconsider a debatable question.

Most questions are decided by a majority vote, but the following questions require a two-thirds vote.

1. To amend the rules.
2. To suspend the rules.
3. To make special order.
4. To take up a question out of its proper order.
5. An objection to the consideration of a question.
6. To extend the limits of debate.
7. To close or limit debate.
8. The previous question.

Enǵlish-Korean
DICTIONARY
of
Parliamentary, Ecclesiastical
and
Some other Terms

A

Abolish, *v.t.* 폐지(廢止)ᄒᆞ다, 철폐(撤廢)ᄒᆞ다.
Abolition, *n.* 폐지, 철폐.
Above. 이샹(以上).
Absence, *n.* 결석(缺席), 흠셕(欠席), 궐셕(闕席).
Absence for cause. 유고(有故)결셕, etc.
Absence without cause or notice. 무고(無故)
결셕, etc.
Absences, Examining committee on. 결셕사찰
위원(査察委員), etc.
Absent, To be. 결셕ᄒᆞ다, etc.
Absent member. 결셕원(員), 결셕회원(會員),
etc.
Absentee, *n* 결셕자(者), 결셕성(生), etc.
Absentee without cause or notice. 무고결셕
쟈, etc.
Academy, *n.* 즁학교(中學校).
Accept, *v.t.* (a petition or an application) 슈
리(受理)ᄒᆞ다.
Acceptance, *n.* 승낙(承諾), 득낙(得諾), 슈리.
Accompanying paper (enclosure). 별지(別紙).
Accountability, *n.* 칙임(責任).
Accusation, *n.* 고소(告訴), 소송(訴訟).
Accusation, Statement of. 고소장(告訴狀).

(1)

Acc—Adv

Accuse, *v.t.* 고소하다, 고발(告發)하다.
Accused person. 피고(被告), 피고인(人).
Accuser, *n.* 고소인(人). (Prosecutor) 원고(原告).
Acknowledgement, *n.* 승낙(承諾).
Act for, To. 대리(代理)하다.
Additional (Supplementary) rules. 부측(附則).
Address, *n.* (1) 강설(講說), 연설(演說). (2) (of a person) 쥬소성명(住所姓名).
Address in response. 답수(答辭).
Address, Public. 강연(講演).
Adjourn, *v.t.* 연회(延會)하다. *v.i.* 폐회(閉會)하다, 휴회(休會)하다.
Adjourn a meeting, To. 폐회(閉會)하다, 휴회하다.
Adjourn for recess, To. 명회(停會)하다.
Adjourn, To fix the time to which to. 폐회기(期)를명(定)하다.
Adjournment, *n.* 연회, 폐회, 휴회, 명회.
Administer, *v.t.* 관리(管理)하다, 베프다, 경영(經營)하다.
Administrate, *v.t.* 집행(執行)하다.
Administration, *n.* (1) 판리. (2) 행정(行政), 집행.
Administration committee. 집행위원(委員).
Administrator, *n.* 판리인(人), 판리자(者).
Admission, *n.* 입회(入會), 입장(入場).
Admission ticket. 입장권(券).
Admit to membership, To. 입회를허(許)하다.
Admonish, *v.t.* 권계(勸戒)하다.
Admonition, *n.* 권계.
Adopt, *v.t.* 처용(採用)하다, 가결(可決)하다.
Adopt as a whole, To. 전부(全部)처용하다.
Adopt by sections, To. 축됴(逐條)처용하다.
Adoption, *n.* 처용, 가결.
Adult department. 장년부(壯年部), 장년반(班).
Advance, *v.t.* 제출(提出)하다.
Advertise, *v.t* 광고(廣告)하다.
Advertisement, *n.* 광고.
Advertisement (bulletin) board. 광고판(板).
Advice, *n.* 권고(勸告), 충고(忠告), 훈계(訓戒).
Advise, *v.t.* 권고하다, 충고하다.

(2)

Adv—Apo

Adviser, *n.* 고문(顧問).
Advocacy, *n.* 변호(辯護).
Advocate, *n.* 변호인(人). *v.t.* 변호하다.
Affair, *n.* 수건(事件), 안건(案件).
Affairs of an assembly or society. 회무(會務).
Affirmative decision. 가결(可決).
Affirmative question or motion. 가결안(案)
Affirmative side. 가편(可便).
Affirmative vote. 가표(可票).
After Christ (A.D.). 셔력긔원후(西曆紀元後), 예수강성후(降生後), 쥬후(主後).
Agree, *v.i.* 승낙(承諾)하다, 허락(許諾)하다.
Agreement, *n.* (1) 승낙, 허락. (2) 찬성(贊成). (3) 계약(契約).
Agreement, To make an. 계약하다.
Aid, *n.* 찬성(贊成). *v.t.* 찬성하다.
Alms, *n.* 구제(救濟).
Alms, To give. 구제하다.
Alternate, *n.* 대리후보(代理候補), 륜츠(輪次), 체번(替番). *v.* (As for associate pastors to take turns in preaching) 체번하다.
Alternate moderator. 륜츠회장(會長).
Amend, *v.t.* 기의(改議)하다; 기정(改正)하다, 슈정(修正)하다.
Amendment, *n.* 기의, 기의안(案); 기안(改案); 기정, 슈정.
Amendment committee. 슈정위원(委員).
Amendment to an amendment. 지기의(再改議).
Amendment, To make an amendment to an. 지기의하다.
Amendment, To move an. 기의하다.
Angel, *n.* 텬수(天使), 수자(使者).
Announce, *v.t.* 공포(公布)하다, 포고(布告)하다, 광고(廣告)하다.
Announcement, *n.* 공포, 포고, 광고; 포빅(告白).
Annual Conference. 년회(年會), 미(每)년회.
Answer, *n.* 디답(對答); 답변(答辯). *v.* 디답을하다; 답변하다.
Answer to a communication. 답변셔(書).
Anti-tobacco Society. 금연회(禁煙會), 단연회(斷煙會).
Apologetics, *n.* 변증론(辯證論).

(3)

Apology, *n.* 사과(謝過).
Apostacy, *n.* 비교(背敎)
Apostate, *n.* 비교자(者).
Apostatize, *v.i.* 비교하다.
Apostle. *n.* 사도(使徒)
Apostle's Creed. 사도신경(信經).
Apostolic Church. 사도 (시, 쎄) 교회[使徒(時)敎會].
Appeal, *n.* (from one court to the next above) 공소(控訴), (second appeal one step up from a 공소), 상고(上告), 상소(上訴). *v.i.* 공소하다, 상고하다, 상소하다.
Appeal, Petition of. 공소장(狀).
Appear, *v.i.* 출두(出頭)하다, 출셕(出席)하다.
Appellant, *n.* 공소인(人), 상고인(人).
Applause, *n.* 박수(拍手), 박장(拍掌).
Applicant, *n.* 지원자(志願者).
Application, *n.* 청원(請願), 지원.
Application, To make an. 청원하다, 출원(出願)하다.
Apply for, To. 지원하다.
Appoint, *v.t.* 지뎡(指定)하다.
Appoint a committee or an officer, To. 쟈벽(自辟)하다.
Appointment, *n.* 지명.
Appointment, To make an official. 임직(任職)하다.
Appointment to office. 임직.
Apportionment, *n.* 임수(任事).
Apportionment committee. 임수부(部).
Approval, *n.* 인허(認許), 인가(認可), 재가(裁可) ; 승인(承認).
Approve, *v.t.* 인허하다, 인가하다, 재가하다, 승인하다.
Approved, To be. 인허받다 or 되다, 인가받다 or 되다 ; 승인(承認)되다.
Argument, To make an end of. 파의(罷議)하다.
Arrangement, *n.* 쥰비(準備), 셜비(設備).
Arrangement committee. 쥰비위원(委員) ; 졀ᄎ(節次)위원, 슌셔(順序)위원, 쥰비회(會).
Arrangements, To make. 쥰비하다.
As follows, To be. 여좌(如左)하다, 좌긔(左記)

(4)

대로.
Ask, *v.* 뭇(問)다.
Assemblage, *n.* 회즁(會衆)
Assemble, *v.i.* 회집(會集)하다, 집회(集會)하다.
Assemblies, Rules of Order for Public. 의회통용규즉(議會通用規則).
Assembly, *n.* 회(會).
Assembly for study. 강습회(講習會).
Assembly hall. 의수당(議事堂).
Assembly, Public. 의회(議會).
Assembly's documents. 회즁문건(會衆文件).
Assent, *n.* 승낙(承諾), 재가(裁可).
Assist, *v.t.* 찬셩(贊成)하다.
Assistance, *n.* 찬셩.
Assistant, *a.* 부(副).
Assistant secretary. 부셔긔(書記).
Assistant treasurer. 부회계(會計).
Associate member. 찬셩원(贊成員), 찬셩회원(會員).
Associate pastor. 동수목수(同事牧師).
Association, *n.* 회(會), 협회(協會), 련합회(聯合會).
Association for carrying out a measure. 긔셩회(期成會).
Assume an office, To. 취임(就任)하다.
Assumption of office. 취임.
Asylum for the blind and dumb. 명아원(盲啞院).
Asylum for the old. 양로원(養老院).
Asylum for the old and for orphans. 양로고ᄋ원(孤兒院).
At once. 죽셕(卽席)에.
Attend, *v.t.* 출셕(出席)하다, 참셕(參席)하다 ; 립회(立會)하다, 출두(出頭)하다.
Attends but has not the privilege of the floor, One who. 방텽원(傍聽員).
Attendance, *n.* 출셕, 참셕 ; 립회 ; 출두.
Attendance as a hearer. 방텽(傍聽).
Attendance, Number in. 출셕수(數).
Attendant, *n.* 출셕원(員), 참셕원, 참셕회원(會員).
Attendant, Late. 만도회원(晚到會員).

(5)

Att—Bef

Attorney, Power of. 위임장(委任狀).
Audit, *n.* 검사(檢査). *v.t.* 검사하다.
Auditing committee. 검사위원(檢査委員).
Auditor, *n.* 검사원(檢査員).
Authority, *n.* 직권(職權).
Authority or Power, To exceed. 월권(越權)하다.
Average, *n.* 평균(平均).
Aye and no. 가부(可否).

B

Back up, To. (support) 후원(後援)하다.
Backing, *n.* (succour) 후원.
Backslide, *v.i.* 퇴보(退步)하다, 타락(墮落)하다.
Backsliding. 퇴보, 타락.
Ballot, *n.* 투표(投票). *v.i.* 투표하다.
Ballot, False. 부정(不正)투표.
Ballot, Secret. 무기명암투표(無記名暗投票), 무기명투표.
Ballot, Opening of the. 개표(開票).
Ballot, To open the. 개표(改票)하다.
Ballots, Counting. 계표(計票).
Ballots, To count. 계표하다.
　Method of counting ballots.
　正 ╫╫. Indicates five ballots.
　╔ ⅢⅠ. Indicates four ballots.
　╥ Ⅱ.　Indicates Two ballots.
Band of Singers. 찬양대(讚揚隊), 찬미대(讚美隊).
Baptism, *n.* 세례(洗禮).
Baptism by effusion. 주수세례(注水洗禮).
Baptism by immersion. 침수세례(浸水洗禮).
Baptism by sprinking. 관수세례(灌水洗禮).
Baptism, Infant. 으헌(兒孩)세례.
Baptist Church. 침례교회(浸禮敎會).
Baptize, *v.* 세례배프다, 세례주다.
Baptized, To be. 세례받다.
Baptized member ⎫세례교인(敎人), 입교인(入
Baptized Christian ⎭敎人).
Before Christ (B.C.). 서력긔원전(西曆紀元前),

(6)

Bel—Bou

예수강성젼(降生前), 쥬젼(主前).
Belief, *n.* 밋음, 신앙(信仰).
Believe, *v.t.* 밋다, 신앙하다.
Believe in Jesus, To. 예수(를) 밋다.
Benediction, *n.* 츅복긔도(祝福祈禱), 츅도(祝禱).
Betroth, *v.t.* 약혼(約婚)하다, 뎡혼(定婚)하다.
Betrothed, To be. 약혼되다, 뎡혼되다.
Betrothal, *n.* 약혼, 뎡혼.
Bible, The. ⎫성경(聖經), 셩셔(聖書).
Bible, The Holy. ⎭
Bible (training) Class. 사경회(査經會).
Bible Class committee. 사경위원(委員).
Bible Institute. 성경학교(聖經學校), 셩셔학원(聖書學院).
Bible Institute, Men's. 남(男)성경학교, 남셩셔학원.
Bible Institute, Women's. 녀(女)성경학교, 녀셩셔학원.
Bible, Reading of the. 성경랑독(聖經朗讀).
Bible, To read the. 성경(을)랑독하다.
Bible School, Daily Vacation. 하긔으동성경학교(夏期兒童聖經學校).
Bible School, Weekday. 쥬간성경학교(週間聖經學校).
Bible Society. 셩셔공회(聖書公會).
Bill, *n.* 법안(法案).
Bill of Religion. 종교(宗敎)법안.
Birthday greeting. 싱일츅하(生日祝賀).
Birthday greeting card. 싱일츅하표(票), 싱일츅하장(狀).
Bishop, *n.* 감독(監督).
Blank, *n.* 식양지(式樣紙), 용지(用紙), 셔식(書式).
Board, *n.* 부(部), 국(局), 회(會).
Board of Directors. 리스회(理事會).
Board, President of a. 국쟝(局長).
Board of treasurers. 탁스(托事)부.
Body, *n.* 단톄(團體).
Born again, To be. 싱성(重生)하다, 거듭나다.
Boundary, *n.* 경계(境界).
Boundary committee. 뎡계위원(定界委員), 경계위원.

(7)

Bou—Car

Boundary, To determine a. 뎡계ᄒᆞ다, 경계 풀덩ᄒᆞ다.
Branch, n. 지부(支部).
Branch Society. 지회(支會).
Bring forward, To. 뎨츌(提出)ᄒᆞ다.
Budget, n. 예산(豫算),"예산안(案).
Budget committee. 예산위원(委員).
Bulletin board. 광고판(廣告板).
Burial ceremony. 장례(葬禮), 장스(葬事).
Business, n. 스건(事件), 스무(事務).
Business committee. 스무위원(委員).
Business hour. 스무시간(時間), 직무(執務)시간.
Business, Order of. 스무슌셔(順序), 스무졀ᄎᆞ(節次).
Business, To attend to. 시무(視務)ᄒᆞ다.
Business, To do. [회무(會務), 스무(事務),etc.] 쳐리(處理)ᄒᆞ다.
Business, Transaction of. 회무쳐리.
By-laws, n. 규측(規則), 셰측(細則).

C

Call, n. 쳥빙(請聘), 쳥요(請邀). v.t 쳥빙ᄒᆞ다, 쳥요ᄒᆞ다.
Call a meeting, To. 쇼집(召集)ᄒᆞ다.
Call, Form of the. 쳥빙셔(書).
Call out, To. 호츌(呼出)ᄒᆞ다.
Call to order, To. 회셕졍돈(會席整頓)식히다, 고육(告肅)ᄒᆞ다.
Called, One who has been (as of a pastor). 피빙쟈(被聘者).
Calling. 쇼집(召集).
Calling out (Summons). 호츌(呼出).
Candidate, n. 지원쟈(志願者), 후보쟈(候補者).
Canon, n. (1) 교회법(敎會法). (2) 경뎐(經典).
Capacity, n. 즈격(資格).
Carried, To be. 가결(可決)되다, 쳐용(採用)되다, 통과(通過)되다, 득승(得勝)ᄒᆞ다.
Carry into effect, To. 실시(實施)ᄒᆞ다.
Carry out, To. 실시(實施)ᄒᆞ다.
Carrying out a measure, Association for. 긔

Cas—Cha

성회(期成會).
Case, n. (of law) 스건(事件), 안건(案件).
Case, Judicial. 지판(裁判)스건.
Catechise, v.t. 문답(問答)ᄒᆞ다.
Catechism, n. 요리문답(要理問答).
Catechism, Larger. 대(大)요리문답.
Catechism, Shorter. 쇼(小)요리문답.
Catechist, n. 뎐도스(傳道師).
Catechumen, n. 학습교인(學習敎人), 학습인, 견습인(見習人).
Catechumenate, Examination for the. 학습문답(學習問答).
Catechumen, To receive as a. 학습세우다.
Catholic Church, Roman. 로마교회(敎會), 로마교, 텬쥬교(天主敎).
Catholic Church, The Holy (Universal). 성공회(聖公會).
Cause, n. 스고(事故), 연고(緣故), 유고(有故).
Cause, With. 유고(有故).
Cause, Without. 무고(無故).
Celebration, n. 츅하(祝賀).
Celebration, Congratulatory. 츅하회(會).
Celebrate, v.t. 츅하ᄒᆞ다.
Censor, v.t. 검열(檢閱)ᄒᆞ다.
Censorship, n. 검열.
Censure, n. 권계(勸戒), 칙망(責望), 징척(懲責). v.t. 권계ᄒᆞ다, 칙망ᄒᆞ다, 징척ᄒᆞ다.
Censure, Infliction of. 시벌(施罰).
Censure, Removal of. 히벌(解罰).
Ceremony, n. 례식(禮式), 의식(儀式), 식(式).
Certificate, n. 증명셔(證明書), 증셔(證書), 면허(免許).
Certificate of dismission. 이명(移名)증셔.
Certificate, Written. 면허장(狀).
Certify, v.t. 면허ᄒᆞ다.
Chair, The. 회장셕(會長席), 의장셕(議長席), 슈셕(首席), 슈회(司會).
Chairman, n. 회장(會長), 의장(議長), 스회쟈(司會者).
Chairman of a committee. 위원장(委員長).
Chairman, Temporary. 림시(臨時)회장.
"Mr. Chairman" "회장" "의장".

Cha—Chu

Chairmanship, *n.* 회장직(會長職), 사회(司會).
Chapel, *n.* 전도당(傳道堂).
Charge, *n.* (1) 위임(委任). (2) 소장(訴狀).
Charge, To give in. 위임(委任)ㅎ다.
Charge, To receive. 위임밧다, 위임되다.
Charge of, To take. 위임을다, 담당(擔當)ㅎ다.
Charity, *n.* 주선(慈善), 자혜(慈惠).
Charity Concert. 주선음악회(音樂會).
Charity Hospital. 주혜병원(病院).
Charity, Work of. 주선사업(事業).
Chastity, *n.* 정조(貞操), 정절(貞節).
Children's Catechism. 으히문답(兒孩問答).
Children's Day. 으히쥬일(兒孩主日).
Children's Sunday School Class. 쇼으회 (小兒會).
Choice, *n.* 전형(銓衡), 선택(選擇).
Choose, *v.t.* 전형ㅎ다, 선택ㅎ다.
Chorus, *n.* 찬양디(讚揚隊), 찬미디(讚美隊).
Chosen, Being. 피션(被選).
Christ, *n.* 긔독(基督), 그리스도.
Christian, *n.* 긔독교인(敎人), 그리스도인, 예수교인. *a.* 긔독교의, 그리스도뎍(的).
Christian Church. 긔독교회(敎會), 그리스도교회, 예수교회.
Christian Endeavour Society. 면려회(勉勵會), 면려청년회(靑年會).
Christian Endeavour Society, Women's. 녀주(女子)면려회.
Christianity, *n.* 긔독교, 그리스도교, 예수교.
Christmas, *n.* 구쥬성탄(救主聖誕), 성탄절(聖誕節). **Christmas Day.** 성탄일(聖誕日).
Church, *n.* 교회(敎會), 긔독교회; (The building) 교회당(堂), 교당, 회당, 예비당(禮拜堂).
Church, Condition of the. 교회상황(狀況).
Church, Early. 초디(初代)교회.
Church friend (Christian). 교우(敎友).
Church government. 교회정치(政治).
Church History. 교회력스(歷史), 교회스(史).
Church member, Becoming a. 입교(入敎).
Church member, To become a. 입교ㅎ다.
Church, Member of the. 교인(敎人).
Church of Jesus. 예수교회, 긔독교회.

(10)

Chu—Com

Church offering. 연보(捐補), 연보전(錢).
Church officers. 교회직원(職員), 교회직임(職任), 교회직분(職分), 제직(諸職).
Church or Congregation, Particular. 지교회(支敎會).
Church, Organized. 조직(組織)교회.
Church, Roll of the. 교적(敎籍), 교인명부(名簿).
Church Service. 예비(禮拜).
Church Session. 당회(堂會).
Church, State (Established). 국교(國敎).
Church, Universal. 전교회(全敎會).
Church, Unorganized. 미조직(未組織)교회, 미성(未成)교회.
Circuit, *n.* 구역(區域), 순행(巡行)구역.
Circular letter. 륜함(輪啣), 륜뎝(輪牒).
Circumstance, *n.* 상황(狀況).
Circumstantial report. 상황보고(報告).
Citation, *n.* 호출장(呼出狀), 쇼환장(召喚狀), 공함(公函).
Cite, *v.t.* 호출ㅎ다.
Clap hands, To. 박슈(拍手)ㅎ다.
Clapping of hands. 박슈.
Class, *n.* 반(班), (of M. E. Church) 속(屬), 강습회(講習會).
Class leader. 반장(長), 속장(屬長).
Class meeting. 반회(會), 속회.
Class, Normal. 사범(師範)강습회.
Clauses. 됴목(條目).
Clerk, *n.* (as of session) 서긔(書記).
Collection, *n.* 연보(捐補), 연보전(錢).
Collection of money. 슈전(收錢), 집금(集金).
Collection, To take up a. 연보ㅎ다.
Collector, *n.* 슈전원(員), 집금인(人).
College, *n.* 대학(大學), 대학교(校), 전문(專門)학교.
Colporteur, *n.* 전서(勸書), 매서(賣書).
Colporteur's itinerary. 전서로뎡, (written) 전서로뎡긔(路程記).
Combined meeting. 련합회(聯合會), 련합공의회(公議會).
Comforter, *n.* (The Holy Spirit). 보혜스(保惠師). [성신(聖神)].

(11)

Com—Con

Commemoration, *n.* 긔념(紀念).
Comment, *v.* 히석(解釋)ᄒ다.
Commentary, *n.* 히석(解釋).
Commission, *n.* 위임(委任).
Commit, *v.t.* 위임ᄒ다.
Commit to deal with, To. 위임처리(委任處理)ᄒ다.
Committee, Chairman of a. 위원장(長).
Committee or committee meeting. 위원회(會).
Committee, or member of a committee. 위원(委員), 임원(任員).
Committee, New. 신위원(新委員)
Committee of the whole. 젼회(全會)위원.
Committee, Selection of a. 위원션뎡(選定).
Committee, Special. 특별(特別)위원, 별위원.
Committee, To select a. 위원션뎡ᄒ다.
Communicant, *n.* 입교인(入敎人), 세례교인(洗禮敎人), 셩찬셩에인(聖餐成員人).
Communicate, *v.* 통지(通知)ᄒ다, 통텹(通牒)ᄒ다.
Communication, *n.* 통지, 통텹.
Communion-table 셩찬상(聖餐床).
Compare with, To. 참고(參考)ᄒ다, 참죠(參照)ᄒ다.
Compilation, *n.* 편즙(編輯).
Compile, *v.t.* 편즙ᄒ다.
Compiler, *n.* 편즙인(人), 편즙쟈(者).
Complain, *v.i.* 항고(抗告)ᄒ다.
Complaint, *n.* 항고.
Complaint, Memorandum of. 항고장(狀).
Complaint, Written. 소장(訴狀).
Completed, To be. 락셩(落成)ᄒ다.
Completion, *n.* (of building operations). 락셩.
Completion Ceremony. 락셩식(式).
Compose, *v.t.* 죠직(組織)ᄒ다.
Concert, *n.* 음악회(音樂會), 음악연주회(演奏會).
Conclusion, *n.* 결돈(結論), 죵결(終結).
Concur, *v.i.* 젼낙(承諾)ᄒ다.
Condition, *n.* 됴건(條件), 샹황(狀況).
Condition of the Church. 교회(敎會)샹황.
Confer, *v.i.* 협의(協議)ᄒ다.

(12)

Con—Con

Conference, *n.* 회(會).
Confess, *v.t.* 쥬복ᄒ다, 고벽ᄒ다.
Confession, *n.* 쥬복(自服), 고벽(告白).
Confide, *v.* 신임(信任)ᄒ다.
Confidence, *n.* 신임.
Confidential, *a.* 비밀(秘密).
Confidential inquiry. 비밀됴사(調査).
Congratulate, *v.t.* 츅하ᄒ다.
Congratulations, *n.* 츅하(祝賀), 츅ᄉ(祝辭).
Congratulations, To offer one's. 츅ᄉ을드리다.
Congratulatory address. 츅ᄉ.
Congratulatory address, To make a. 츅ᄉᄒ다.
Congratulatory celebration. 츅하회(會), 츅하식(式).
Congratulatory letter. 츅하쟝(狀).
Congratulatory telegram. 츅뎐(祝電).
Congregation, *n.* 회즁(會衆).
Congregational Church. 죠합교회(組合敎會).
Congregational Government. 죠합졍치(政治).
Congregational meeting. 공동쳐리회(共司處理會), 공동의회(議會).
Conscience, *n.* 량심(良心).
Consecrate, *v.t.* 헌신(獻身)ᄒ다.
Consecration, *n.* 헌신.
Consecration meeting. 헌신예비(禮拜).
Consent, *n.* 허락(許諾), 승낙(承諾). *v.i.* 허락ᄒ다, 승낙ᄒ다.
Consent of the assembly. 회즁(會衆)의공허(公許).
Consider, *v.* 심의(審議)ᄒ다.
Consideration, *n.* 심의.
Constitution, *n.* 헌법(憲法), 헌쟝(憲章).
Constitution, Committee for the formation of a. 헌법위원(委員).
Constitution of the Presbyterian Church. 쟝로교회(長老敎會)헌법.
Constitutional, *a.* 헌법샹(上).
Contract, *n.* 계약(契約).
Contract, Termination (dissolution) of a. 히약(解約).
Contract, To terminate (dissolve) a. 히약ᄒ다.
Contribute, *v.t.* 츌연(出捐)ᄒ다.

(13)

Con—Cri

Contribution, *n.* 의연(義捐), 의연금(金).
Contributions, To collect. 의연모집(募集)ᄒᆞ다.
Control, *n.* 관리(管理), 관할(管轄). *v.t.* 관리ᄒᆞ
다, 감독(監督)ᄒᆞ다.
Control, Direct. 직할(直轄), 직접(直接)관할.
Controller, *n.* 관리인(人).
Convene, *v.t.* 쇼집(召集)ᄒᆞ다.
Convene a meeting, To. 회(會)를쇼집ᄒᆞ다.
Convener of a meeting. 쇼집자(者).
Convention, *n.* 회(會).
Conversion to another faith. 기종(改宗).
Convert, *n.* (religious) 기종자(者).
Converted to another faith, To be. 기종ᄒᆞ다.
Convocation, *n.* 쇼집(召集).
Co-pastor, *n.* 동사목ᄉᆞ(同事牧師).
Copy, Written. 등본(謄本).
Copy of census-register. 민적(民籍)등본.
Copy off, To. 이록(移錄)ᄒᆞ다.
Correct, *v.t.* 슈뎡(修正)ᄒᆞ다, 교졍(校正)ᄒᆞ다.
Correct an error, To 졍오(正誤)ᄒᆞ다.
Correction, *n.* 슈졍, 교졍, 졍오.
Correspondence course. 통신과(通信科).
Council, *n.* 협의회(協議會), 회(會).
Counsel, *n.* 협의(協議).
Counsellor, *n.* 고문(顧問).
Course, *n.* 과(科).
Course, Elective. 션과(選科).
Course of study, Higher. 고등과(高等科).
Course, Regular. 본과(本科), 원과(原科).
Course, Special. 별과(別科), 특(特)별과.
Court, Church (Ecclesiastical). 교회재판소(敎
會裁判所), 교회법뎡(敎會法庭).
Court, Higher. 상회(上會).
Court, Inferior. 하회(下會).
Court, Highest. } 최고법뎡(最高法庭).
Court, Supreme.
Co-worker, *n.* 공직자(共職者).
Cradle-roll department. 영ᄋᆞ부(嬰兒部).
Credentials, *n.* 신임장(信任狀) ; 증서(證書), 쳔
셔(薦書).
Critic, *n.* 비평가(批評家).
Criticism, *n.* 비평(批評).

(14)

Cri—Ded

Criticize, *v.t.* 비평ᄒᆞ다.
Current or ordinary expenditure. 경상비(經常
費).

D

Date, *n.* 일부(日附), 월일(月日), 시일(時日),
일ㅈ(日子).
Date and place. 시일과(급)장소(及場所), 시일
장소.
Date at which an assembly or a meeting
opens. 회긔(會期), 회일(會日).
Date for a meeting, To fix a. 회긔를뎡(定)ᄒᆞ다.
Date of opening a meeting. 기회(開會)일ㅈ.
Date, To set a. 뎡긔(定期)ᄒᆞ다.
Deacon, *n.* 집ᄉᆞ(執事).
Deacon, Acting. 시무(視務)집ᄉᆞ.
Deacon, Ordained. 장립(將立)집ᄉᆞ.
Deacon, Unordained. 셔리(署理)집ᄉᆞ.
Deaconess, *n.* 녀집ᄉᆞ(女執事).
Deal with, To. 쳐리(處理)ᄒᆞ다.
Dean, *n.* 학감(學監).
Debate, *n.* 의ᄉᆞ(議事), 이론(異論), 토의(討議),
토론(討論), 변론(辯論). *v.* 토의ᄒᆞ다, 토론ᄒᆞ
다, 변론ᄒᆞ다.
Decide, *v.t.* 결뎡(決定)ᄒᆞ다, 결의(決議)ᄒᆞ다, 쳐
단(處斷)ᄒᆞ다, 판결(判決)ᄒᆞ다, 판단(判斷)ᄒᆞ
다, 판뎡(判定)ᄒᆞ다.
Decide by vote, To. 가부취결(可否取決)ᄒᆞ다.
Decide in favor, To. 가결(可決)ᄒᆞ다.
Decided, To be 결뎡되다.
Decision, *n.* 결뎡, 결의, 쳐결(採決), 쳐단, 판단,
판뎡.
Decision, Judicial. 판결(判決).
Decision, Immediate. 직결(直決), 즉결(即決).
Decision, To give an immediate. 직결ᄒᆞ다, 즉
결ᄒᆞ다.
Decision, Wrong. 오결(誤決).
Decline, *v.t.* 수면(辭免)ᄒᆞ다, ᄉᆞ퇴(辭退)ᄒᆞ다.
Declining, *n.* ᄉᆞ면, ᄉᆞ퇴.
Dedication, *n.* (of church). 헌당(獻堂), 봉헌
(奉獻).

(15)

Ded—Dir

Dedication, Ceremony of. 헌당식(式), 봉헌식.
Dependent, *n.* 피고(被告).
Delay, *v.t.* 연긔(延期)하다.
Delegate, *n.* 총뎌(總代).
Delegate, Alternate. 더뎌(代理)총뎌.
Delegate, Special. 특파원(特派員).
Delegate to General Assembly. 총회(總會)총뎌.
Delegate to Presbytery. 로회(老會)총뎌.
Deliberate, *v.t.* 심의(審議)하다.
Deliberation, *n.* 심의.
Demission, *n.* 스직(辭職).
Demit, *v.t.* (The ministry or eldership). 스직하다.
Demonstrate, *v.t.* 변명(辯明)하다.
Demonstration, *n.* 변명.
Denial, *n.* 부인(否認).
Denomination, *n.* 교파(敎派), 종파(宗派).
Deny, *v.t* 부인(否認)하다. 「거절(拒絶)」.
Department, *n.* 부(部), 국(局), 과(科).
Department, Member of a. 부원(員).
Depose, *v.* 구공(口供)하다, 공술(供述)하다, 공종(供證)하다.
Deposition 구공, 공술, 공종.
Deprivation, *n.* 탈직(奪職).
Deprive, *v.t.* 탈직하다.
Deputyship 더뎌(代理).
Design, *n.* 방침(方針), 방척(方策).
Designate, *v.t.* 지뎡(指定)하다.
Designation, *n.* 지뎡.
Desire, *n.* 지원(志願), *v t.* 지원하다.
Despatch, Special. 특파(特派).
Despatch specially, 'To. 특파하다.
Despatched person, special. 특파원(員).
Determination, *n.* 결뎡(決定).
Determine, *v.* 결뎡하다.
Determined, To be. 결뎡되다.
Devotional meeting. 경건회(敬虔會).
Digression, *n.* 탈선(脫線).
Direct control. 직할(直轄), 직접관할(直接管轄).
Direct, *v.t.* 지시(指示)하다, 지휘(指揮)하다, 장리(掌理)하다.

(16)

Dir—Dra

Directing committee. 지시위원(委員).
Direction, *n.* 지시, 지휘.
Director, *n.* 간스(幹事), 리스(理事).
Directors, Board of. 리스회(會).
Directory, *n.* 쥬소성명부(住所姓名簿).
Directory for Worship. 례비모범(禮拜摸範).
Disbursement, *n.* 지출(支出).
Disciple, *n.* 뎨즈(弟子), 문도(門徒).
Discipline, *n.* 징계(懲戒).
Discipline, Book of. 권징됴례(條例).
Discourse, *n.* 강셜(講說).
Discuss, *v.t.* 토론(討論)하다, 토의(討議)하다.
Discussion, *n.* 토론, 토의.
Discussion, Impartial. 공론(公論), 공의(公議).
Discussion, Subject for. 의뎨(議題), 토론예목(題目).
Dismiss, *v.t.* (from a post or an office). 면직(免職)하다, 출직(黜職)하다, 히임(解任)하다.
Dismissal, *n.* (from office). 면직, 출직, 히임.
Disobedience, *n.* 불복(不服).
Disobey, *v.* 불복하다.
Dispensation, *n.* 시뒤(時代).
Disproof, *n.* 반증(反證).
Disprove, *v.t.* 반증을따.
Dispute, *n.* 변론(辯論). *v.* 변론하다.
Dissatisfaction, *n.* 불복(不服).
Dissatisfied, To be. 불복하다.
Dissent, *n.* 불복. *v.i* 불복하다.
District, *n.* 구역(區域).
District Conference. 구역회(會).
District of "Kwunchal". 권찰(勸察)구역.
Divide, *v.t.* 분설(分設)하다.
Division, *n.* (of church 분셜.
Divorce, *n.* 리혼(離婚). *v.t.* 리혼하다.
Doctor, *n.* 의스(醫師), 의원(醫員).
Doctrine, *n.* 교리(敎理), 도리(道理).
Doctrine, Christian. 긔독교(基督敎)교리, 그뤼스도교교리.
Doctrine, Fundamental. 긔본(基本)교리.
Documents, *n.* 셔류(書類), 문셔(文書).
Documents, Assembly's. 회즁문진(會中文件).
Draft, To prepare a. 긔초(起草)하다, 긔안(起

(17)

Dra—Ena

案)ᄒᆞ다.
Draft, Committee to prepare a first. 긔초위원
(委員).
Draft, First. 긔초.
Draft, Revision or amendment of a. 긔졍안
(改正案), 긔졍건(件).
Draw up (the first copy), **To.** 긔초(起草)ᄒᆞ
다, 됴졔(調製)ᄒᆞ다.
Drop the matter, To. 파의(罷議)ᄒᆞ다.
Dropping the matter. 파의.
Duration of office. 임긔(任期).
Duty, *n.* 의무(義務), 쳐임(責任), 직무(職務),
직임(職任), 직분(職分).
Duty, Special. 젼임(專任).

E

Early Church. 초ᄃᆡ교회(初代敎會).
Early leaving (meeting, school, etc.). 조퇴
(早退).
Early leaving member. 조퇴회원(會員).
Early, To leave. 조퇴ᄒᆞ다.
Easter Day. 부활쥬일(復活主日).
Ecclesiastical court. 교회법뎡(敎會法庭), 교회
지판소(裁判所).
Ecclesiastical law 교회법(敎會法).
Edit, *v.t.* 편즙(編輯)ᄒᆞ다.
Editing, *n.* 편즙.
Editor, *n.* 편즙인(人), 편즙자(者), 긔자(記者).
Editor in chief. 쥬필(主筆).
Editorial committee. 편즙위원(委員).
Educate, *v.t.* 교육(敎育)ᄒᆞ다.
Education, *n.* 교육.
Educational department. 교육부(部), 학무국
(事務局).
Educational association. 교육회(會).
Elder, *n.* 쟝로(長老), (in M. E. Church) 쟝로
ᄉᆞ(師).
Eligibility, *n.* 피션권(被選權).
Enact, *v.t* 졔뎡(制定)ᄒᆞ다.
Enactment, *n.* 졔뎡.

(18)

Enc—Exe

Enclosure, *n.* 별지(別紙).
Engage to marry, To. 약혼(約婚)ᄒᆞ다, 뎡혼(定
婚)ᄒᆞ다.
Engagement, *n.* 약혼, 뎡혼.
Enter a Society, To. 입회(入會)ᄒᆞ다.
Entire number. 젼수(全數).
Entire assembly. 만쟝(滿場).
Entrance, *n.* 입회, 입쟝(入場).
Episcopal government. 감독졍쳬(監督政軆).
Episcopal power. 감독권(監督權).
Episcopalian Church. 감독교회(監督敎會).
Epworth League. 엡웟쳥년회(靑年會).
Equipment, *n.* 셜비(設備).
Era, Christian. 셔력긔원(西曆紀元).
Establish, *v.t.* 셜립(設立)ᄒᆞ다.
Establish newly, To. 신셜(新設)ᄒᆞ다.
Establishment, *n.* 셜립.
Estimate, *n.* 예산(豫算). *v.t.* 예산ᄒᆞ다.
Estimate, Rough. 개산(槪算).
Estimates, Table of. 예산표(表).
Estimate, Written. 예산셔(書).
Evangelist, *n.* (ordained) 젼도목ᄉᆞ(傳道牧師).
Evidence, *n.* 증거(證據).
Evidence, Insufficient. 증거불츙분(不充分).
Examination, *n.* (1) 시험(試驗), 시취(試取).
(2) 검사(檢査), 심사(審査), 됴사(調査); 검열
(檢閱).
Examination, Final judicial. 죵심(終審).
Examine. *v.t.* (1) 시험ᄒᆞ다. (2) 시취ᄒᆞ다, 검사
ᄒᆞ다, 심사ᄒᆞ다, 됴사ᄒᆞ다; 검열ᄒᆞ다.
Examiner, *n.* 검사원(員), 검사인(人).
Examining committee. (1) 시취위원(委員).
(2) 검사위원, 됴사위원; 검열위원.
Examining committee (on absences). 결셕사
찰위원(缺席査察委員).
Exceed authority, To. 월권(越權)ᄒᆞ다.
Exchange of pulpits. 강단교환(講壇交換).
Exchange pulpits, To. 강단교환ᄒᆞ다.
Excommunicate, *v.t.* 츌교(黜敎)ᄒᆞ다.
Excommunication, *n.* 츌교.
Execute, *v.t.* 실시(實施)ᄒᆞ다, 실힝(實行)ᄒᆞ다.
Execution, *n.* 실힝, 실시.

(19)

Exe—Fix

Executive committee. 실행위원(委員).
Exhort, *v.t.* 권면(勸勉)ᄒ다.
Exhortation, *n.* 권면.
Exhorter, *n.* (in M. E. Church) 권ᄉ(勸事).
Exhorter, Woman. 녀권ᄉ(女勸事).
Expel, *v.t.* 퇴장(退場)식이다.
Expenditure, *n.* 경비(經費).
Expenditure, Current or ordinary. 경상비(經常費).
Expenditure, Temporary. 림시비(臨時費).
Expense, *n.* 경비(經費), 비(費), 비용(費用).
Expense of a society. 회비(會費).
Explain, *v.* 히셕(解釋)ᄒ다, 셜명(說明)ᄒ다, 변명(辨明)ᄒ다.
Explanation, *n.* 히셕, 셜명, 변명.
Exposition, *n.* 히셕(解釋).
Expound, *v.t.* 히셕ᄒ다.
Extension Sunday School for non-Christians. 확장쥬일학교(擴張主日學校).
Extract, *n.* 쵸본(抄本).
Extraordinary, *a.* 림시(臨時), 비상(非常).

F

Faculty, *n.* 직원(職員).
Faculty meeting. (of school) 직원회(會), 교ᄉ회(敎師會).
Faith, *n.* 밋음, 신앙(信仰).
Family worship. 가뎡례ᄇ(家庭禮拜), 가족(家族)례ᄇ, 쵝속(眷屬)례ᄇ.
Farewell meeting. 젼별회(餞別會), 송별회(送別會).
Father, The. 셩부(聖父).
Fees, *n.* 회금(會金).
Feeling 감상(感想), 늣김(感), 졍(情).
Fill up, To 보결(補缺)ᄒ다.
Finance, *n.* 지졍(財政), 회계(會計).
Financial committee. 지졍위원(委員).
Financial report. 지졍보고(財政報告), 회계(會計)보고.
Fixed period. 뎡긔(定期).

(20)

Flo—Gen

Floor, One who has the privilage of the. 언권원(言權員), 언권쟈(言權者).
Floor, The. 언권(言權), 론셕권(論席權), 셕권(席權).
Floor, To get the. 언권을엇다.
Follows, To be as. 여좌(如左)ᄒ다, 좌긔(左記)대로.
Foreign Missions. 외디젼도(外地傳道), 외국션교(外國宣敎).
Foreign Missions, Board of. 외디젼도국(局), 외국션교국.
Form, *n.* 셔식(書式), 식양(式樣). *v.t.* 조직(組織)ᄒ다.
Form, According to. 졍식(正式), 졍식으로.
Formal, *a.* 졍식(正式), 졍식의.
Formally, *adv.* 졍식으로, 공식(公式)으로.
Formalities, *n.* 슈쇽(手續).
Formality, *n.* 졔식, 공식.
Former, *a.* 죵젼(曾經). As 죵젼교쟝(校長) the former principal.
Forward, *v.t.* 파견(派遣)ᄒ다, 파송(派送)ᄒ다.
Found, *v.t.* 셜립(設立)ᄒ다, 창립(創立)ᄒ다.
Foundation, *n.* (1) 셜립, 창립. (2) 지단(財團).
Foundation, Commemoration of. 창립긔념(紀念).
Foundational committee 지단부(部).
Foundational (juridical) person. 지단법인(法人).
Friday, *n.* 금요일(金曜日), 례ᄇ오일(禮拜五日).
Friendly meeting. 곤친회(懇親會).
Furlough, *n.* 휴가.
Full number. 셩ᄉ(成數).
Future plan. 경영ᄉ건(經營事件).
Fundamental principles of teaching. 교슈원측(敎授原則).

G

Gathering, *n.* 회(會), 모힘.
Gavel, *n.* 꼬퇴(叩槌), 회쟝퇴(會長槌).
General Assembly. 총회.

(21)

Gen—Hol

General Assembly, Expense of. 총회비(費).
General Assembly of the Presbyterian Church of Chosen. 죠션쟝로교회총회(朝鮮長老教會總會).
General Conference. 총의회(總議會).
General rule. 총측(總則).
Governing Power. 치리권(治理權).
Government, n. 졍치(政治), 제도(制度).
Government, Church. 교회(教會), 졍치(政治).
Gospel, n. 복음(福音).
Gospel Hall. 복음당(堂), 젼도관(傳道舘).
Grace, n. (1) 은혜(恩惠). (2) (at table) 식긔도(食新禱).
Graded Lessons. 계단공과(階段工課).
Greeting, n. 쵹수(祝辭).
Guidance, n. 인도(引導), 안니(案內).
Guide, n. 인도인(人), 인도쟈(者), 안닉인, 안닉쟈. v.t. 인도ᄒᆞ다, 안닉ᄒᆞ다.
Guide-book 안닉셔(書).

H

Habit, n. 습관(習慣), 형슈(行習), (bad) 버릇.
Hands on, To lay. 안슈(按手)ᄒᆞ다.
Hands. Laying on of. 안슈.
Handshaking, n. 악슈(握手).
Hands, To shake. 악슈ᄒᆞ다.
Hearer, n. 방텽인(傍聽人).
Hearer, To attend as a. 방텽(傍聽)ᄒᆞ다.
Heavenly Father. 텬부(天父).
Helper, n. 조수(助手), (in M. E. Church) 젼도ᄉᆞ(傳道師).
Helper, Woman. (Exhorter) 녀젼ᄉᆞ(女勸事).
Heresy, n. 이단(異端).
Heretic, n. 이단인(人).
High or Higher. 고등(高等).
High school. 고등학교(學校).
Higher Course of study. 고등과(科).
Hold, v.t. (a ceremony) 거힝(擧行)ᄒᆞ다, (a meeting) 긔회(開催)ᄒᆞ다.
Hold a meeting, Failure to. 류회(流會).

(22)

Hol—Ins

Hold a meeting, To fail to. 류회ᄒᆞ다.
Hold office, To 취직(就職)ᄒᆞ다.
Hold plural appointments at the same time, To. 겸임(兼任)ᄒᆞ다.
Hold the same office at the same time, (Two or more persons). 동임(同任)ᄒᆞ다.
Hold up the hand, To. 거슈(擧手)ᄒᆞ다.
Holding, For a society to have plural office. 예겸(例兼)ᄒᆞ다.
Holding, Plural office. 겸임(兼任).
Holding up the hands. 거슈(擧手).
Holiday, n. 휴가(休暇).
Holy Spirit. 셩신(聖神).
Home department. (of Sunday school) 가뎡부(家庭部).
Home Missions. 너디젼도(內地傳道), 너디션교(內地宣教).
Home Missions, Board of. 너디젼도국(局), 너디션교국.
Homiletics, n. 강도학(講道學).
Hospital, n. 병원(病院), 의원(醫員).
Hospital, Charity. 쟈혜(慈惠) 병원.
Hospital, Christian. 긔독(基督) 병원.

I

Idea, n. 의견(意見).
Immediate decision. 직결(直決), 즉결(即決).
Immediately, adv. 즉셕(即席)에.
Impartial discussion. 공론(公論), 공의(公議).
Impartial opinion. 공론.
Impression, n. 소감(所感).
Inauguration, n. 취임식(就任式).
Income, n. 슈입(收入).
Independent Church. 쟈유교회(自由教會).
Indicate, v.t. 지시(指示)ᄒᆞ다.
Indication, n. 지시.
Infant department. 유동부(兒童部).
Inform, v.t. 통지(通知)ᄒᆞ다, 고빅(告白)ᄒᆞ다.
Information, n. 통지, 고빅.
Inspect, v.t. 검사(檢查)ᄒᆞ다.

(23)

Ins—Ite

Inspecting committee. 검열위원(檢閱委員).
Inspection, *n.* 검사.
Inspector, *n.* 검사원(員), 검사인(人).
Installation, *n.* 위임식(委任式).
Installation, Ceremony of. 위임식.
Installed, To be. 위임(委任)받다, 위임되다.
Institute, *n.* 학원(學院), 학교(學校), (of Sunday School) 강습회(講習會). *v.i.* 설명(設定)하다.
Institute, Local teacher training. 강습회.
Institute, Right to. 설명권(權).
Institution, *n.* 설명(設定).
Instructor, *n.* 선성(先生), 교수(教師).
Intellect, *n.* 지력(智力), 지(智).
Intention, *n.* 의향(意向).
Intercessor, *n.* (Jesus Christ) 중보(中保), 중계(仲裁).
Intermediate department. 중등부(中等部), 중등반(班).
International Sunday School (I. S. S.). 만국쥬일학교(萬國主日學校).
International Sunday School Association. 만국쥬일학교회(會).
International Sunday School Conference. 만국쥬일학교대회(大會).
Interpret, *v.t.* (1) 히셕(解釋)하다. (2) 통변(通辯)하다, 통역(通譯)하다.
Intepretation, *n.* (1) 히셕. (2) 통변, 통역.
Interpreter, *n.* 통변, 통역, 통역자(通譯者).
Introduce, *v.t.* 쇼개(紹介)하다, 천(薦)하다, 천거(薦擧)하다.
Introduction, *n.* 쇼개, 천, 천거(薦擧).
Introduction, Letter of. 쇼개장(狀), 천셔(書).
Investigation, *n.* 쳔형(銓衡).
Invitation, *n.* 돈빙(招聘).
Invite, *v.t.* 토빙하다.
Irregular, *a.* 불규측(不規則).
Irregularity, *n.* 불규측.
Issue, *n.* 발힝(發行), 발간(發刊). *v.t.* 발힝하다, 발간하다.
Items, *n.* 됴건(條件), 됴목(條目).
Items of an account. 닉역(內譯).

(24)

Iti—Lat

Itinerant pastor. 순힝목사(巡行牧師), 순회목사(巡週牧師).
Itinerary, *n.* 순힝, 순회.

J

Jesus, *n.* 예수, 야소(耶蘇).
Join, *v.t.* 참가(參加)하다, 가입(加入)하다.
Joining. 입회(入會), 가입.
Judge, *v.t.* 지판(裁判)하다, 판결(判決)하다.
Judgement, *n.* 지판, 판결.
Judgement by default. 결셕(缺席)판결.
Judgement in writing. 판결셔(書).
Judicatory, *n.* 쳐리회(處理會).
Judicatory, Higher. 상회(上會), 상급회(上級會).
Judicatory, Lower. 하회(下會).
Judicial Commission. 지판국(裁判局).
Judicial decision. 판결(判決).
Junior department. 쇼년부(少年部), 쇼년반(少年班).
Jurisdiction, *n.* 쳔한(權限).

K

Kindergarten, *n.* 유치원(幼稚園).
Kneeling in prayer. 꿰리긔도(跪拜祈禱), 무릎을꿇고긔도흠.
"Kwunchal" Leader of a group of Christians (in the Presbyterian Church). 쳔찰(勸察).
"Kwunchal", District of. 쳔찰구역(區域).
"Kwunchal", Meeting of. 쳔찰회(會).

L

Laity, *n.* 평신도(平信徒), 평교인(平敎人).
Last meeting. 젼회(前會).
Late, To be. 만도(晚到)하다.
Late attendant. 만도회원(會員).

(25)

Law—Lor

Law case. 소송사건(訴訟事件).
Laws, n. 법(法).
Laws and regulations. 법규(法規).
Lay on the table, To. 존안(存案)하다.
Layman, n. 평신도(平信徒), 평교인(平敎人).
Lead, v. 인도(引導)하다.
Leader, n. 령수(領袖); 인도인(人), 인도자(者), 수회자(司會者).
Leave, v.t. 퇴장(退場)하다.
Leave early, To. 조퇴(早退)하다.
Leave of absence. 휴가(休暇).
Leave of absence, Pastor who has. 휴가목사 (牧師).
Leave of one's own accord. 자퇴(自退)하다.
Leave one's seat, To. 퇴석(退席)하다, 퇴좌(退座)하다.
Leave the room, To. 퇴석하다.
Leaving early (meeting, school, etc.). 조퇴 (早退).
Lecture, n. 강설(講說), 강연(講演), 연설(演說). v.t. 강연하다.
Lecture, Meeting for. 강연회(會), 연설회(會).
Lecture, To give a. 강연하다, 연설하다.
Lecturer, n. 연사(演士).
Left early, Member who has. 조퇴회원(早退會員).
Leper hospital. 라병원(癩病院), 문둥병원.
License, n. 면허(免許), 면허장(狀). v.t. 면허하다, 면허주다.
Licensed, To be. 면허얻다, 면허받다.
Licentiate, n. 강도사(講道師).
Look after, To. 감독(監督)하다.
Lookout committee. 계사부(計査部).
Lord's Day. 유일(主日), 예비일(禮拜日).
Lord's Prayer. 쥬긔도(主祈禱), 쥬긔도문(文).
Lord's Supper. 만찬(晩餐), 셩(聖)만찬, 셩찬(聖餐).
Lord's Supper, To administer the. 셩찬(을)베프다.

(26)

Mai—Mem

M

Maintain, v.t. 유지(維持)하다.
Maintenance, n. 유지.
Maintenance, Method of 유지방법(維持方法).
Majority, n. 과반수(過半數), 반수이상(半數以上).
Maker of a motion. 졔츌자(提出者), 립안자(立案者), 뎨안자(提案者).
Manage, v. 쳐리(處理)하다, 장리(掌理)하다, 판리(管理)하다, 지비(支配)하다.
Management, n. 쳐리, 장리, 지비, 관리, 판리부(部).
Manager, n. 리스(理事), 간스(幹事), 판리인(人), 총무(總務).
Marriage, n. 결혼(結婚), 혼인(婚姻), 셩혼(成婚).
Marriage ceremony. 혼례(婚禮), 혼례시(式).
Marriage ceremony, To conduct. 혼례를행(行)하다.
Marry, v. 결혼하다, 혼인하다.
Martyr, n. 슌교자(殉敎者).
Martyr, To die as a. 슌교하다.
Matyrdom, n. 슌교(殉敎).
Matter, To drop the. 롸의(罷議)하다.
Matters, n. 스항(事項), 안건(案件).
Meet again, To. 지회(再會)하다.
Meet together, To. 집회(集會)하다.
Meeting, n. 회(會), 집회(集會), 회집(會集), 고집, 회석(會席).
Meeting, Joint. 련합회(聯合會), 련합공의회(公議會).
Meeting place. 집회장소(塲所), 회집쳐(處).
Meeting, Room for a. 회의실(會議室).
Meeting, Seats in a. 회석(會席).
Meeting, Smaller or subordinate. 쇼회(小會).
Meeting, The first general. 창립총회(創立總會).
Member, n. 회원(會員).
Member of the church. 교인(敎人).

(27)

Mem—Mod

Member, Honorary. 명예(名譽)회원.
Member, Regular. 원(原)회원, 정원(正員).
Membership, *n.* 회원조격(資格).
Membership, To transfer or remove. 이명(移名)ᄒᆞ다.
Membership, Transfer or removal. 이명, 이전(移轉)
Memory drill. 암송련습(暗誦練習).
Methodist Episcopal Church, Southern. 남감리교회(南監理敎會).
Methodist Episcopal Church. 감리교회, 미감미교회(美監理敎會).
Minister, *n.* 목ᄉᆞ(牧師).
Ministry, *n.* 성직(聖職).
Minority, *n.* 미반수(未半數), 반수미만(半數未滿), 반수이하(以下), 쇼수(少數).
Miuute-book. 회록(會錄).
Minutes, *n.* 회록.
Minutes of the previous meeting. 전회(前會)회록, 전회록.
Minutes or record, To examine the. 회록검사(檢査)ᄒᆞ다.
Minutes, To amend the. 회록교명(校正)ᄒᆞ다.
Minutes, To approve. 회록채용(採用)ᄒᆞ다, 회록을밧다.
Minutes, To keep. 회록ᄒᆞ다.
Minutes, To read the. 회록랑독(朗讀)ᄒᆞ다).
Minutes, To record. 회록긔저(記載)ᄒᆞ다.
Mission. *n.* (1) 미션회(會), 선교회(宣敎會). (2) 파견(派遣).
Mission field. 선교구역(宣敎區域).
Missions, Board of. 선교국(局).
Missionary, *n.* 선교ᄉᆞ(宣敎師).
Missionary's district. 선교ᄉᆞ구역(宣敎師區域).
Missionary society. 전도국(傳道局).
Mistake, *n.* 오착(誤錯), 차오(錯誤).
Mistake in writing. 오록(誤錄), 오셔(誤書).
Mistake, To make a. 그릇(오착)ᄒᆞ다.
Misunderstand, *v.t.* 오히(誤解)ᄒᆞ다.
Misunderstanding, *n.* 오히.
Moderator (of session, etc.), *n.* 회장(會長).
"Mr. Moderator" "회장".

(28)

Mon—Oat

Monument, *n.* 긔념비(紀念碑).
Morality, *n.* 도덕(道德).
Motion, *n.* 동의(動議), 의안(議案).
Motion, Original. 원동의(原動議).
Motion, Substitute. 딕의(代議)동의.
Motion, To offer a. 동의ᄒᆞ다.
Motion, To state the. 동의(를)셜명(說明)ᄒᆞ다.
Motion, To withdraw a. 동의(를)취쇼(取消)ᄒᆞ다, 동의(를)취하(取下)ᄒᆞ다, 청의(撤議)ᄒᆞ다.
Move, *v.t.* 동의ᄒᆞ다(動議).
Mover, *n.* 동의쟈(者).

N

Name, *n.* 씨명(氏名), 성명(姓名), 일홈. *v.t.* 지명(指名)ᄒᆞ다.
Name, Honorable. 방명(芳名).
Name, To strike off a. 져명(除名)ᄒᆞ다.
Negative, *n.* 부결(否決). *v.t.* 부결ᄒᆞ다.
Negative side. 부편(否便).
Negative vote. 부표(否票).
New Testament. 신약(新約).
New Testament, The complete. 신약전서(全書).
Next meeting. 릭회(來會), 츠회(次會).
Nominate, *v.t.* 공천(公薦)ᄒᆞ다, 천(薦)ᄒᆞ다, 지명(指名)ᄒᆞ다.
Nominating committee. 공천위원(委員).
Nomination, *n.* 공천, 천, 지명.
Nomination by acclamation. 호천(呼薦).
Nomination, Method of. 천션법(薦選法).
Non-attendance, *n.* 결석(缺席), 흠석(欠席), 궐석(闕席).
Normal class. 소범강습회(師範講習會).
Notice, *n.* 통지셔(通知書).
Number, Full. 성수(成數).

O

Oath, *n.* 멩셔(盟誓), 밍셰.
Oath, To take an. 밍셔ᄒᆞ다.

(29)

Obj—Ope

Object, *n.* 옥뎍(目的), 의향(意向).
Object of a meeting. 회(會)의옥뎍.
Object, *v.t.* 반듸(反對)ᄒᆞ다, 항의(抗議)ᄒᆞ다, 항거(抗拒)ᄒᆞ다.
Objection, *n.* 반듸, 항의, 항거, 이돈(異論), 이의(異議).
Objector, *n.* 반듸쟈(反對者).
Obligation, *n.* 본분(本分).
Off of the subject, To be. 탈션(脫線)ᄒᆞ다.
Offer, *v.t.* 데명(提呈)ᄒᆞ다.
Offering, Church. 연보(捐補), 연보젼(錢), 헌금(獻金).
Office, *n.* (1) ᄉᆞ무(事務), 직무(職務), 지임(職任). (2) 국(局), ᄉᆞ무국, ᄉᆞ무소(所).
Office at the same time (two or more persons), To hold the same. 동임(同任)ᄒᆞ다.
Office, Being in. 봉직(奉職).
Office, Holding an. 직직(在職).
Office or travelling secretary. 간ᄉᆞ(幹事).
Office-room. ᄉᆞ무실(室).
Office, Tenure of. 직직.
Office, To be in. 봉직ᄒᆞ다.
Office, To hold. 취직(就職)ᄒᆞ다.
Office, To take (Chairman). 승셕(昇席)ᄒᆞ다.
Office, While in. 직직즁(中).
Officer, *n.* 직원(職員), 임원(任員).
Officer, New. 신임원(新任員), 신임위원(新任委員).
Officers of a church, Meeting of all the. 제직회(諸職會).
Officers of the churches in a specified territory, Meeting of all the. 도(都)제직회.
Old and New Testament. 신구약(新舊約).
Old Testament, The. 구약(舊約).
Old Testament, The Complete. 구약젼셔(全書).
Open a meeting, To. 긔회(開會)ᄒᆞ다.
Open letter. 공긔쟝(公開狀).
Open to the public, To. 공긔(公開)ᄒᆞ다.
Opening a meeting, Ceremony of. 긔회셕(開會式).
Opening a meeting, Date of. 긔회일(日).
Opening exercise. 긔회식.

(30)

Ope—Par

Opening of a meeting. 긔회.
Openness, *n.* 공긔(公開).
Opinion, *n.* 의견(意見).
Opinion, Different. 이돈(異論), 이의(異議).
Oppose, *v.* 반듸(反對)ᄒᆞ다.
Opposition, *n.* 반듸.
Ordain, *v.t.* 임직(任職)ᄒᆞ다, 쟝립(將立)ᄒᆞ다.
Ordained, To be. 쟝립받다, 임직(任職)되다.
Order, *n.* (1) 순셔(順序). (2) 셩직(聖職).
Order of business. 순셔.
Order of the day. 의ᄉᆞ일졍(議事日程).
Orders, Special. 특별(特別)규측.
Ordination, *n.* 임직(任職), 안슈례(按手禮), 쟝립(將立).
Ordination of pastor. 목ᄉᆞ(牧師)임직.
Ordination reception. 임직환영(歡迎).
Organ (instrument), *n.* (as of government) 긔관(機關), (Paper or magazine) 긔관[신문혹쟝지(新聞或雜誌)].
Organization, *n.* 셜립(設立), 창립(創立), 조직(組織).
Organization, Method of. 조직법(法).
Organize, *v.t.* 셜립ᄒᆞ다, 창립ᄒᆞ다, 조직ᄒᆞ다, 긔회(開催)ᄒᆞ다.
Organizer, *n.* 셜립쟈(者).
Organizing committee. 창립위원(委員).
Original book. } 원문(原文).
Original writing. }
Orphan asylum. } 고ᄋᆞ원(孤兒院).
Orphanage, *n.* }
Orthodoxy, *n.* 졍교(正敎).
Outlay of money. 경비(經費).
Overture, *n.* 의의(獻議).
Overture committee. 헌의부(部).

P

Papal Government. 교황졍치(敎皇政治).
Pardon, Begging. 샤과(謝過).
Pardon, To beg. 샤과ᄒᆞ다.
Parish, *n.* 목ᄉᆞ구역(牧師區域).

(31)

Par—Per

Part in, To take. 참가(參加)ᄒᆞ다.
Part, To take. 참예(參預)ᄒᆞ다, 참여(參與)ᄒᆞ다.
Part with, To take. 참석(參席)ᄒᆞ다.
Participation, n. 참가, 참석.
Particular church or congregation. 지교회(支敎會).
Party, n. 단톄(團體), 당파(黨派) ; 회(會).
Pass, v.t. 통과(通過)ᄒᆞ다, 가결(可決)ᄒᆞ다.
Passing (a motion), n. 통과, 가결.
Pastor, n. 목ᄉᆞ(牧師), 감독(監督).
Pastor, Assistant. 조ᄉᆞ(助事)목ᄉᆞ.
Pastor, Associate. 동ᄉᆞ(同事)목ᄉᆞ.
Pastor emeritus. 원로(元老)목ᄉᆞ.
Pastor, Honorably retired. 공로(功勞)목ᄉᆞ, 은퇴(隱退)목ᄉᆞ (in M. E. Church).
Pastor in charge. 위임(委任)목ᄉᆞ.
Pastor without charge. 무임(無任)목ᄉᆞ.
Pastoral theology. 목회학(牧會學), 목회신학(神學).
Payment, n. 지출(支出), 지불(支拂).
Penal regulations. 벌측(罰則).
Perform, v.t. 거힝(擧行)ᄒᆞ다.
Period of service. 임긔(任期).
Period of years. 년긔(年期).
Periodical committee. 뎡긔위원(定期委員).
Permanent, a. 영구(永久), 흥존(恒存), 샹무(常務), 샹비(常備), 샹설(常設), 샹치(常置).
Permanent committee. 영구위원(委員), 샹비위원.
Permanent judicial commission. 샹비지판국(裁判局), 샹셜지판국.
Permanent officer. 영구임원(任員), 샹무임원.
Permission, n. 허락(許諾), 승낙(承諾) ; 면허(免許).
Permission, To get. 허락밧다.
Permit, n. 인허, 인가, v.t. 허락ᄒᆞ다, 승낙ᄒᆞ다, 면허ᄒᆞ다, 면허주다.
Peroration, n. 결론(結論).
Personality, n. 인격(人格).
Pertaining to.........year. 년도(年度).
　Example : 이년도(二年度) For the second year.

(32)

Pet—Pra

Petition, n. 청원(請願), 신청(申請), 출원(出願).
Petition, Written. 청원셔(書), 원셔, 신청셔.
Petition, To prepare a. 청원ᄒᆞ다.
Physical education (or training) department. 태육회(體育會), 태육부(部).
Physician, n. 의ᄉᆞ(醫師), 의원(醫員).
Place, n. 쟝소(場所), 위치(位置).
Place for a meeting. 회셕(會席), 회집쟝소(會集場所).
Place of, To take the. 더리(代理)ᄒᆞ다.
Plan, n. 경영(經營), 방침(方針), 방책(方策). v.t. 경영ᄒᆞ다.
Plan, Future. 경영ᄉᆞ건(事件).
Plans, Committee to make. 경영위원(委員).
Platform, Speaker's. 강단(講壇).
Play, n. 유희(遊戲).
Plural office holding. 겸임(兼任).
Plurality, n. 다수(多數), 다뎜(多點), 최(最)다수.
Point at issue (in question). 론뎜(論點).
Pope, n. 교황(敎皇), 교왕(敎王).
Position, n. 쟝소(場所), 위치(位置).
Post or position, To take up a. 취임(就任)ᄒᆞ다.
Postpone, v.t. 연긔(延期)ᄒᆞ다, 류안(留案)ᄒᆞ다.
Postponement, n. 연긔, 류안.
Postponement to a certain time. 뎡긔(定期)연긔.
Postponement, Indefinite. 무긔(無期)연긔.
Power, n. 직권(職權) ; 셰력(勢力).
Powers, Committee with full. 전권위원(全權委員).
Powers, Full. 전권(全權).
Powers, Limits or extent of. 권한(權限).
Pray, v.i. 긔도(祈禱)ᄒᆞ다.
Prayer, n. 긔도.
Prayer, Kneeling in. 궤비(跪拜)긔도.
Prayer meeting. 긔도회(會), 긔젼회(祈禱會).
Prayer meeting, Early morning. 새벽긔도회.
Prayer, Private. 亽(私)긔도.
Prayer, Public. 공(公)긔도.
Prayer, Secret. 은밀(隱密)긔도.
Prayer, Silent. 묵(默)긔도.

(33)

Pra—Pre

Prayer, Standing in. 긔립(起立)긔도, 니러서셔 긔도홈.
Prayer, To offer. 긔도ᄒ다.
Prayer with laying on of hands. 안슈(按手)긔도.
Preach, *v.t.* (a sermon) 강도(講道)ᄒ다, 젼도(傳道)ᄒ다.
Preacher, *n.* 젼도ᄉ(師), 젼도인(人), 목ᄉ(牧師).
Preaching, *n.* 젼도.
Preaching band. 젼도ᄃ(隊).
Preaching, Personal. 기인(個人)젼도.
Preaching place. 젼도쳐(處).
Preaching room. 젼도실(室), 젼도사랑(舍廊).
Preaching, Street. 로방(路傍)젼도, 거리젼도.
Preaching to individual. 기인젼도.
Precedent, *n.* 젼예(前例), 션예(先例).
Preparation, *n.* 준비(準備).
Preparation, To make. 준비ᄒ다.
Prepare, *v.* 준비ᄒ다.
Prerogative (privilege). 특권(特權).
Presbyterial government. 쟝로졍치(長老政治).
Presbyterian Church. 쟝로교회(長老敎會).
Presbyterian Church, Constitution of. 쟝로교 헌법(憲法).
Presbyterian Church, Government of the. 쟝 로교졍치(政治).
Presbyterian Church of Chosen, General Assembly of the. 죠션쟝로교총회(總會).
Presbytery, *n.* 로회(老會).
Present, *v.t.* 제츌(提出)ᄒ다, 졔뎡(提呈)ᄒ다.
Present, To be. 츌셕(出席)ᄒ다, 참셕(叅席)ᄒ다; 립회(立會)ᄒ다.
Present office or duty. 현임(現任), 현임직분(職分).
Present together, To be. 동참(同叅)ᄒ다.
Preside over, To. ᄉ회(司會)ᄒ다.
President (of school), *n.* 총쟝(總長), 교쟝(校長).
Previous meeting. 젼회(前會).
Previous question. 의뎐뎡지쳥(議論停止請), 션결문제(先決問題).

(34)

Pre—Pro

Previous question, To move the. 의뎐뎡지(흘 기을)동의ᄒ다, 션결문제(를)동의ᄒ다.
Primary department. 초등부(初等部), 초등반(班).
Primary school. 쇼학교(小學校).
Principal, *n.* 학교쟝(學校長), 교쟝.
Print, *v.* 인쇄(印刷)ᄒ다.
Printed form. 용지(用紙).
Printer, *n.* 인쇄쟈(者).
Printing, *n.* 인쇄.
Privilege, 권리(權利).
Privilege of the floor. 셕권(席權).
Privilege, Question of. 특권문뎨(特權問題), 권리문데.
Probationer, *n.* 견습인(見習人), 시보(試補).
Problem, *n.* 문뎨(問題), 안건(案件).
Proceedings, *n.* 의ᄉ(議事), 쳐리수션(處理事件).
Process, *n.* 슈속(手續).
Process, Judicial. 지판(裁判)슈속.
Proclaim, *v.t.* 공포(公布)ᄒ다, 발포(發布)ᄒ다, 션언(宣言)ᄒ다.
Proclamation, Public. 공포, 발표, 션언.
Program (or programme), *n.* 슌셔(順序), 졀ᄎ(節次), 슌셔지(紙), 슌셔셔(書).
Program, Committee on. 슌셔위원(委員), 졀ᄎ위원.
Project, *v.t.* 발긔(發起)ᄒ다.
Projection, *n.* 발긔.
Project method. 설계교슈법(設計敎授法).
Projector, *n.* 발긔인(人), 발긔쟈(者).
Promoter, *n.* 찬성인(贊成人), 찬성쟈(者); 발긔인.
Proof, *n.* 증거(證據), 립증(立證).
Property, *n.* 쟈산(財産).
Proposal, *n.* 메안(提案), 의안(議案), 발긔(發起).
Propose, *v.t.* 데의(提議)ᄒ다, 제츌(提出)ᄒ다; 발긔ᄒ다.
Proposition, *n.* 데의, 의안.
Prosecute, *v.t.* 긔소(起訴)ᄒ다.
Prosecuting committee. 긔소위원(委員).

(35)

Pro—Put

Prosecution, *n.* 긔소.
Prosecutor, *n.* 긔소인(人), 긔소자(者), 원고(原告).
Prospectus, *n.* 규측셔(規則書), 취지셔(趣旨書), 발긔서(發起書).
Protest, *n.* 이의(異議), 항의(抗議), 항변(抗辯).
Protest against, To. 항의ᄒᆞ다.
Protest, Judicial. 징변셔(呈辯書).
Protest, Written. 이의셔(書), 항의셔, 항변셔.
Protestant, *n.* 깅졍교도(更正敎徒).
Protestantism, *n.* 깅졍교.
Prove, *v.t.* 증거(證據)ᄒᆞ다, 립증(立證)ᄒᆞ다.
Provide, *v.* 판비(辦備)ᄒᆞ다.
Proviso, *n.* }
Provisory clause. } 단셔(但書).
Psychology, *n.* 심리학(心理學).
Public discussion. 공의(公議).
Public letter. 공함(公函).
Public opinion. 공론(公論).
Public prayer. 공긔도(公祈禱).
Public, To open to. 공기(公開)ᄒᆞ다.
Public worship. 공동예비(共同禮拜), 공즁예비(公衆禮拜), 공례비(公禮拜).
Publication, *n.* 발힝(發行), 간힝(刊行), 발잔(發刊), 출판(出版), 출판물(物).
Publication committee. 출판위원(委員).
Publicity, *n.* 공기(公開).
Publish, *v.t.* 발힝ᄒᆞ다, 간힝ᄒᆞ다, 발잔ᄒᆞ다, 출판ᄒᆞ다.
Publisher, *n.* 발힝자(發行者), 발힝인(人).
Pulpit, *n.* 강단(講壇), 강ᄃᆡ(講臺).
Punish, *v.t.* }
Punishment, To inflict. } 셔벌(施罰)ᄒᆞ다.
Punishment, *n.* 셔벌. Opp. 힝벌(解罰).
Purport, *n.* 취지(趣旨).
Purpose, To state the. 취지셜명(說明)ᄒᆞ다.
Purpose, *n.* 취지, 목뎍(目的).
Put away (a wife), To. 기쳐(棄妻)ᄒᆞ다, 니혼(離婚)ᄒᆞ다.
Put off, To. 연긔(延期)ᄒᆞ다.

(36)

Qua—Rec

Q

Qualified, *p.a.* 조격잇ᄂᆞᆫ.
Qualification, *n.* 조격(資格).
Qualification for membership. 회원(會員)조격.
Qualified person, Well. 뎍임자(適任者).
Question, *n.* 문(問), 문뎨(問題), 질문(質問), 의안(議案).
Questions and answers. 문답(問答).
Question or motion which has been passed. 가결안(可決案).
Questioning, *n.* 문답법(法).
Quorum, *n.* 뎡수(定數), 뎡원(定員), 셩수(成數).

R

Rally Day. 진흥쥬일(振興主日).
Rank, *n.* 계급(階級).
Read, *v.t.* 랑독(朗讀)ᄒᆞ다.
Reading, *n.* 랑독.
Readmission, *n.* 지입회(再入會).
Reappointed, To be. 복직(復職)되다.
Reappointment, *n.* 복직, 복임(復任), 지임(再任).
Reason, *n.* 리유(理由), 도리(道理).
Reasons, Written statement of. 리유셔(書).
Recall, *v.t.* 철폐(撤廢)ᄒᆞ다, 철회(撤回)ᄒᆞ다, 쇼환(召喚)ᄒᆞ다.
Recant, *v.t.* 취쇼(取消)ᄒᆞ다.
Recantation, *n.* 취쇼.
Receipts and disbursements. 저젼출납(財錢出納), 금젼(金錢)출납.
Receive, *v.t.* (a petition or application) 슈리(受理)ᄒᆞ다; 졉슈(接受)ᄒᆞ다; 환영(歡迎)ᄒᆞ다.
Receive guests, To. 졉빈(接賓)ᄒᆞ다, 응졉(應接)ᄒᆞ다.
Reception, *n.* 졉빈, 환영.
Recess, *n.* 명회(停會), 휴회(休會), 즁지(中止), 휴식(休息), 휴게(休憩).

(37)

Rec—Reg

Recess time. 휴식시간(時間).
Recess, To take. 휴지ᄒᆞ다, 휴식ᄒᆞ다.
Recommend, v.t. 쳔(薦)ᄒᆞ다.
Recommendation, n. 쳔, 유쳔(推薦).
Recommendation or introduction, Letter of. 쳔셔(薦書).
Reconsider, v.t. 지론(再論)ᄒᆞ다.
Reconsideration, n. 지론, 지의(再議).
Record (of one's life), n. 리력(履歷). v.t. 긔록(記錄)ᄒᆞ다, 등록(登錄)ᄒᆞ다, 긔록(記錄)ᄒᆞ다.
Record, Written. 리력셔(書).
Record-book. 회록(會錄).
Recorded, To be wrongly. 오록(誤錄) 되다.
Records, n. 회록, 의ᄉ록(議事錄), 문부(文簿).
Records and books. 쟝부.
Records, To keep. 회록ᄒᆞ다.
Records, To read. 회록랑독(朗讀)ᄒᆞ다.
Recreation, n. 휴양.
Reelect, v.t. 지션(再選)ᄒᆞ다, 기션(改選)ᄒᆞ다.
Reelection, n. 지션, 기션.
Reelection, Time of. 기션긔(期).
Refer to, To. 쳥교(稟考)ᄒᆞ다.
Reference, n. 문의(問議).
Reference of a judicial case to an upper court by a lower, asking that the case be tried there. 의탁판결(依托判決).
Reform, v.t. 기혁(改革)ᄒᆞ다.
Reformation, n. 기혁.
Reformation, Religious. } 종교기혁(宗敎改革).
Reformation, The. }
Reformer, n. 종교기혁쟈(宗敎改革者).
Refutation, n. 항론(抗論), 반박(反駁).
Refute, v.t. 항론ᄒᆞ다, 반박ᄒᆞ다.
Regenerate, v.i. 즁셩(重生)ᄒᆞ다, 거듭나다.
Regeneration, n. 즁셩, 거듭남, 지셩(再生).
Register, v.t. 입록(入錄)ᄒᆞ다, 등록(登錄)ᄒᆞ다, 긔록(記錄)ᄒᆞ다, 긔입(記入)ᄒᆞ다.
Register of names. 명부(名簿).
Regular meeting. 뎡긔회(定期會), 통샹회(通常會), 평샹회(平常會).
Regular course. 본과(本科), 원과(原科).
Regular payment. 회금(會金).

(38)

Reg—Rep

Regulations, n. 규뎡(規定), 규졍(規程), 규측(規則), 규측셔(書), 규식(規式), 규례(規例).
Reject, v.t. 부결(否決)ᄒᆞ다.
Rejection, n. 부결.
Relationship, Committee on friendly. 교셥위원(交涉委員).
Relief, n. 구제(救濟).
Relief, Board of Ministerial. 목ᄉ구제부(牧師救濟部).
Relief department. 구제부(部).
Relief society. 구제회(會).
Religion, n. 종교(宗敎), 교(敎), 도(道).
Religion of Christ. 긔독교(基督敎), 그리스도종교, 그리스도교.
Religion, To preach. 션교(宣敎)ᄒᆞ다.
Religious education. 종교교육(敎育).
Religious education, Board (or committee) of. 종교교육부(敎育部).
Religious education, Director of. 종교교육지도쟈(支導者).
Religious living. 종교셩활(生活).
Religious training. 종교훈련(訓練).
Religious worker. 교역쟈(敎役者), 교회ᄉ역쟈(敎會事役者).
Remain in office, To. 잉임(仍任)ᄒᆞ다.
Remaining in office. 잉임.
Remonstrance, n. 항의(抗議).
Remonstrate against, To. 항의ᄒᆞ다.
Removal, n. 면직(免職).
Removal of suspension. 허벌(解罰). Opp. 시벌.
Remove, v.t. 면직ᄒᆞ다.
Repent, v. 회긔(悔改)ᄒᆞ다.
Repentance, n. 회긔.
Reply, n. 디답(對答), 답변(答辯), 답수(答辭). v.i. 답변ᄒᆞ다.
Reply, Written. 답변셔(書).
Report, n. 보고(報告), 통지(通知). v. 보고ᄒᆞ다, 통지ᄒᆞ다.
Represent, v.t. 디표(代表)ᄒᆞ다.
Representation, n. 디리(代理).
Representative, n. 디표, 디표쟈(者)).
Reproof, n. 권계(勸戒), 징칙(懲責), 징벌(懲

(39)

Rep—Rev

Reprove, v.t. 견계하다, 징척하다, 징벌하다.
Request, Special. 특청(特請).
Request, To make a special. 특청하다.
Rescind, v.t. 폐지(廢止)하다.
Resign, v. 수면(辭免)하다.
Resign from office, To. 수직(辭職)하다.
Resignation, n. 수면, 수직.
Resignation, Acceptance of a person's. 수직 허박(許薄)
Resignation by letter. 수직원(願).
Resignation for cause. 유고(有故)수직.
Resignation from old age or disability. 로쇠 (老衰)수직.
Resignation of all (the officers). 총(總)수직.
Resignation, To accept. 수면밧다.
Resolution, n. 결의(決議).
Resolve, v.t. 결의하다.
Responsibility, n. 칙임(責任).
Responsibility for any work or office, To take part of. 분임(分任)하다.
Responsible for, To be. 담임(擔任)하다, 담당 (擔當)하다.
Rest, n. 휴식(休息), 휴게(休憩), 휴양(休養). v.i. 휴식하다, 휴양하다.
Rest place. 휴식처(處), 휴게소(所) 휴양소.
Rest temporarily from office, To 휴직(休職)하다.
Rest year. 안식년(安息年).
Resting from office, Temporarily. 휴직.
Resume a seat, To. 복좌(復座)하다, 복석(復席)하다.
Resume one's office, To. 복직(復職)하다.
Resumption of office. 복직, 복임(復任).
Retire from office. To. 퇴직(退職)하다.
Retired pastor. 퇴직목사(牧師).
Retired pastor, Honourably. 은퇴목수(隱退牧師).
Return to office, To. 복좌(復座)하다, 복석(復席)하다.
Reverse a decision or an order, To. 물서(勿施)하다.

(40)

Rev—Sac

Review, n. 복심(複審). v.t. 검사(檢查)하다.
Review and control. 검사와교제(校止).
Review, To pass in. 검사밧다.
Revise, v.t 기정(改正)하다.
Revised Verson (of Bible). 기정역(改正譯).
Revising committee. 기정위원(委員).
Revision, n. (of rules, programs, etc.) 기정, 슈정(修正).
Revival, n. 부흥(復興).
Revival meeting. 부흥회(會).
Rewards, n. 상금(賞品).
Rewrite, v.t. 이록(移錄)하다.
Right, n. 천리(權利).
Right of speaking. 언천(言權).
Rite, n. 의식(儀式).
Ritual, n. 례식(禮式).
Ritualistic, a 의식뎍(儀式的).
Roll-call, n. 호명(呼名). 덤명(點名), 죠명(照名).
Roll of honour. 명예명부(名譽名簿).
Roll of the church. 교젹(敎籍).
Rolls, n. 명부(名簿).
Roll, To call the. 덤명하다, 호명하다, 죠명하다.
Rule, v.t. 치리(治理)하다.
Rules, n. 장졍(章程), 규측 規則), 규뎡(規定), 가졍(規程), 뎡관(定欵).
Rules and by-laws for assembly. 회규(會規), 회측(會則).
Rules and regulations. 장졍규측.
Rules of order. 세측.
Rules, regulations, etc., Committee on. 규측위원(委員).
Ruling, n. 치리(治理).
Ruling authority. 치리천(權).
Ruling elder. 치리장로(長老).

S

Sabbath, n. 안식일(安息日), 례비일(禮拜日), 쥬일(主日).
Sacrament, n. 성례(聖禮).
Sacrament, To administer a. 성례를힝(行)하다,

(41)

Sal—Sec

성예를 비드다.
Salvation, *n.* 구원(救援).
Salvation Army. 구세군(救世軍).
Salvationist, *n.* 구세군인(救世軍人).
Sanction, 재가(裁可). *v.t.* 재가하다.
Sanction, Official. 인허(認許).
Sanction, To give. 인허하다.
Sanction, To obtain the 인허맛다, 인허엇다.
Save, *v.t.* 구원(救援)하다.
Saved, To be. 구원엇다.
Saviour, *n.* 구쥬(救主).
School, *n.* 학교(學校), 학당(學堂).
School, Boys'. 남(男)학교.
School, Common. 보통(普通)학교.
School, Girls'. 녀(女)학교.
School, Higher. 고등(高等)학교.
School, Middle. 즁(中)학교.
School, Primary. 쇼(小)학교.
School, Private. 수립(私立)학교.
School, Public. 공립(公立)학교.
School-board. 학무국(學務局), 학무위원(學務委員).
Scriptures, *n.* 성경(聖經), 셩셔(聖書).
Seal, *n.* 인(印), 도장(圖章).
Seated in good order, Being. 좌석졍돈(座席整頓).
Seated in good order, To be. 좌석졍돈하다.
Seat, *n.* 좌석(座席).
Seats for the public. 방텽석(傍聽席).
Secede, *v.i.* 탈퇴(脫退)하다.
Seceder, *n.* 탈퇴자(者).
Secession, *n.* 탈퇴.
Second a motion, To. 저쳥(再請)하다.
Seconder, *n.* 저쳥자(再請者); 찬셩자(贊成者).
Secret, *n.* 비밀(秘密).
Secret business. 비밀수건(事件).
Secret meeting. 비밀회(會).
Secretary, *n.* 셔긔(書記), 간수(幹事), 총무(總務).
Secretary, Assistant. 부(副)셔긔.
Secretary for the records or minutes. 회록(會錄)셔긔.

(42)

Sec—Spe

Secretary, General (S. S.). 총무.
Secretary, Temporary. 림시(臨時)셔긔.
Sections, *n.* 됴목(條目).
Sections and clauses. 관항(欵項).
Select, *v.t.* 션릭(選擇)하다, 쳔형(銓衡)하다.
Selection, *n.* 션릭, 쳔형.
Selective course. 션과(選科).
Send, *v.t.* 파송(派送)하다.
Senior department. 고둥부(高等部), 고둥반(高等班).
Separate paragraph. 별항(別項), 별긔(別記).
Septuagint, *n.* 칠십인역셩경(七十人譯聖經).
Sergeant at arms. 수찰(司察).
Sermon, *n.* 강도(講道), 설교(說敎).
Serve in, To. 봉직(奉職)하다.
Service, Order of. 례비셔슌(禮拜順序).
Session, *n.* 회긔(會期).
Session, Church. 당회(堂會).
Session, Member of the. 당회원(堂會員).
Session, Moderator of the. 당회장(堂會長).
Session without a moderator. 당회위당회(虛位會).
Sessional records. 당회록(錄).
Settle, *v.t.* 히결(解決)하다, 결뎡(決定)하다.
Settled, To be. 히결되다, 락착(落着)되다, 결뎡되다.
Settlement, *n.* 히결, 락착, 결뎡.
Shake hands, To. 악수(握手)하다.
Sign and seal, To. 셔명날인(署名捺印)하다.
Sign jointly, To. 련셔(連署)하다.
Signature and seal. 셔명날인.
Signature, Joint. 련셔.
Sitting, *n.* 회긔(會期).
Situation, *n.* 장쇼(場所), 위치(位置).
Social gathering. 됴친회(懇親會), 근담회(懇談會).
Social position (standing). 신분(身分).
Society, *n.* 회(會), 협회(協會); 샤회(社會).
Solution, *n.* 히결(解決).
Solve, *v.t.* 히결하다.
Son (of God), **The.** 셩자(聖子).
Speaker, *n.* 연수(演士).

(43)

Spe—Sum

Speaker's platform. 강단(講壇), 연단(演壇).
Special, *a.* 특별(特別). 림시(臨時).
Special meeting. 특별회(會), 림시회 ; (특별모
　림).
Specification, *n.* 셜명셔(說明書).
Speech, *n.* 연셜(演說) ; 언론(言論).
Speech, To give a. 연셜한다.
Spot, On the. 즉셕(卽席)에.
Stamp, *n.* 인(印), 도장(圖章).
Stamp, Postage. 우표(郵票) [우편졉슈(切手)].
Stand for, To. 디표(代表)한다.
Standing, *a.* 샹비(常備), 샹셜(常設), 샹치(常
　置), 샹무(常務).
Standing, Good. 무흠(無欠).
Standing committee. 샹비위원(委員).
Standing rules. 샹규(常規), 일뎡흔규측(一定흔
　規則).
State one's views or opinions, To. 진졍(陳情)
　한다.
Stated supply. 림시목수(臨時牧師).
Station, *n.* 밋숀지회(支會), 스테숀회(會).
Station in life. 신분(身分).
Statistical table. 통계표(統計表).
Statistics, *n.* 통계(統計).
Steps, To take. 슈속(手續)한다.
Steward, *n.* (in M. E. Church) 유수(有司).
Stipulations, *n.* 규규(規程).
Story (for children), *n.* 동화(童話).
Story telling. 동화법(法).
Subdivision, *n.* 지부(支部).
Submit to inspection, To. 검사(檢査)밧다.
Subscribe, *v.* 출연(出捐)한다.
Subscription, *n.* 의연(義捐), 의연금(金).
Subscription, To solicit. 의연모집(募集)한다.
Subsidiary motion. 보조동의(補助動議).
Substitute motion. 디리동의(代理動議).
Substitution, *n.* 디리(代理).
Suffrage, *n.* 션거권(選擧權). 투표권(投票權).
Suggest, *v.t.* 에의(提議)한다.
Suggestion, *n.* 에의.
Sum total. 총계(總計), 총합(總合), 도합(都合).
Summon, *v.t.* 호츌(呼出)한다.

(44)

Sum—Sys

Summons, *n.* 호츌.
Sunday, *n.* 일요일(日曜日), 쥬일(主日).
Sunday School. 쥬일학교(學校), 일요학교
Sunday School Association, (Korea). (죠션)
　쥬일학교련합회(聯合會)
Sunday School Association subsidiary to the
　Korea S. S. A., District auxiliary. 쥬일학교
　협의회(協議會).
Sunday School Conference. 쥬일학교대회(大
　會).
Sunday School (including ages 5 to 17), The
　whole Children's. 유년(幼年)쥬일학교.
Sunday School for non-Christians, Extension.
　확쟝(擴張)쥬일학교.
Sunday School Lesson. 쥬일학교공과(工課)
Sunday School Organization. 쥬일학교조직(組
　織).
Superintend, *v.t.* 쟝리(掌理)한다.
Superintendent, District. 감리수(監理師).
Superintendent, School. 학감(學監).
Superior, *a.* 고등(高等).
Supervise, *v.t.* 감독(監督)호다.
Support, *n.* 유지(維持), 후원(後援). *v.t.* 유지
　한다, 후원한다.
Supporters, Meeting of. 후원회(會).
Suspend, *v.t.* 쳐벌(責罰)한다, 덩지(停止)한다,
　참교(懲敎)뎡지한다. (a matter) 존안(存案)
　한다.
Suspend a meeting, To. 뎡회(停會)한다.
Suspend from office, To. 뎡직(停職)한다.
Suspended member. 쳐벌밧은교인.
Suspended, To be. 쳐벌밧다.
Suspension, *n.* 쳐벌, 참교뎡지, 뎡지.
Suspension of a meeting. 뎡회, 휴회.
Suspension, Removal of. 히벌(解罰). Opp.
　셔벌.
Suspension, To be restored from. 히벌되다.
Suspension, To remove. 히벌한다.
Swear, *v.t.* 멍셔(盟誓)한다.
Synod, *n.* 대회(大會).
System, *n.* 제도(制度), 졔(制) ; 조직(組織).
Systematic, *a.* 조직뎍(組織的).

(45)

T

Table, 표(表), 일람표(一覽表).
Table (as of statistics), Accompanying. 별표 (別表).
Table, To lay on the. 존안(存案)흐다.
Table, To take from the. 긔안(起案)흐다.
Take over a portion of any work, To. 분담 (分擔)흐다.
Take part of responsibility for any work, To. 분임(分任)흐다.
Tardiness, n. 지쳠(遲滯), 만도(晚到).
Teacher, n. 교수(敎師), 션성(先生).
Teacher training course. 교수양셩과(養成科).
Teaching of Christ. 긔독교(基督敎), 그리스도교.
Teaching, Method of. 교슈방법(敎授方法).
Teller, n. 계표원(計票員), 투표됴사원(投票調査員).
Temperance committee. 계독부(戒毒部).
Temperance society. 졀쳬회(節制會), 금쥬회(禁酒會).
Temporary, a. 림시(臨時).
Temporary office. 림시임원(任員).
Term of office. 임긔(任期).
Term, Three years. 삼년조(三年組).
Testify, v. 립증(立證)흐다, 증거(證據)흐다.
Testimonial, n. 증셔(證書).
Testimony, n. 증거(證據), 립증.
Text, n. (Scripture from which a sermon is preached. Or an original copy from which other copies are made.) 본문(本文), 원문(原文).
Thanksgiving-day n. 감사일(感謝日), 감사졀일 (節日).
Theological Seminary. 신학교(神學校).
Theology, n. 신학(神學).
Thursday, n. 목요일(水曜日), 예비사일(禮拜四일).
Tie vote. 가부동수(可否同數).
Time, n. 시일(時日).
Time or times, n. 회(回).

(46)

Examples : The first time. 뎨일회(第一回), 쳣회.
Once. 일회(一回).
Twice. 이회(二回).
Three times. 삼회(三回).
Token, n. 긔념품(紀念品).
Total, n. 총계(總計), 도합(都合).
Training, n. 교육(敎育), 훈련(訓練).
Transact, v.t. 쳐리(處理)흐다.
Transaction, n. 쳐리.
Transaction of business. 회무(會務)쳐리.
Transcribe, v.t. 이록(移錄)흐다.
Transfer n. (of a pastor), 이임(移任), 젼임 (轉任). (of membership) 이명(移名), v.t. 이임흐다, 젼임흐다; 이명흐다.
Treasurer, n. 회계(會計).
Treasurer, Assistant. 부(副)회계.
Treasurer, Local (branch). 지(支)회계.
Treasurer, Temporary. 림시(臨時)회계.
Treat, v.t. 쳐리(處理)흐다.
Treatment, n. 쳐리.
Trustees, Board of. 탁수부(托事部).
Tuesday, n. 화요일(火曜日), 예비이일(禮拜二日).

U

Unanimous, a. 만쟝일치(滿場一致).
Unanimous affirmative vote. 젼수가결(全數可決).
Unconditional, a. 무됴건(無條件).
Unconditional permission. 무됴젼허락(許諾).
Unconditionally, adv. 무됴젼으로.
Uniform Lessons. 통일공과(統一工課).
Union, n. 합셩(合設).
Unite, v.t. 합셜흐다.
University, n. 대학(大學), 종합(綜合)대학.
Unqualified, a. 쟈격(資格)업는, 무(無)쟈격.
Uphold, n.t. 후원(後援)흐다.
Usher, n. 수찰(司察).

(47)

Vac—Vot

V

Vacancy, *n.* 허위(虛位); (as in a committee) 결원(缺員).
Vacancy by election, Filling a. 보결선거(補缺選擧).
Vacant church. 허위교회(虛位敎會).
Vacant district. 허위구역(區域).
Vice, *a.* 부(副).
Vice-chairman. 부회장(會長).
View, *n.* 소견(所見), 의견(意見).
Visitation, *n.* 시찰(視察).
Visitation committee. 시찰위원(委員), 시찰부(部).
Visitation committee, Field of the. 시찰구역(區域).
Visitation committee, Meeting of the. 시찰회(會).
Visitation, To make a. 시찰하다.
Visitor. 뤼빈(來賓).
Visitor's seat. 뤼빈석(席).
Viva voce. 구션(口選).
Volunteer, *n.* 지원자(志願者).
Volunteer for, To. 지원하다.
Vote, *n.* 투표(投票). *v.* 투표하다, 가부(可否)하다, 선거(選擧)하다.
Vote aye, To. 가(可)라흐다, 녜라흐다.
Vote by show of hands, To. 거슈(擧手)투표흐다, 거슈쳐결(採決)흐다.
Vote, Negative. 부표(否票).
Vote no, To. 부(否)라흐다, 아니라흐다.
Vote, One who has received the second highest. 츠덤자(次點者).
Vote, Rising. 긔립쳐결(起立採決).
Vote, Right to. 투표권(權).
Vote, Scattered. 산표(散票).
Vote, Standing. 긔립쳐결(起立採決).
Vote, The. 투표례.
Vote, To put to. 투표결(票決)흐다.
Vote, To receive the second highest. 츠덤(次點)밧다.

(48)

Vot—Wor

Vote, To take a second. 지표(再票)흐다.
Voter, *n.* 투표자(者).
Votes, Number of. 투표수(數), 표수.
Votes, Highest number of. 다수(多數), 다덤(多點).
Votes, Second highest number of. 츠덤(次點).
Voting, *n.* 쳐결(採決), 투표.
Voting by acclamation. 발성쳐결(發聲採決).
Voting, Result of. 투표결과(結果).
Voting slips. 투표지(紙).
Voucher, *n.* 증거서류(證據書類); 증인(證人).
Vow, *n.* 밍셔(盟誓), 딩세.

W

Waive (give up) one's right, To. 쳔리포기(權利抛棄)흐다.
Warrant, *n.* 위임장(委任狀), 더리(代理)위임장.
Wedding ceremony. 혼례(婚禮), 혼례식(式).
Wednesday, *n.* 슈요일(水曜日), 례비삼일(禮拜三日).
Wednesday Prayer Meeting. 삼일긔도회(三日祈禱會), 슈요야(夜)긔도회.
Welcome, *n.* 환영(歡迎), *v.t.* 환영흐다.
Welcome, Meeting of. 환영회(會).
Will, *n.* 뜻지(意志), 의(意).
Will of meeting. 회즁의견(會衆意見).
Withdraw, *v.t.* 쳘폐(撤廢)흐다, (as of a complaint) 취하(取下)흐다.
Withdraw from, To. 탈회(脫會)흐다.
Withdrawal, *n.* 탈회.
Withdrawal, Notice of. 탈회계(屆).
Witness, *n.* 증인(證人).
Witness to, To bear. 증거(證據)흐다.
Woman's Missionary Society. 녀션교회(女宣敎會).
Work, *n.* 직무(職務), 사업(事業).
Work together, To. 동사(同事)흐다.
World's Sunday School Association. 세계쥬일학교련합회(世界主日學校聯合會).
World-wide Week of Prayer. 만국통공긔도회

(49)

Wor—You

(萬國通共祈禱會).
Worship, *n.* 례ᄇᆡ(禮拜). *v.* 례ᄇᆡᄒᆞ다, 숭ᄇᆡ(崇
拜)ᄒᆞ다.
Worship, Directory for. 례ᄇᆡ모범(模範).
Worship, Meeting for. 례ᄇᆡ회(會).

Y

Yea and nay.⎫ 가부(可否).
Yes and no. ⎭
Yeas or nays. 가부간(可否間), 가부편(便).
Young Men's Christian Association (Y. M.
C. A.). 긔독교쳥년회(基督敎靑年會), 그리스도
교쳥년회.
Young Women's Christian Association (Y.
W. C. A.). 녀즈(女子)긔독교쳥년회, 녀즈그리
스도교쳥년회.
Young People's Association. 쳥년회(靑年會).
Young People's department. 쳥년부(靑年部),
쳥년반(靑年班).
Young People's Preaching Society. 쳥년젼도
회(傳道會).

PART II

Korean-English

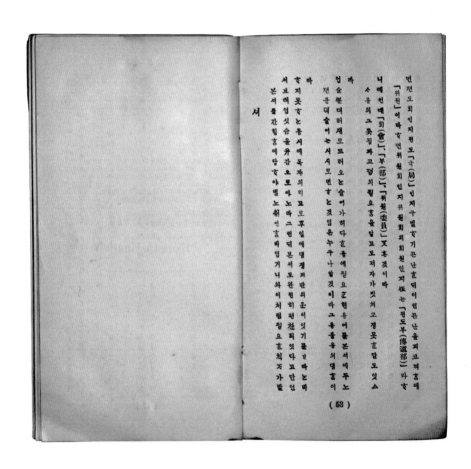

면젼도회인지젼도「국(局)」인지구별하기간난ᄒᆞ더이럿ᄯᅳᆫ난울펴코져홈에

「위원」이라ᄒᆞ면위원회인지위원회의회원인지ᄯᅩ는「젼도부(傳道部)」라ᄒᆞ

니예컨대「회(會)」니「부(部)」니「위원(委員)」이ᄯᅩ홋것이라

수용의그ᄯᅳᆺ될ᄯᅡ교졍의필요홈을알ᄆᆞ도더자가잇처고졍못홈말도잇스

라

전문대슐어ᄂᆞᆫ서서로변ᄒᆞᄂᆞᆫ것임은누구나알것이라그용홈의뎡홈이

업슬ᄲᅮᆫ머리재로드러오노슐어가ᄒᆞ다홈홈에될요호현용어둘본서에두노

라

(53)

셔

마

지못ᄒᆞᄂᆞᆫ동시에독자의이고후일에뎡졍쟈판의운이잇기를ᄇᆞᆯ라ᄂᆞᆫ바

서ᄂᆞ며업ᄉᆞᆷ을유감오로아노라그런더본서도완젼히젼찬되엿다고단언

본서를잔힝홈에당ᄒᆞ야별노ᄒᆞᆼ박업거니와이쳐렴필요홈쳑ᄌᆞ가발

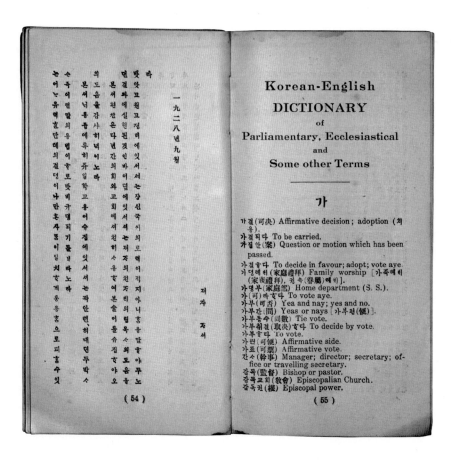

Korean-English
DICTIONARY
of
Parliamentary, Ecclesiastical
and
Some other Terms

가

가결(可決) Affirmative decision; adoption (채용).

가결되다 To be carried.

가결안(案) Question or motion which has been passed.

가결호다 To decide in favour; adopt; vote aye.

가뎡례비(家庭禮拜) Family worship [가족례비(家族禮拜), 권속(眷屬)례비].

가명부(家庭部) Home department (S. S.).

가(可)라호다 To vote aye.

가부(可否) Yea and nay; yes and no.

가부간(間) Yeas or nays [가부편(便)].

가부동수(同數) Tie vote.

가부취결(取決)호다 To decide by vote.

가부호다 To vote.

가편(可便) Affirmative side.

가표(可票) Affirmative vote.

간수(幹事) Manager; director; secretary; office or travelling secretary.

감독(監督) Bishop or pastor.

감독교회(敎會) Episcopalian Church.

감독권(權) Episcopal power.

(55)

라

밧앗고원고뎡의에잇서서는장신국씨의로력이젹지아니ᄒᆞ믈말ᄒᆞ야두노

뎐결과에실현된것이바아덤에잇서서는젹지의친지비의톄목수의도움을

본서뎐션은다년간의회와교회에서친히수용ᄒᆞ여본슐이을슈집ᄒᆞ야오

의도음을감사히녀이노라

본서너용즁에루히쥬일학교용어슈집에잇서서는과안년헌대덤두박스

一九二八년九월

저자 자서

수독어련말의용법이호로밧비규뎡되기를ᄇᆞ라노라

논어노유력호단에의결뎡이나만혼사통이일처ᄒᆞ게응용홈으로피ᄒᆞ수잇

(54)

감독－검열

감독정치(政治) Episcopal goverment.
감독ㅎ다 To look after; supervise; control.
감리ᄉ(監理司) District superintendent.
감리교회(監理敎會) Methodist Episcopal Church (미감리교회).
감사일(感謝日) Thanksgiving-day [감사절일(感日)].
감상(感想) Feeling.
개산(槪算) Rough estimate.
강단(講壇) Pulpit; speaker's platform.
강단교환(交換) Exchange of pulpits [강뎌교환(講臺交換)].
강단교환ㅎ다 To exchange pulpits.
강도(講道) Sermon [셜교(說敎)].
강도ᄉ(師) Licentiate.
강도학(學) Homiletics.
강도ㅎ다 To preach (a sermon).
강뎌(講臺) Pulpit.
강셜(講說) Address; lecture; discourse.
강습회(講習會) Assembly for study; class; local teacher training institute.
ᄉ범(師範)강습회Normal class.
강연(講演) Lecture; public address; speech.
강연회(會) Meeting for lectur?.
강연ㅎ다 To give a lecture; lecture.
거슈(擧手) Holding up the hand.
거슈투표(投票) To vote by a show of hands.
거슈ㅎ다 To hold up the hand.
거힝(擧行)ㅎ다 To perform; hold (a ceremony), [힝(行)ㅎ다].
검사(檢査) Audit; examination; inspection.
검사밧다 To pass in review; submit to inspection.
검사위원(委員) Auditing or examining committee. [검열(檢閱)위원].
검사와교졍(校正) Review and control
검사원(員) Auditor; examiner; inspector [검사의(人)].
검사ㅎ다 To audit; examine; inspect.
검열(檢閱) Inspection; examination; censorship.
검열ㅎ다 To inspect; examine; censor.

(56)

견습－경영

견습인(見習人) Catechumen; probationer. [시보(試補)] (in E. M. Church).
결뎡(決定) Decision; determination; settlement [락착(落着)].
결뎡되다 To be decided; be determined; be settled.
결뎡ㅎ다 To decide; determine; settle.
결론(結論) Conclusion; peroration.
결석(缺席) Absence; non-attendance [흠셔 or 혈셕(闕席)].
결석사찰위원(査察委員) Examining committee for absentees.
결석원(員) Absent member; absentee [결석자(者)].
결석판결(判決) Judgment by default.
결석ㅎ다 To be absent.
결의(決議) Resolution; decision.
결의ㅎ다 To resolve; decide.
결원(缺員) Vacancy (as in a committee).
결혼(結婚) Marriage [혼인(婚姻)]. See 혼례.
결혼ㅎ다 To marry.
겸임(兼任) Plural office holding.
겸임ㅎ다 To hold plural appointments at the same time.
계급(階級) Rank.
계단공과(階段工課) Graded Lessons.
계독부(戒毒部) Temperence committee.
계사부(計査部) Lookout committee.
계약(契約) Contract; agreement.
계약ㅎ다 To make an agreement.
계표(計票) Counting ballots.
계표원(員) Teller.
계표ㅎ다 To count ballots.
경젼회(敬虔會) Devotional meeting; prayer meeting.
경계위원(境界委員) Boundary committee. See 뎡계.
경뎐(經典) Canon.
경비(經費) Expenditure; expense; outlay of money.
경샹비(經常費) Current ordinary expenditure.
경영(經營) Plan; preparation.

(57)

경영−공포

경영위원(委員) Committee to make plans.
고등(高等) High ; higher ; superior.
고등과(科) Higher course of study.
고등반(班) Senior department [고등부(部)].
고등학교(學校) High school.
고문(顧問) Adviser ; counsellor.
고백(告白) Announcement ; information ; confession (of faith).
고백하다 To confess ; inform.
고소(告訴) Complaint ; accusation.
고소인(人) Complaint ; accuser.
고소장(狀) Statement of complaint or accusation.
고소하다 To complain ; accuse.
고숙(告勳)하다 To call to order.
고아원(孤兒院) Orphanage ; orphan asylum.
고퇴(叩槌) Gavel [회장퇴(會長槌)].
공기도(公祈禱) Public prayer.
공개(公開) Openness ; publicity.
공개하다 To open to the public.
공개장(狀) Open letter.
공동예비(共同禮拜) Public worship [공동예티 (公衆禮拜); 공례비(公禮拜)].
공동처리회(共同處理會) Congregational meeting [공동의회(共同議會)].
공론(公論) Public opinion ; impartial opinion ; impartial discussion [공의(公議)].
공소(控訴) Appeal (from one court to the next above).
공소인(人) Appellant.
공소장(狀) Statement of appeal.
공소하다 To appeal.
공식(公式) Formality. (정식).
공식으로 Formally.
공식의 Formal.
공의(公議) Public discussion.
공직자(共職者) Co-worker [동사자(同事者)].
공천(公薦) Nomination (천).
공천위원(委員) Nominating committee.
공천하다 To nominate.
공포(公布) Announcement [포고(布告)]; public proclamation [발포(發布); 선언(宣言)].

(58)

공포−교회

공포하다 To announce ; make known ; proclaim.
공함(公函) Citation [소환장(召喚狀)]; public letter.
교(敎) Doctrine ; religion. [도(道)].
교회(敎會) Church (회당 ; 교회당 ; 례비당 ; 교회).
교리(敎理) Doctrine.
  기독교(基督敎)교리 Christian doctrine.
  기본(基本)교리 Fundamental doctrine.
교섭(交涉) Negotiation ; friendly relation.
교섭하다 To negotiate ; have friendly relation.
교섭위원(交涉委員) Committee on friendly relationship ; Committee for negotiation.
교수방법(敎授方法) Methods of teaching.
교사(敎師) Teacher.
교사양성과(養成科) Teacher training course.
교역자(敎役者) Religious worker. [교회사역자 (敎會事役者)].
교우(敎友) Church friend (Christian).
교육(敎育) Education ; training.
교육부(部) Educational department [학무부 (學務部)].
교육회(會) Educational society.
교육하다 To educate.
교인(敎人) Member of the church ; Christian.
교적(敎籍) Roll of the church. [교인명부(敎人 名簿)].
교체(交替) Succeeding in office. [교대(交代)].
교체하다 To succeed one another in office.
교파(敎派) Denomination. [종파(宗派)].
교회(敎會) Church.
교회당(堂) Church (the building).
교회역사(歷史) Church history. [교회사기(史 紀)].
교회법(法) Canon; ecclesiastical law.
교회법뎡(法庭) Church or ecclesiastical court. [교회지판소 敎會裁判所)].
교회정치(政治) Church government.
교회직임(職任) Church officers. [직원(職員); 직분(職分)].
교회형편(形便) Condition of the church. [교

(59)

회상화(狀況)].
교황(教皇) Pope. [교왕(教王)].
교황졍치(政治) Papal government.
구공(口供) Confession ; deposition [공술(供述)；공증(供證)]; testimony.
구공하다 To confess ; depose.
구션(口選) Viva voce.
구션하다 To elect by acclamation.
구세군(救世軍) Salvation Army.
구세인(人) Salvationist.
구셰쥬(救世主) The Saviour. [구쥬(救主)].
구스건(舊事件) Old business.
구약(舊約) The Old Testament.
구약젼셔(全書) The complete Old Testament.
구역(區域) District ; circuit. [슌힝(巡行)구역].
구역회(會) District conference.
구원(救援) Salvation.
구원하다 To save. 구원엇다 To be saved.
구제(救濟) Alms. [시졔(施濟)]; relief.
구제부(部) Relief department.
구제회(會) Relief association.
구제하다 To give alms ; relieve.
구쥬셩탄(救主聖誕) Christmas [셩탄졀(聖誕節)]. Christmas Day. [셩탄일(聖誕日)].
국(局) Board ; office.
국쟝(長) President of a board ; chief of an office.
국교(國敎) State (Established) Church.
규뎡(規定) Rules ; regulations.
규예(規例) Ordinance ; regulations ; by-laws [규식(規式)].
규졍(規程) Rules ; regulations ; stipulations.
규측(規則) Rules ; by-laws ; regulations.
규측셔(書) Regulations ; prospectus.
규측위원(委員) Committee on rules, regulations, etc.
특별(特別)규측 Special orders.
그릇(誤錯)하다 To make a mistake.
그리스도 See 긔독.
금연회(禁烟會) Anti-tobacco society. [단연회(斷烟會)].

(60)

금요일(金曜日) Friday. [례빅오일(禮拜五日)].
금쥬회(禁酒會) Temperance society. [졀졔회(節制會)].
긔관(機關) Organ or instrument(as of government).
긔관[신문휴잡지(新聞或雜誌)]. Organ (paper or magazine).
긔념(紀念, 記念) Commemoration.
긔념물(物) Token.
긔념비(碑) Monument.
긔도(祈禱) Prayer; (at table) grace[시긔도(食新禱)].
긔도회(會) Prayer meeting.
긔도하다 To pray ; offer prayer ; say grace (before or after a meal).
공(公)긔도 Public prayer.
묵(默)긔도 Silent prayer [묵도(默禱)].
ᄉ(私)긔도 Private prayer.
안수(按手)긔도 Prayer with lay on of hands.
은밀(隱密)긔도 Secret prayer.
츅복(祝福)긔도 Benediction [츅도(祝禱)].
긔독(基督) Christ (그리스도).
긔독교(敎) Christianity ; religion of Christ ; teaching of Christ. (그리스도교).
긔독교의 Christian.
긔독교인(人) Christian. (그리스도인).
긔독교쳥년회(靑年會) Young Men's Christian Association. (Y. M. C. A.) (基督靑年會).
녀주긔독교쳥년회(女子基督敎靑年會) Young Women's Christian Association. (Y. W. C. A.) [녀즈긔독교쳥년회(女子基督敎靑年會)].
긔독교회(會) Christian Church ; Church.
긔른(起論)하다 To take from the table.
긔립(起立) Standing up.
긔립긔도(起立祈禱) Standing in prayer.
긔립하다 To stand up.
긔부금(寄附金) Donation, gift of money.
긔셩회(期成會) Association for carrying out a measure.
긔소(起訴) Prosecution.
긔소위원(委員) Prosecuting committee.

(61)

긔소—긔표

긔소쟈(者) Prosecutor [긔소인(起訴人)].
긔소ᄒ다 To prosecute.
긔수(記事)ᄒ다. See 회록.
긔안(起案)ᄒ다 To prepare a draft.
긔원(紀元) Christian era [예수강싱(耶穌降生)].
셔력(四曆)긔원젼(前) Before Christ (B. C.). [쥬젼(主前)].
셔력(四曆)긔원후(後) After Christ (A. D.). [쥬후(主後)].
긔쟈(記者) Editor.
긔초(起草) First draft.
긔초위원(委員) Committee to prepare a first draft.
긔초ᄒ다 To draft; prepare a draft. [긔안(起案)ᄒ다].
곤친회(懇親會) Friendly meeting; social gathering. [친목회(親睦會); 곤담회(懇談會)].
긔션(改選) Re-election.
긔션긔(期) Time of re-election.
긔션ᄒ다 To reelect; elect (in the place of the person previously chosen).
긔안(改案) Amendment [긔의안(改議案)].
긔의(改議) Amendment.
긔의ᄒ다 To amend; move an amendment.
긔인젼도(個人傳道) Personal preaching; preaching to individual.
긔졍(改正) Revision; amendment. (of rules, programme, etc.) (슈졍).
긔졍안(案) Draft revision or amendment. [긔졍젼(件)].
긔졍역(譯) Revised version (of Bible).
긔졍위원(委員) Revising committee.
긔졍ᄒ다 To revise; amend.
긔죵(改宗) Conversion to another faith. [반졍(反正)].
긔죵쟈(者) Religious convert.
긔죵ᄒ다 To be converted to another faith.
긔회(開催)ᄒ다 To organise; hold (a meeting).
긔표(開票) Opening of the ballot.
긔표부(簿) Polling book.
긔표ᄒ다 To open the ballot.

(62)

긔혁—권사

긔혁(改革) Reformation.
죵교(宗敎)긔혁 Religious reformation; the Reformation.
죵교긔혁쟈(者) Reformer.
긔혁ᄒ다 To reform.
긔회(開會) Opening of a meeting.
긔회식(式) Ceremony of opening a meeting; opening exercise.
긔회일ᄌ(日字) Date of opening a meeting.
긔회ᄒ다 To open a meeting; begin a meeting; hold a meeting.
긔졍교(更正敎) Protestantism.
긔셰교도(徒) Protestant.
과(科) Course; department.
과반수(過半數) Majority.
관리(管理) Administration; management [지비(支配)]; control [관할(管轄)].
관리부(部) Management; governing body.
관리인(人) 관리쟈(者) } Administrator; manager; controller.
관리ᄒ다 To administrate; manage; control.
관항(欵項) Sections and clauses.
광고(廣告) Announcement; advertisement.
광고판(板) Advertisement board; bulletin board.
광고ᄒ다 To announce; advertise.
권고(勸告) Advice [죵고(忠告)].
권고ᄒ다 To advise.
권리(權利) Right; privilege [특권(特權)].
권리문데(問題) Question of privilege.
권리포기(抛棄)ᄒ다 To waive (give up) one's right.
권면(勸勉) Exhortation.
권면ᄒ다 To exhort.
공(公)권면 Public exhortation.
ᄉ(私)권면 Private exhortation.
권셔(勸書) Colporteur [매셔(賣書)].
권셔로졍긔(路程記) Colporteur's (written) itinerary.
권쇽예비(眷屬禮拜) See (가뎡예비).
권ᄉ(勸師) Exhorter (in M. E. Church).

(63)

권 ─ 다수

녀권사 (女勸師) Woman exhorter; woman helper.

권징됴례 (勸懲條例) Book of Discipline.

권찰 (勸察) "Kwunchal," leader of a group of Christians (in the Presbyterian Church).

권찰구역 (區域) District of a "Kwunchal".

권찰회 (會) Meeting of "Kwunchal".

권한 (權限) Jurisdiction, limits or extent of powers.

궤비긔도 (跪拜祈禱) Kneeling in prayer. (무릎을 꿇고긔도홈).

나

남감리교회 (南監理敎會) Southern Methodist Church.

남성경학교 (男聖經學校). See 성경학교.

남장로교회 (南長老敎會). See 쟝로교회.

남학교 (男學校). See 학교.

녀권사 (女勸師). See 권사.

녀선교사회 (女宣敎師會) Women's Missionary Society. [녀전도회 (女傳道會)].

녀집사 (女執事) Deaconess.

녀쥬거독청년회 See 긔독교.

년긔 (年期) Period of years.

년도 (年度) Pertaining to—year. *Example:* 이년도 (二年度) For the second year.

년회 (年會) Annual Conference. (뎌년회).

네 (可) 唯라ᄒᆞ다 To vote aye.

늣김 (感) Feeling.

닉역 (內譯) Items of an account.

닉디전도 (內地傳道) Home Missions. [닉디선교 (內地宣敎)].

닉디전도국 (局) Board of Home Missions.

다

다수 (多數) Plurality; most votes. [다념 (多

(64)

단셔 ─ 뎡직

點)].

죵 (從) 다수 According to plurality vote.

단서 (但書) Proviso; provisory clause.

단톄 (團體) Body (of persons); party.

담임 (擔任) ᄒᆞ다 To take charge of; be responsible for [담당 (擔當); 담칙 (擔責)].

답변 (答辯) Answer; reply.

답셔 (書) Answer to a communication; written reply.

답ᄉᆞ (答辭) Reply; address in response.

당션 (當選) 되다 To be elected.

당파 (黨派) Party.

당회 (堂會) Church session.

당회록 (錄) Sessional records.

당회원 (員) Member of the session.

당회쟝 (長) Moderator of the sesson.

대요리문답 (大要理問答) The Larger Catechism.

대회 (大會) Synod; large convention (of Sunday School).

뎍임쟈 (適任者) Well qualified person.

뎜명 (點名) ᄒᆞ다 Roll-call. [호명 (呼名); 조명 (照名)].

뎜됴 (點) To call the roll.

뎨안 (提案) Proposal.

뎨의 (提議) Suggestion; proposition.

뎨의쟈 (者) Proposer.

뎨의ᄒᆞ다 To suggest; propose.

뎨졍 (提呈) ᄒᆞ다 To present; offer.

뎨ᄌᆞ (弟子) Disciple. [문도 (門徒)].

뎨츌 (提出) ᄒᆞ다 To present; propose; bring forward; advance.

뎡계 (定界) Boundary.

뎡계위원 (委員) Boundary committee.

뎡계ᄒᆞ다 To determine a boundary.

뎡긔 (定期) Fixed period.

뎡긔위원 (委員) Periodical committee.

뎡긔회 (會) Regular meeting.

뎡긔ᄒᆞ다 To set a date.

뎡수 (定數) Quorum. [뎡원 (定員)].

뎡지 (停止) Suspension.

뎡지ᄒᆞ다 To suspend.

뎡직 (停職) ᄒᆞ다 To suspend from office.

(65)

뎡한—티답

뎡한(定限)ᄒ다 To fix a date.
뎡회(停會) Suspension of a meeting; adjournment; recess. [휴회(休會)].
뎡회ᄒ다 To adjourn a meeting; suspend a meeting; adjourn for recess.
도덕(道德) Morality.
도리(道理) Reason; doctrine.
도합(都合) Total.
동의(動議) Motion.
동의를셜명(說明)ᄒ다 To state the motion.
동의를취쇼(取消)ᄒ다 To withdraw a motion. [동의취하(動議取下); 철의(撤議)].
동의쟈(者) Mover.
동의ᄒ다 To move; offer a motion.
원(原)동의 Original motion.
동임(同任)ᄒ다 To hold the same office at the same time (two or more persons).
동참(同參)ᄒ다 To be present together.
동화(童話) Story (for children).
동화법(法) Story telling.
됴건(條件) Condition; items.
됴목(條目) Clauses; sections; items.
됴사(調査) Examination; investigation.
됴사위원(委員) Examining committee.
됴사ᄒ다 To examine; investigate.
득낙(得諾)ᄒ다 To get permission.
득승(得勝)ᄒ다 To be carried. (최ᄅᆞᆼ되다; 가결ᄒ다).
등록(登錄)ᄒ다 To record; register.
등본(謄本) Written copy.
호젹(戶籍)등본 Copy of a census register. [민젹(民籍)등본].
디방회(地方會) District conference. [구역회(區域會)].
디리(代理) Substitution; deputyship; representation.
디리동의(動議) Substitute motion. [디안(代案)].
디리총디(總代) Alternate delegate.
디리ᄒ다 To act for; take the place of.
디답(對答) Answer; reply.
디답ᄒ다 To answer; reply.

(66)

티의—론셕

디의(代議) See 디리동의.
디표(代表) Representative. [디표쟈(者)].
디표ᄒ다 To represent; stand for.

라

라병원(癩病院) Leper hospital. (ᄂᆞᆼ둉병원)
락션(落選)되다 To fail of an election.
락셩(落成) Completion (of building operation).
락셩식(式) Completion ceremony.
락셩ᄒ다 To be completed; be finished.
랑독(朗讀) Reading.
랑독ᄒ다 To read.
량심(良心) Conscience.
련셔(連署) Joint signature.
련셔ᄒ다 To sign jointly.
련합회(聯合會) Joint meeting [련합공의회(聯合公議會)]; association.
례겸(例兼) For a society to have plural office holding.
례비(禮拜) Worship; church service.
례비당(堂) Church (Worship House) [회당(會堂); 교회당(敎會堂)].
례비모범(模範) Directory for Worship.
례비슌셔(順序) Order of service. [졀ᄎᆞ(節次)].
례비일(日) Sabbath; Lord's Day [쥬일(主日)].
례비회(會) Meeting for worship.
례비ᄒ다 To worship [슝비(崇拜)ᄒ다].
례식(式式) Ceremony; ritual.
령슈(領袖) Leader.
로마교(羅馬敎) Roman Catholic Church [로마교회(羅馬敎會); 텬쥬교].
로방젼도(路傍傳道) Street preaching.
로쇠ᄉᆞ직(老衰辭職) Resignation from old age or disability.
로회(老會) Presbytery.
로회총디(總代) Delegate to Presbytery.
로회비(費) Expense of the Presbytery.
론뎜(論點) Point at issue (in question).
론셕권(論席權) The floor [셕권(席權)].

(67)

류안－한국

류안(留案) Postponement [연긔(延期)].
류안하다 To postpone.
류회(流會) Failure to hold a meeting.
류회하다 To fail to hold a meeting.
륜츠(輪次) Alternate.
륜츠회장(會長) Alternate moderator.
륜람(輪覽) Circular [륜텹(輪牒)].
리력(履歷) Record (of one's life).
리력셔(書) Written record.
리스(理事) Director ; manager.
리스제(制) Director system.
리스회(會) Board of directors.
리유(理由) Reason.
리유셔(書) Written statement of reasons.
리혼(離婚) Divorce.
리혼하다 To divorce ; put away (a wife) [기쳐 (棄妻)하다].
림시(臨時) Temporary ; special ; extraordinary ; unusual [특별(特別)].
림시슈(牧師) Stated supply.
림시비(費) Unusual expenditure.
림시셔긔(書記) Temporary secretary.
림시위원(任員) Temporary officer.
림시회(會) Special meeting [특별회(特別會)].
림시회계(會計) Temporary treasurer.
림시회장(會長) Temporary chairman.
립증(立證) Proof ; testimony.
립증하다 To prove ; testify.
립회(立會)하다 To be present ; attend.
린빈(來賓) Visitor.
린빈셕(席) Visitor's seat.
린회(來會) Next meeting [츠회(次會)].

마

만국쥬일학교(萬國主日學校) International Sunday School.
만국쥬일학교대회(大會) I. S. S. Conference.
만국쥬일학교회(會) I. S. S. Association.
만국통공긔도회(萬國通共祈禱會) World-wide

(68)

만도－목회

Week of Prayer.
만도(晩到) Tardiness [지챵(遲參)].
만도회원(會員) Late attendant.
만도하다 To be late.
만장(滿場) Entire assembly.
만장일치(一致) Unanimous.
만찬(晩餐) Lord's Supper. [셩만찬(聖晩餐)].
면려회(勉勵會) Christian Endeavour Society
면려쳥년회(勉勵靑年會)].
녀즈(女子)면려회 Woman's C. E. S.
면직(免職) Dismission (from office); deposition ; removal.
면직되다 To be dismissed.
면직하다 To dismiss ; remove.
면허(免許) Permission ; license ; certificate.
면허밧은교스(敎師) Certified teacher.
면허엇다 To be licensed.
면허장(狀) Written permit, license, or certificate.
면허하다 To permit ; license ; certify.
명부(名簿) Register of names ; rolls.
명예(名譽)명부 Roll of honour.
모힘(集合) See 회 or 회.
목뎍(目的) Object ; purpose.
목스(牧師) Pastor ; minister ; preacher.
목스구역(區域) Parish ; district.
목스구제부(救濟部) Board of Ministerial Relief.
목스쟝립(將立) Ordination.
공로(功勞)목스 Honorably retired pastor.
[우회(隆退)목스 in M. E. Church].
동스(同事)목스 Associate pastor ; co-pastor.
디방(地方)목스 Pastor at large (in charge of existing churches of a large field).
무임(無任)목스 Pastor without charge.
림시(臨時)목스 Stated supply.
위임(委任)목스 Pastor in charge.
원로(元老)목스 Emeritus pastor.
젼도(傳道)목스 Ordained evangelist (to establish new churches).
조스(助事)목스 Assistant pastor.
목요일(木曜日) Tuesday [례티四일(禮拜四日)].
목회학(牧會學) Pastoral theology [목회신학(牧

(69)

무고―밍아

會神學)].
무고(無故) Without cause.
무고결석, 흠석(欠席, 缺席) Absence without cause.
무고결석자(者) One who is absent without cause.
무긔명투표(無記名投票) Secret ballot.
무뎡수(無定數) Unlimited as to the number.
무됴건(無條件) Unconditional.
무됴건으로 Unconditionally.
무됴건허락(許諾) Unconditional permission.
무슌(無順) Not in order ; out of order ; disorderly.
무흠(無欠) Good standing.
문뎨(問題) Question ; problem ; subject.
문답(問答) Question and answers.
문답힘(法) Questioning.
문답ᄒ다 To catechise.
문부(文簿) Records and books ; records.
문의(問議) Reference ; question.
물시(勿施)ᄒ다 To reverse a decision or an order. [취쇼(取消)].
뭇(問)다 To ask ; inquire of [질문(質問)ᄒ다].
묵긔도(默祈禱) Secret prayer.
미감리교회(美監理敎會) Methodist Episcopal Church.
미반수(未半數) Minority. [반수미만(半數未滿), 쇼수(少數)].
미비ᄉ건(未備事件) Unprepared business. [미비건(未備件)].
미셩교회(未成敎會) Unorganized Church [미조직교회(未組織敎會)].
미진ᄉ건(未盡事件) Unfinished business [미진건(未盡件)].
밋친회(밋신會) Mission. [션교회(宣敎會)].
미원지회(支會) Station. [스페션회(會)].
밋다 To believe : 예수 믈 밋다 To believe in Jesus. (신앙ᄒ다).
밋음(信) Belief ; faith. [신앙(信仰)].
밍셔(盟誓) Vow ; oath (밍세).
밍셔ᄒ다 To take an oath ; swear.
밍아원(盲啞院) Asylum for the blind and dumb.

(70)

박슈―별표

바

박슈(拍手) Clapping of hands ; Applause. [박장(拍掌)].
박슈ᄒ다 To clap hands.
반(班) Class.
반쟝(長) Class leader.
반회(會) Class meeting.
반뎌(反對) Opposition ; objection ; dissent.
반뎌ᄒ다 To oppose ; object ; dissent.
반증(反證) Disproof.
반증ᄒ다 To disprove.
반수이상(半數以上) Majority (과반수).
반수이하(半數以下) Minority (미반수) [반수미만(半數未滿)].
발간(發刊) Publication [간힝(刊行)] ; issue. [발힝(發行)].
발간ᄒ다 To publish ; issue.
발긔(發起) Proposal ; projection.
발긔셔(書) Prospectus.
발긔인(人) Projector ; promoter.
발긔ᄒ다 To propose ; project.
발힝(發行) Publication ; issue. See 간힝.
발힝쟈(者) Publisher [발힝인(人)].
방명(芳名) Honorable name.
방침(方針) Plan ; design [방책(方策)].
방텽(傍聽) Attendance as a hearer.
방텽셕(席) Seats for the public.
방텽인(人) Hearer.
방텽원(員) One who attends but has not the privilege of the floor.
방텽ᄒ다 To attend as a hearer.
벌측(罰則) Penal regulations.
법(法) Laws.
법안(法案) Bill.
종교(宗敎)법안 Bill of religion.
법규(法規) Laws and regulations.
별지(別紙) Accompanying paper ; enclosure.
별표(別表) Accompanying table (as of statistics).

(71)

별항―부

별항(別項) Separate paragraph [별거(別記)].
변론(辯論) Dispute ; debate.
변론ᄒᆞ다 To dispute ; debate.
변명(辯明) Explanation ; demonstration.
변명ᄒᆞ다 To explain ; demonstrate.
변증론(辯證論) Apologetics.
변호(辯護) Advocacy.
변호인(人) Advocate [변호자(辯護者), 변호ᄉᆞ (辯護士)].
변호ᄒᆞ다 To advocate.
병원(病院) Hospital [의원(醫院)].
자혜(慈惠)병원 Charity Hospital.
긔독(基督)병원 Christian Hospital.
보결(補缺) Filling a vacancy.
보결ᄒᆞ다 To fill up.
보고(報告) Report.
보고서(書) Written report.
추가(追加)보고 Supplementary report.
보고ᄒᆞ다 To report.
보조동의(補助動議) Subsidiary motion.
보혜ᄉᆞ(保惠師) Comforter (the Holy Spirit).
복음(福音) Gospel.
복음당(堂) Gospel Hall.
복직(復職) Reappointment ; resumption of office. [복임(復任), 재임(再任)].
복직되다 To be reappointed.
복직ᄒᆞ다 To resume one's office.
복좌(復座)ᄒᆞ다 To return to office ; resume a seat [복석(復席)].
본능(本能) Instunct.
본과(本科) Regular course [원과(原科)].
본문(本文) Text (from which a sermon is preached, or the original copy from which other copies are made.) [원문(原文)].
본분(本分) Duty ; obligation.
봉직(奉職) Being in office
봉직ᄒᆞ다 To be in office ; serve in.
부(副) Vice ; assistant.
부서긔(書記) Assistant secretary.
부회계(會計) Assistant treasurer.
부회장(會長) Vice-chairman.
부(部) Department ; Board [국(局)].

(72)

부원―사경

부원(員) Member of a department or board.
부결(否決) Rejection ; negative.
부결되다 To be lost.
부결ᄒᆞ다 To reject ; negative.
부(否)ᄆᆞ라ᄒᆞ다 To vote no.
부인(否認) Denial.
부인ᄒᆞ다 To deny.
부덩투표(不正投票) False ballot (casting two or more ballots).
부측(附則) Additional (supplementary) rules.
부편(否便) Negative side.
부표(否票) Negative vote.
부흥(復興) Revival.
부흥회(會) Revival meeting.
부활쥬일(復活主日) Easter Day.
분담(分擔)ᄒᆞ다 To take over a portion of any work.
분셜(分設) Division (as of a church).
분셜ᄒᆞ다 To divide.
분임(分任)ᄒᆞ다 To take part of the responsibility for any work or office.
불규측(不規則) Irregularity.
불규측ᄒᆞ다 Irregular.
불복(不服) Dissatisfaction ; disobedience.
불복ᄒᆞ다 To be dissatisfied ; dissent ; disobey.
비(費) Expense ; expenditure. [비용(費用)].
비밀(秘密) Secret ; confidential.
비밀ᄉᆞ건(事件) Secret business.
비밀됴ᄉᆞ(調査) Confidential inquiry.
비밀회(會) Secret meeting.
비평(批評) Criticism.
비평가(家) Critic.
비평ᄒᆞ다 To criticize.
ᄇᆡ교(背敎) Apostacy.
ᄇᆡ교자(者) Apostate.
ᄇᆡ교ᄒᆞ다 To apostatize.

사

ᄉᆞ경회(査經會) Bible [training] class.
ᄉᆞ경회위원(委員) Bible class committee.

(73)

작제—서전

삭제(削除)하다 To rescind ; omit [따(漏)하다].
산표(散票) Scattered vote.
삼년조(三年組) Three year term.
삼일긔도회(三日祈禱會) Wednesday prayer-meeting. [슈요야긔도회(水曜夜祈禱會)].
새벽긔도회(早朝祈禱會) Early morning prayer-meeting.
상픔(賞品) Rewards.
상황(狀況) Circumstance ; condition.
상황보고(報告) Circumstancial report.
특별(特別)상황 Special circumstances.
사과(謝過) Apology ; begging pardon.
사과하다 To beg pardon.
상고(上告) Appeal (Second appeal one step up from a 공소). [공소(控訴)].
상고인(人) Appellant.
상고하다 To appeal.
상규(常規) Standing rules [뎡규(定規)].
상비(常備) Standing ; permanent. [상설(常設); 상치(常置); 상무(常務)].
상비위원(委員) Standing or permanent committee
상비지판국(裁判局) Permanent judicial commission.
상소(上訴) Appeal (general word through all the courts).
상회(上會) Superior court ; higher judicatory. [상급회(上級會)].
서긔(書記) Secretary, clerk (as of session,). 회록(會錄)서긔 Secretary for the records or minutes.
서류(書類) Documents [문서(文書)].
서명날인(署名捺印) Signature and seal [셔압(署押)].
서명날인하다 To sign and seal.
서식(書式) Blank [식양지(式樣紙)]; 용지(用紙) : form [식양(式樣)].
서약(誓約) Vow ; oath.
서약서(書) Written oath.
서약하다 To take an oath.
서천(席捲) The floor ; privilege of the floor. [론(論)서천].

(74)

선거—세계

선거(選擧) Election.
선거권(權) Suffrage ; the vote (투표권).
선거방법(方法) Method of election.
선거법(法) Election law.
선거인(人) Elector ; voter.
선거하다 To elect ; vote.
보결(補缺)선거 Filling a vacancy by election.
총(總)선거 General election.
선결문뎨(先決問題) Previous question. [의론덩지동의(議論停止動議)].
선결문뎨(를)동의(動議)하다 To move the previous question.
선고(宣告) Adjudication.
선고하다 To adjudicate.
선교구역(宣敎區域) Mission field ; missionary's circuit.
선교국(局敎局) Board of Mission.
선교사(宣敎師) Missionary.
선교수구역(區域) Missionary's district.
선교회(宣敎會) Mission.
선교(宣敎)하다 To preach religion.
선과(選科) Elective course.
선도사(宣道師) Evangelist. [뎐도자(傳道者)].
선생(先生) Teacher ; instructor. (교사).
선릭(選擇) Selection ; choice.
선릭하다 To select ; choose.
설계교슈법(設計敎授法) Project method.
설교(說敎) Sermon [강도(講道)].
설덩(設定) Establishment ; institution.
설덩권(權) Right to establish ; right to institute.
설덩하다 To establish ; institute
설립(設立) Foundation ; establishment ; organization.
설립자(者) Founder ; organizer.
설립하다 To establish ; organize.
설명(說明) Explanation
설명서(說明書) Specification.
설명하다 To explain.
설비(設備) Equipment.
세계쥬일학교회(世界主日學校會) World's Sunday School Association.

(75)

셰력―소감

셰력(勢力) Power.
셰예(洗禮) Baptism.
셰예교인(敎人) Baptized member ; communicant.
셰예문답(問答) Examination for baptism.
셰예밧다 To be baptized.
셰예주다 To baptize ; administer baptism. (셰 력베프다)
주슈셰예(注水洗禮) Baptism by effusion.
침슈셰예(浸水洗禮) Baptism by immersion.
관슈셰예(灌水洗禮) Baptism by sprinkling.
셰측(細則) By-laws ; rules of order.
셩경(聖經) The Bible ; Holy Bible ; scriptures [셩셔(聖書)].
셩경공과(工課) Scripture lesson.
셩경공부회(工夫會) Bible class [셩경연구회(聖經研究會)].
셩경랑독(朗讀) Reading of the Bible.
셩경랑독ᄒ다 To read the Bible.
셩경학교(學校) Bible Institute [셩셔학원(聖書學院)].
남(男)셩경학교 Men's Bible Institute.
녀(女)셩경학교 Women's Bible Institute.
셩공회(聖公會) The Holy Catholic Church (Universal).
셩예(聖禮) Sacrament.
셩예를힝ᄒ다 To administer a sacrament.
셩부 聖父) The Father.
셩셔공회(聖書公會) Bible Society.
셩슈(成數) Full number ; quorum (뎡수).
셩신(聖神) The Holy Spirit.
셩직(聖職) Order ; ministry [교직(敎職)].
셩ᄌ(聖子) The Son (of God).
셩찬(聖餐)The Lord's Supper [셩만찬(聖晚餐)].
셩찬긔(器) Vessels for the administration of the Lord's Supper.
셩찬(을)베프다 To administer the Lord's Supper.
셩찬상(床) Communion table.
셩찬참예인(參預人) Communicant.
셩혼(成婚) Marriage. See 결혼.
쇼감(所感) Impression.

(76)

소송―슌회

소숑(訴訟) Accusation.
소숑ᄉ건(事件) Law case.
소장(訴狀) Charge ; written complaint.
쇼년반(少年班) Junior department [쇼년부(少年部)].
쇼수(少數) Minority. (미반수).
쇼요리문답(小要理問答) The Shorter Catechism.
쇼ᄋ회(小兒會) Children's Sunday School Class.
쇼개(紹介) Introduction.
쇼개장(狀) Letter of introduction.
쇼개ᄒ다 To introduce.
쇼집(召集) Calling ; convocation.
쇼집장(長) Convener of a meeting.
쇼집ᄒ다 To call a meeting ; convene.
쇼회(小會) Small or subordinate meeting.
쇽(屬) Class (of M. E. Church).
쇽장(長) Class-leader.
쇽회(會) Class-meeting.
슈리(受理) Acceptance.
슈리ᄒ다 To accept ; receive (a petition or an application) ; take up (an appeal).
슈셕(首席) "The Chair" (the chairman) [회장셕(會長席)].
슈속(手續) Process ; formalities.
슈속ᄒ다 To take steps.
슈요일(水曜日) Wednesday [예비삼일(禮拜三日)].
슈입(收入) Income.
슈젼(收錢) Collection of money [집금(集金)].
슈젼원(員) Collector [집금인(集金人)].
슈졍(修正) Amendment (rules or programme); correction [교졍(校正)].
슈졍위원(委員) Amendment committee.
슈졍ᄒ다 To amend ; correct.
슌교(殉敎) Martyrdom.
슌교자(者) Martyr.
슌셔(順序) Programme ; order of business ; order.
슌셔지(紙) Programme [슌셔셔(順序紙)].
슌회(巡廻) Itinerary [슌힝(巡行)].

(77)

순회—신학

순회목사(牧師) Itinerant pastor [순행목사(巡行牧師)].
습관(習慣) Habit.
승낙(承諾) Acceptance ; acknowledgment.
승낙하다 To concur ; assent ; agree.
승석(昇席)하다 To take office (chairman).
승인(承認) Approval.
승인되다 To be approved.
승인하다 To approve.
시명(氏名) Name [일홈, 성명(姓名)].
시무(視務)하다 To attend to business.
시벌(施罰) Punishment : infliction of censure. opp. 혜벌.
시벌하다 To punish ; inflict punishment.
시일(時日) Date [일즈(日子)] ; time.
시일급장소(時日及場所) Date and place. [시일급장소(時日及場所)].
시찰(視察) Visitation.
시찰구역(區域) Field of the visitation committee.
시찰위원(委員) Visitation committee.
시찰회(會) Meeting of the visitation committee.
시찰하다 To make a visitation.
시취(試取) Examination [시험(試驗)].
시취위원(委員) Examining committee.
시취하다 To examine.
신구약(新舊約) Old and New Testament ; The Holy Bible. [신구약성경(新舊約聖書)].
신분(身分) Social position (standing) ; station in life.
신설(新設) New establishment.
신설하다 To establish newly.
신사건(新事件) New business.
신앙(信仰) Faith ; belief.
신약(新約) The New Testament.
신약전서(全書) The Complete New Testament.
신임(信任) Confidence.
신임장(狀) Credentials.
신임하다 To confide.
신임위원(新任員) New offices ; new committees [신임위원(新任委員)].
신학(神學) Theology.

(78)

신학—사회

신학교(校) Theological seminary.
실시(實施) Carrying into effect.
실시하다 To carry out ; execute (rules).
실행(實行) Execution.
실행위원(實行委員) Executive committee [실행부(實行部)] ; 집행위원(執行委員) ; 사무위원(事務委員)].
실행하다 To execute.
심리학(心理學) Psychology.
심사(審査) Examination ; investigation ; inquiry.
심사위원(委員) Committee of inquiry.
심사하다 To examine ; inquire.
심의(審議) Consideration ; deliberation.
심의하다 To consider ; deliberate.
스전(事件) Business ; affair ; case (in law).
스도(使徒) Apostle.
스도시(敎)교회(敎會) Apostolic Church.
스도신경(信經) Apostles' creed.
스면(辭免) Declining [스퇴(辭退)] ; resignation.
스면밧다 To accept a resignation.
스면하다 To decline ; resign.
스무(事務) Office ; business.
스무국(局) Office ; business office.
스무소(所) Office.
스무시간(時間) Business hours.
스무실(室) Office room.
스무위원(委員) Business committee.
스무처리(處理)하다 To do business.
스직(辭職) Resignation ; demission.
스직원(願) Petition for a person's resignation ; resignation (by letter) [스표(辭表)].
스직허락(許諾) Acceptance of a person's resignation.
스직하다 To resign from office ; demit (the ministry or eldership).
유고(有故)스직 Resignation for cause.
흥(總)스직 Resignation of all (the officers).
스찰(司察) Usher ; sergeant at arms.
스항(事項) Matters ; items.
스회(司會) Chairmanship ; "the Chair".

(79)

수회—연긔

수회자(者) Chairman ; leader [인도인(引導人)].
수회흐다 To preside over : take the chair.
성일츅하(生日祝賀) Birthday greeting.
성일츅하표(票) Birthday greeting card. [성일 츅하장(狀)].

아

아니라(否)ᄒ다 To vote no.
악슈(握手) Handshaking.
악슈흐다 To shake hands.
안건(案件) Case ; matter ; affair ; problem.
안내(案內) Guidance.
안내셔(書) Guide-book.
안내ᄒ다 To guide.
안슈(按手) Laying on of hands.
안슈츅복(祝福) Benediction [츅도(祝禱)].
안슈례(禮) Ordination.
안슈흐다 To lay hands on.
안식년(安息年) Rest year.
안식일(安息日) Sabbath.
암숑련습(暗誦練習) Memory drill.
약혼(約婚) Engagement ; betrothal.
약혼흐다 To engage, to marry ; betroth [뎡혼 (定婚)].
약혼되다 To be betrothed.
양로고오원(養老孤兒院) Asylum for the old and for orphans.
양로원(養老院) Asylum for the old.
언권(言權) The floor ; right of speaking [발언권(發言權)].
언권원(員) One who has the privilege of the floor. [언권자(言權者)].
언권(을)엇다 To get the floor.
언론(言論) Speech.
엡윗청년회(엡윗靑年會) Epworth League.
여좌(如左)ᄒ다 To be as follows. [좌긔(左記)대로].
연긔(延期) Postponement.
연긔흐다 To postpone ; put off ; delay.

(80)

연보—위임

연긔(定期)연긔 Postponement to a certain time.
무긔(無期)연긔 Indefinite postponement.
연보(捐補) Church offering ; collection. [연보 전흑금 or (捐補錢或金), 헌금(獻金)].
연보흐다 To take up a collection.
연셜(演說) Lecture ; address ; speech.
연셜회(會) Meeting for lecture.
연셜흐다 To lecture ; make a speech.
연ᄉ(演士) Lecture ; speaker [변ᄉ(辯士)].
연긔(延期)흐다 To adjourn (a meeting).
예산(豫算) Estimate ; budget.
예산셔(書) Written estimate.
예산위원(委員) Budget committee ; estimate committee.
예산표(表) Table of estimates.
예산흐다 To estimate.
예수 Jesus [야소(耶蘇)].
예수교(敎) Doctrine of Jesus ; Christianity [긔독교 or 그리스도교(基督敎)].
(죠션) 예수교셔회(書會) (Korean) Christian Literature Society.
예수교인(人) Christian.
예수교회(會) Church of Jesus ; Christian Church [긔독교회(基督敎會) or 그리스도교회].
영구임원(永久任員) Permanent officer [샹무임(常務員)].
영오부(嬰兒部) Cradle-roll department.
오결(誤決) Wrong decision.
오록(誤錄) Mistake in writing [오셔(誤書)].
오록되다 To be wrongly recorded.
오착(誤錯) Mistake. [착오(錯誤), 그릇].
오해(誤解) Misunderstanding.
오해흐다 To misunderstand.
외디젼도(外地傳道) Foreign Missions. [외국션교(外國宣敎)].
외디젼도국(局) Board of Foreign Missions.
용지(用紙) Printed form.
우표(郵票) Postage-stamp. [우편졉슈(郵便切手)].
위임(委任) Commission ; charge.
위임목ᄉ(牧師) Pastor in charge.

(81)

위엄—의식

위엄밧다 To receive charge ; be installed [위엄되다].

위임식(式) Installation ; ceremony of installation.

위임장(狀) Power of attorney ; warrant. [대 리위임장(代理委任狀)].

위임처리(處理)ᄒ다 To commit to deal with ; commit to treat.

위임ᄒ다 To commit ; give in charge.

위원(委員) Committee ; member of a committee.

위원선뎡(選定) Selection of a committee.

위원선뎡ᄒ다 To select a committee.

위원장(長) Chairman of a committee.

위원회(會) Committee meeting.

전회(全會)위원 Committee of the whole.

특별(特別)위원 Special committee.

유고(有故) Cause [ᄉ고(事故)].

유고결석(缺席) Absence for cause.

유고셔(書) Notice of absence.

유고사직(辭職) Resignation for cause.

유년반(幼年班) Beginners' department [유치부 (幼稚部)].

유사(有司) Steward (in M. E. Church).

유지(維持) Support ; maintenance.

유지방법(方法) Method of maintenance.

유지ᄒ다 To support ; maintain.

유치원(幼稚園) Kindergarten.

유회(遊戱) Play.

은책(隱責) Secret censure.

은혜(恩惠) Grace.

음악회(音樂會) Concert [음악연주회(演奏會)].

자션(慈善)음악회 Charity concert.

의(意) Will [의지(意志)].

의견(意見) Opinion ; idea. [의ᄉ(意思)].

의견셔(書) Dissent.

의뎨(議題) Subject for discussion.

의론(議論) See 토론.

의론뎡지동의(停止動議) Previous question.

의지(意志) Will.

의무(義務) Duty.

의식(儀式) Rite ; ceremony.

의식뎍(的) Ritualistic.

(82)

의ᄉ—인쇄

의ᄉ(議事) Proceedings ; debate.

의사당(堂) Assembly hall.

의사일뎡(日程) Order of the day.

의ᄉ(醫師) Doctor ; physician. [의원(醫員)].

의안(議案) Proposition ; proposal ; motion ; question.

의안뎨출자(提出者) Maker of a motion.

의연(義捐) Contribution ; subscription. [의연금(義捐金)].

의연(을)모집(募集)ᄒ다 To collect contribution ; solicit subscription.

의탁판결(依托判決) Reference of a judicial case to an upper court by a lower, asking that it be tried there.

의향(意向) Intention ; object. [지향(志向)].

의회(議會) Public assembly.

의회통용규측(通用規則) Rules of Order for Public Assemblies.

이견셔(異見書) Dissent.

이단(異端) Heresy.

이단인(人) Heretic.

이록(移錄)ᄒ다 To rewrite ; copy off ; transcribe.

이론(異論) Different opinion ; objection ; debate.

이명(移名) Transfer or removal of membership. [이전(移轉)].

이명증셔(證書) Certificate of dismission.

이명ᄒ다 To transfer or remove membership.

이의(異議) Different opinion ; objection ; protest ; dissent.

이의셔(書) Written protest.

이임(移任) Transfer (of a pastor).

이임ᄒ다 To transfer.

인(印) Seal ; stamp. [도장(圖章)].

인격(人格) Personality.

인도(引導) Guidance.

인도인(人) Guide ; leader [인도자(引導者)].

인도ᄒ다 To guide ; lead.

인쇄(印刷) Printing.

인쇄자(者) Printer [인쇄인(人)].

인쇄ᄒ다 To print.

(83)

인허(認許) Official sanction ; approval ; permit. [인가(認可)].

인허밧다 or 엇다 To obtain the sanction ; be adproved.

인허ᄒᆞ다 To give sanction ; approve.

일부(日附) Date [월일(月日)].

임긔(任期) Duration of office ; period of service : term of office.

임수(任수) Apportionment.

임수부(部) Apportionment committee.

임직(任職) Ordination [장립(將立)]; appointment to office.

임직되다 To be ordained ; be appointed.

임직ᄒᆞ다 To ordain ; made an official appointment.

임직환영(歡迎) Ordination reception.

입교(入敎) Becoming a church member.

입교인(人) Member of the church ; baptized Christian ; communicant.

입교ᄒᆞ다 To become a church member.

입류(入錄)ᄒᆞ다 To record ; register. [등록(登錄); 긔록(記錄)].

입장(入場) Admission ; entrance.

입장권(券) Admission ticket.

입회(入會) Entrance ; joining ; admission.

입회불허(許)ᄒᆞ다 To admit to membership.

입회금(金) Entrance fee.

입회ᄒᆞ다 To enter or join a society.

잉임(仍任)ᄒᆞ다 To remain in office [류임(留任)].

ᄋᆞ동부(兒童部) Infant department.

ᄋᆞ히문답(兒孩問答) Children's Catechism.

ᄋᆞ히세례(兒孩洗禮) Infant baptism.

원고(原告) Accuser ; prosecutor.

원로목수(元老牧師) Pastor emeritus.

원문(原文) Original book ; original writing ; the text [본문(本文)].

원서(願書) Petition (written). [청원서(請願書)].

원측(原則) Fundamental principles.

교슈(敎授)원측 Fundamental principles of teaching.

월권(越權)ᄒᆞ다 To exceed authority or power.

(84)

자

장년반(壯年班) Adult department. [장년부(壯年部)].

장례(葬禮) Burial (funeral) ceremony. [장ᄉᆞ(葬事)].

장례식(式) Funeral rites. [장식(葬式)].

장로(長老) Elder.

장로ᄉᆞ(師) Elder (in M. E. Church).

장로교회(長老敎會) Presbyterian Church. [장로회(長老會)].

장로교회정치(政治) Government of the Presbyterian Church.

장로교회헌법(憲法) Constitution of the Presbyterian Church.

(죠선)장로교회총회(總會) General Assembly of the Presbyterian Church (of Chosen).

남장로교회 Southern Presbyterian Church.

북장로교회 Northern Presbyterian Church.

장리(掌理)ᄒᆞ다 To manage ; direct ; superintend.

장립밧다 or 되다 To be ordained.

장립식(式) Ordination ceremony.

장립ᄒᆞ다 To ordain.

장소(場所) Place ; situation ; position. [쳐소(處所), 위치(位置)].

장정(章程) Rules.

장정규측(規則) Rules and regulations.

장정긔초위원(起草委員) Committee on the formation of a constitution.

전교회(全敎會) Universal Church.

전권(全權) Full powers.

전권위원(委員) Committee with full powers.

전도(傳道) Preaching.

전도당(堂) Chapel.

전도ᄃᆡ(隊) Preaching band.

전도목ᄉᆞ(牧師) Ordained evangelist.

전도사쳐(舍廳) Preaching room. [전도실(傳道室)].

전도ᄉᆞ(師) Catechist ; preacher ; helper (in

(85)

전도—정오

M. E. Church).
전도인(人) Preacher ; evangelist.
전도처(處) Preaching place.
전도회(會) Missionary Society.
전도하다 To preach.
전례(前例) Precedent. [선예(先例)].
전별회(餞別會) Farewell meeting. [송별회(送別會)].
전수(全數) Entire member.
전수가결(可決) Unanimous affirmative vote.
전임(專任) Special duty.
전임(轉任) Transfer.
전임하다 To transfer.
전형(銓衡) Selection ; choice ; investigation.
전형하다 To select ; choose.
전회(前會) Last meeting ; previous meeting.
전회록(錄) Minutes of the previous meeting.
절제회(節制會). See 금주회.
절차(節次). See 순서.
절차위원(委員) Committee on programme, arrangement committee. [순서위원(順序委員)] 수무(事務) 절차 Order of business.
접빈(接賓) Reception. [응접(應接)].
접빈실(室) Reception room. (응접실).
접빈위원(委員) Reception committee.
접빈하다 To receive guests.
제정(制定) Enactment.
제정하다 To enact.
제도(制度) System [제(制)] ; government.
이사제(理事制) Director system.
제명(除名)하다 To strike off a name.
제한(制限) Limitation.
제한하다 To limit.
제직(諸職) Church officers [제직원(員)].
제직회(會) Meeting of all officers of a church.
도(都)제직회 Meeting of all officers of the churches in the specified territory.
정(情) Feeling.
정교(正教) Orthodoxy.
정식(正式) According to form (정식으로).
정오(正誤) Correction.
정오하다 To correct an error.

(86)

정원—쥬일

정원(正員) Regular member [원회원(原會員)].
정조(貞操) Chastity [정절(貞節)].
정치(政治) Government.
조성교회(組成教會) Organized church [조직교회(組織教會)].
조수(助手) Helper [전도수(傳道師)].
조직(組織) Organization ; system.
조직뎍(的) Systematic.
조직법(法) Organization method.
조직하다 To organize ; compose ; form.
조퇴(早退) Early leaving (meeting, school, etc.).
조퇴회원(會員) Member who has left early.
조퇴하다 To leave early.
조합교회(組合教會) Congregational Church. [회즁(會衆)교회]
존안(存案)하다 To lay on the table ; suspend (a matter).
종교(宗教) Religion.
종교교육(教育) Religious education.
종교교육부(部) Board (or committee) of religious education.
종교교육지도쟈(指導者) Director of religious education.
종교성활(生活) Religious living.
종교훈련(訓練) Religious training.
죠명(照名) Roll-call [호명(呼名) ; 뎜명(點名)].
죠명하다 To call the roll.
죵결(終結) Conclusion.
쥬간성경학교(週間聖經學校) Week day Bible School.
쥬긔도(主祈禱) Lord's Prayer [쥬긔도문(主祈禱文)].
쥬소성명(住所姓名) Address (of a person).
쥬소성명부(簿) Directory (list of names and addresses).
쥬일(主日) Lord's Day ; Sabbath Day [례비일(禮拜日)] ; Sunday [일요일(日曜日)].
쥬일례비 Sunday service.
쥬일져녁례비 Sunday evening service.
쥬일학교(學校) Sunday School (일요학교).
쥬일학교공과(工課) Sunday School Lesson.

(87)

쥬일―죵셔

쥬일학교대회(大會) Sunday School Conference.
(죠션)쥬일학교련합회(聯合會) (Korea) Sunday School Association.
쥬일학교죠직(組織) Sunday School organization.
쥬일학교죠반(班) Organized class.
쥬일학교협의회(協議會) District auxiliary Sunday School Association subsidiary to the Korea S. S. A.
유년(幼年)쥬일학교 The whole children's Sunday School including ages 5 to 17.
으히(兒後)쥬일 Children's Day.
진흥(振興)쥬일 Rally Day.
확장(擴張)쥬일학교 Extension Sunday School for non-Christians.
쥬필(主筆) Editor in chief.
쥬젼, 쥬후(主前, 主後) See 거원.
쥰비(準備) Preparation ; arrangement [셜비(設備)].
쥰비위원(委員) Arrangement committee.
쥰비회(會) Arrangement meeting.
쥰비ᄒᆞ다 To prepare ; make arrangements.
즁등반(中等班) Intermediate department [즁등부(中等部)].
즁셩(重生) Regeneration [거듭남, 지셩(再生), 신셩(新生)].
즁셩ᄒᆞ다 To be regenerated ; be born again. (거듭나다).
즁보(中保) Intercessor (Jesus Christ). [즁지(仲裁)].
즁지(中止) Recess. See 뎡지.
즁지ᄒᆞ다 To take a recess.
즉셕(即席)에 Immediately ; on the spot ; at once.
증거(證據) Evidence ; proof ; testimony.
증거셔류(書類) Voucher.
증거불츙분(不充分) Insufficency of evidence.
증거ᄒᆞ다 To prove ; testify ; bear witness to.
증경(曾經) Former.
증셔(證書) Testimonial ; certificate. [증명셔(證明書)].

(88)

종인―집회

종인(證人) Witness ; voucher. [종거인(證據人)].
지교회(支敎會) Particular church or congregation.
지뎡(指定) Appointment ; designation.
지뎡ᄒᆞ다 To appoint ; designate.
지력(智力) Intellect [지(智)].
지명(指名) Nomination ; naming.
지명ᄒᆞ다 To nominate ; name.
지부(支部) Branch ; subdivision.
지시(指示) Indication ; direction [지휘(指揮)].
지시위원(委員) Directing committee.
지시ᄒᆞ다 To indicate ; direct.
지원(志願) Desire ; application.
지원쟈(者) Candidate ; applicant ; volunteer.
지원ᄒᆞ다 To desire ; apply for ; volunteer for.
지출(支出) Disbursement ; payment [지출(支拂)].
지회(支會) Branch society.
직결(直決) Immediate decision. [즉결(即決)].
직결ᄒᆞ다 To give an immediate decision.
직권(職權) Power ; authority.
직무(職務) Duty ; work [사업(事業)].
직임(職任) Duty ; office.
직원(職員) Officer ; faculty.
직원회(職員會) Faculty meeting (of school).
직할(直轄) Direct control. [직접관할(直接管轄)].
진졍(陳情)ᄒᆞ다 To state one's views or opinions.
진졍셔(書) Petition.
질문(質問) Question.
집무(執務) Business [회무(會務)].
집무시간(時間) Business (office) hours.
집ᄉᆞ(執事) Deacon.
녀(女)집ᄉᆞ Deaconess.
셔리(署理)집ᄉᆞ Unordained deacon ; substitute deacon.
시무(視務)집ᄉᆞ Active deacon.
안슈(按手)집ᄉᆞ Ordained deacon [쟝립(將立)집ᄉᆞ].
집회(集會) [회집(會集)]. See 회(會).
집회ᄒᆞ다 To meet together ; assemble.

(89)

집회—지청

집회장소(場所) Meeting-place [회집처(會集處)].
집행(執行) Administration.
집행위원(委員) Administration committee.
집행하다 Te administrate.
징계(懲戒) Discipline.
징책(懲責) Censure ; reproof.
징책하다 To censure ; reprove.
자선(慈善) Charity [자혜(慈惠)].
자선사업(事業) Works of charity.
자격(資格) Qualification ; capacity.
자격업는 Unqualified.
자격잇는 Qualified.
자벽(自辟)하다 To appoint a committee or an officer [임명(任命)].
자복(自服) Confession.
자유교회(自由敎會) Independent Church.
자퇴(自退)하다 To leave of one's own accord.
재가(裁可) Sanction ; approval ; assent.
재가하다 To sanction ; approve.
재개의(再改議) Amendment to an amendment.
재개의하다 To make an amendment to an amendment.
재단(財團) Foundation.
재단법인(法人) Foundational (juridical) person.
재단부(部) Foundational committee [재단위원(委員)].
재론(再論) Reconsideration. [지의(再議)].
재론하다 To reconsider.
재산(財産) Property.
재선(再選) Reelection.
재선하다 To reelect.
재입회(再入會) Readmission
재전출납(財錢出納) Receipts and disbursements. [금전출납(金錢出納)].
재정(財政) Finance.
재정위원(委員) Financial committee.
재정보고(報告) Financial report [회계보고(會計報告)].
재직(在職) Holding an office ; tenure of office.
재직중(中) While in office.
재청(再請)하다 To second a motion.
재청자(者) Seconder.

(90)

지판—창립

지판(裁判) Judgment [판결(判決)].
지판국(局) Judicial commission. [지판회(裁判會)].
지판수속(手續) Judicial process.
지판사건(事件) Judicial case.
지판하다 To judge.
지회(再會)하다 To meet again.
지표(再票)하다 To take a second vote ; second count of votes.
정론(爭論) Dissension.
진변서(評辯書) Judicial protest.
좌석(座席) Seats.
좌석정돈(整頓) Being seated in good order.
좌석정돈하다 To be seated in good order.

차

착오(錯誤) Mistake ; error. [오착(誤錯)].
찬성(贊成) Aid ; assistance ; agreement.
찬성원(員) Associate member. [찬성회원(贊成會員)].
찬성자(者) Promoter ; supporter. [찬성인(人)].
찬성하다 To aid ; assist.
찬양대(讚揚隊) Band of singers ; chorus. [찬미대(讚美隊)].
참가(參加) Participation.
참가하다 To take part in ; join.
참고(參考)하다 To compare with ; refer to [참조(參照)].
참교명지(參敎停止) Suspension.
참교명지하다 To suspend [집회명지(集會停止)].
참석(參席) Attendance ; participation.
참석원(員) Attendant. [참석회원(會員)].
참석하다 To attend ; be present ; take part with.
참예(參預) Participation. [참여(參與)].
참예하다 To take part.
창립(創立) Organization ; foundation.
창립긔렴(記念) Commemoration of the foundation.

(91)

창립—총계

창립위원(委員) Organizing committee.
창립총회(總會) The first general meeting.
창립호다 To organize ; found.
쳐리(處理) Management ; transaction ; treatment.
쳐리사건(事件) Proceedings.
쳐리회(會) Judicatory ; court.
쳐리호다 To manage ; transact ; treat ; deal with ; do business.
쳔(薦) Nomination ; recommendation ; introduction. [쳔거(薦擧), 츅쳔(推薦)].
쳔셔(書) Letter of recommendation or introduction ; credentials. [증셔(證書)].
쳔호다 To nominate ; recommend ; introduce.
쳔션법(薦選法) Method of nomination.
쳘폐(撤廢) Removal ; abolition.
쳘폐호다 To remove ; withdraw ; abolish.
쳘회(撤還)호다 To recall [쳘회(撤回), 소환(召還)].
쳥년반(靑年班) Young people's department. [쳥년부(靑年部)].
쳥년젼도회(靑年傳道會) Young people's missionary society.
쳥년회(靑年會) Young people's association.
쳥빙(請聘) Call ; invitation. [쳥요(請邀)].
쳥빙셔(書) Form of the call.
쳥빙호다 To invite ; call.
쳥원(請願) Application ; petition. [신쳥(申請), 출원(出願)].
쳥원셔(書) Application ; written petition.
쳥원호다 To make an application ; prefer a petition.
초등반(初等班) Primary department. [초등부(初等部)].
초디교회(初代敎會) Early Church.
쵸본(抄本) Extract.
호젹(戶籍)쵸본 Abstract of a census-register. 민젹쵸본(民籍抄本)].
최고법뎡(最高法庭) Highest court ; supreme court.
최다수(最多數) Plurality.
총계(總計) Total ; sum total. [총합(總合)].

(92)

총디—출판

총디(總代) Representative ; delegate.
총무(總務) Manager ; secretary, (S. S.) general secretary.
총션거(總選擧) See 션거.
총소직(總辭職) See 스직.
총의회(總議會) General Conference.
총측(總則) General rules.
총회(總會) General Assembly.
죠션쟝로교회(朝鮮長老敎會)총회 General Assembly of the Presbyterian Church of Chosen.
총회비(費) Expense of the General Assembly.
총회총디(總代) Delegate to the General Assembly.
츅뎐(祝電) Congratulatory telegram.
츅도(祝禱) Benediction. [츅복긔도(祝福祈禱)].
츅스(祝辭) Congratulatory address ; Congratulations ; greetings.
츅스올드리다 To offer one's congratulations.
츅스호다 To make a congratulatory address.
츅하(祝賀) Congratulation ; celebration.
츅하쟝(狀) Congratulatory letter ; birthday greeting.
츅하회(會) Congratulatory celebration. [츅하식(式)].
츅하호다 To congratulate ; celebrate.
출교(黜敎)Excommunication.
출교호다 To excommunicate.
출두(出頭)호다 To attend ; appear.
출셕(出席) Attendance ; presence.
출셕수(數) Number in attendance.
출셕원(員) Attendant.
출셕호다 To attend ; be present.
출연(出捐)호다 To subscribe ; contribute.
출원(出願) See 쳥원.
출직(黜職) Dismissal ; deprivation. [파직(罷職), 달임(奪任)].
출직호다 To dismiss from a post or place ; deprive of office.
출판(出版) Publication.
출판물(物) Publication.
출판위원(委員) Publication committee.

(93)

출판ᄒᆞ다 To publish.
취쇼(取消) Recantation.
취쇼ᄒᆞ다 To recant.
취임(就任) Assumption of office.
취임식(式) Inauguration.
취임ᄒᆞ다 To assume an office ; take up a post or position.
취지(趣旨) Purpose ; purport.
취지셔(書) Prospectus.
취지셜명(說明)ᄒᆞ다 To state the purpose.
취직(就職)ᄒᆞ다 To take or hold office.
치리(治理) Ruling ; discipline.
치리권(權) Governing power ; ruling authority.
치리쟝로(長老) Ruling elder.
치리회(會) Judicatory.
치리ᄒᆞ다 To rule ; discipline.
칠십인역셩경(七十人譯聖經) Septuagint.
침례교회(浸禮敎會) Baptist Church.
ᄎᆞ뎜(次點) Second highest votes.
ᄎᆞ뎜을밧다 To receive the second highest vote.
ᄎᆞ뎜자(者) One who has received the second highest vote.
ᄎᆞ회(次會) Next meeting.
ᄎᆡ결(採決) Decision ; voting.
발셩(發聲)ᄎᆡ결 Voting by acclamation.
긔립(起立)ᄎᆡ결 Rising vote ; standing vote.
ᄎᆡ용(採用) Adoption.
ᄎᆡ용ᄒᆞ다 To adopt.
젼부(全部)ᄎᆡ용ᄒᆞ다 To adopt as a whole.
축됴(逐條)ᄎᆡ용ᄒᆞ다 To adopt by sections.
ᄎᆡᆨ망(責望) Censure.
ᄎᆡᆨ망ᄒᆞ다 To censure.
ᄎᆡᆨ벌(責罰) Suspension.
ᄎᆡᆨ벌밧다 To be suspended.
ᄎᆡᆨ벌밧은사ᄅᆞᆷ Suspended member. [ᄎᆡᆨ벌밧은교인(敎人)].
ᄎᆡᆨ벌ᄒᆞ다 To suspend.
ᄎᆡᆨ임(責任) Responsibility ; accountability ; duty.

(94)

타

탁ᄉᆞ부(托事部) Board of trustees.
탈션(脫線) Digression.
탈션ᄒᆞ다 To be off the subject.
탈직(奪職) Deprivation.
탈직ᄒᆞ다 To deprive of office.
탈회(脫退) Secession.
탈회자(者) Seceder.
탈회ᄒᆞ다 To secede.
탈회(脫會) Withdrawal.
탈회계(屆) Notice of withdrawal.
탈회ᄒᆞ다 To withdraw from.
텬부(天父) Heavenly Father.
텬ᄉᆞ(天使) Angel [ᄉᆞ쟈(使者)].
텬쥬교(天主敎) Roman Catholic Church [로마교(羅馬敎)].
톄육부(體育部) Physical education (or training) department (톄육회).
톄번(替番)ᄒᆞ다 To alternate (as for associate pastors to take turns in preaching).
톄임(遞任)되다 To be changed (of officers).
토론(討論) Debate ; discussion. [토의(討議)].
토론회(會) Debating society.
토론ᄒᆞ다 To debate ; discuss.
퇴보(退步) Backslide.
퇴보ᄒᆞ다 To backslide.
퇴셕(退席)ᄒᆞ다 To leave one's seat [퇴쟈(退座)] ; leave the room.
퇴쟝식이다 To expel.
퇴직(退職)ᄒᆞ다 To retire from office.
퇴회(退會). See 탈회.
통계(統計) Statistics.
통계부(部) Statistical committee. [통계위원(委員)].
통계표(表) Statistical table.
통과(通過) Passing (a motion) [가결(可決)].
통과ᄒᆞ다 To pass.
통과되다 To be carried.

(95)

통변(通辯) Interpretation [통역(通譯)]; interpreter [통역, 통역자(者)].
통상회(通常會) Regular meeting [평상회(平常會), 뎡긔회(定期會)].
통신결의(通信決議)ᄒᆞ다 To transact business by correspondence.
통신과(通信科) Correspondence course.
통일공과(統一工課) Uniform Lessons.
통지(通知) Communication [통텹(通牒)]; information ; report.
통지서(書) Notice.
통지ᄒᆞ다 Communicate ; inform ; report.
투표(投票) Vote, halloting.
투표결과(結果) Result of voting.
투표권(權) right to vote ; the vote.
투표됴사원(調查員) Teller [계표원(計票員)].
투표자(者) Voter.
투표지(紙) Voting slips.
투표ᄒᆞ다 To vote ; ballot.
긔립(起立)투표 Vote by rising.
발성(發聲)투표 Vote by acclamation.
특권(特權) Prerogative (privilege).
특원관매(問題) Question of privilege.
특별과(特別科) Special course [별과(別科)].
특쳥(特請) Special request.
특청ᄒᆞ다 To make a special request.
특파(特派) Special despatch.
특파원(員) Specially despatched person ; special delegate.
특파ᄒᆞ다 To despatch specially.

파

파견(派遣) Dispatch ; mission.
파견ᄒᆞ다 To dispatch ; send ; forward. [파송(派送)].
파의(罷議)ᄒᆞ다 To make an end of an argument ; drop the matter. [명론(停論)].
파직(罷職) Deposition (from office) [면직(免職)].

(96)

파직ᄒᆞ다 To depose from office.
판결(判決) Judicial decision.
판결서(書) Judgment in writing.
판결ᄒᆞ다 To decide ; judge.
판단(判斷) Decision [판뎡(判定)].
판단ᄒᆞ다 To decide.
판비(辦備)ᄒᆞ다 To provide.
편즙(編輯) Editing ; compilation.
편즙위원(委員) Editing committee [편즙부(編輯部)].
편즙인(人) Editor ; compiler [편즙자(編輯者)].
편즙ᄒᆞ다 To edit ; compile.
폐지(廢止) Abolition.
폐지ᄒᆞ다 To abolish ; rescind.
폐회(閉會) Adjournment. [산회(散會)].
폐회긔(期)물뎡(定)ᄒᆞ다 To fix the time to which to adjourn.
폐회ᄒᆞ다 To adjourn.
평균(平均) Average.
평신도(平信徒) Laity ; layman. [평교인(平敎人)].
평론(評論) Review ; criticism [비평(批評)].
평론ᄒᆞ다 To review ; criticize.
표결(票決)ᄒᆞ다 To put to vote.
표션(票選)ᄒᆞ다 To elect by voting.
표수(票數) Number of votes [투표수(投票數)].
피고(被告) Defendant ; accused person [피고인(被告人)].
피빙쟈(被聘者) One who has been called (as of pastor).
피션(被選) Being elected ; being chosen [피릭(被擇)].
피션권(權) Eligibility ; right to be elected.
피션되다 To be elected.
피션자(者) The person elected.

하

하긔ᄋ동셩경학교(夏期兒童聖經學校) Daily Vacation Bible School.

(97)

하회—허위

하회(下會) Inferior court : lower judicatory.
학감(學監) Dean ; school superintendent.
학교(學校) School [학당(學堂)] ; institute [학원(學院)].
학교장(長) Principal ; president [총장(總長)].
고등(高等)학교 High school.
공립(公立)학교 Public school.
남(男)학교 Boys' school.
녀(女)학교 Girls' school.
보통(普通)학교 Common school.
대(大)학교 College ; university [종합대학(綜合大學)].
쇼(小)학교 Primary school.
수립(私立)학교 Private school.
수범(師範)학교 Normal school.
전문(專門) College.
졸(中)학교 Middle school ; academy.
학무국(學務局) School-board [학무위원(學務委員)].
학습문답(學習問答) Examination for the catechumenate.
학습서다 To become a catechumen.
학습세우다 To receive as a catechumen.
학습인(人) Catechumen [학습교인(學習敎人)].
합설(合設) Union (of churches).
합설하다 To unite.
항고(抗告) Complaint.
항고장(狀) Memorandum of complaint.
항고하다 To complain.
항돈하다 To refute.
항의(抗議) Protest [항변(抗辯)] ; remonstrance ; objection [항거(抗拒)].
항의셔(書) Written protest [항변셔(抗辯書)].
항의하다 To protest against ; remonstrate against ; object to.
허가(許可) See 인허.
허락(許諾) Permission ; consent ; agreement [승낙(承諾)].
허락밧다 To get permission.
허락하다 To permit ; consent.
허위(虛位) Vacancy.
허위교회(敎會) Vacant church.

(98)

허위—회계

허위구역(區域) Vacant district.
허위당회(堂會) Session without a moderator.
헌금(獻金) See 연보.
헌당(獻堂) Dedication (of a church).
헌당식(式) Ceremony of dedication.
헌법(憲法) Constitution [헌장(憲章)].
헌법상(上) Constitutional.
헌법위원(委員) Committee for the formation of a consitution.
헌신(獻身) Consecration.
헌신례비(禮拜) Consecration meeting.
헌신하다 To consecrate.
헌의(獻議) Overture.
헌의부(部) Committee on overtures.
현임(現任) Present office or duty [현임직분(現任職分)].
협의(協議) Counsel.
협의회(會) Council.
협의하다 To confer.
협회(協會) Society ; association.
호천(呼薦) Nomination by acclamation.
호출(呼出) Calling out, summons [초환(召喚)].
호출장(狀) Citation.
호출하다 To call out ; summon ; cite.
혼례(婚禮) Marriage ceremony ; wedding ceremony. [혼례식(婚禮式)].
혼례홀힝(行)하다 To conduct a marriage ceremony.
회(回) Time or times.
뎨일(第一)회 The first time.
이(二)회 Twice.
일(一)회 Once.
삼(三)회 Three times.
회(會) Meeting ; gathering ; assembly ; congress ; conference ; convention ; council ; board ; society ; association ; party ; committee.
회의목뎍(目的) Object of a meeting.
회계(會計) Treasurer ; finances.
회계보고(報告) Financial report ; report of the treasurer.
지(支)회계 Local (or branch) treasurer.

(99)

회규(會規) Rules and by-laws for an assembly [회측(會則)].
회금(會金) Fees; regular payment.
회긔(會期) Session; sitting; date at which an assembly or a meeting opens.
회긔를뎡(定)ᄒᆞ다 To fix the date for a meeting.
회ᄀᆡ(悔改) Repentance.
회ᄀᆡᄒᆞ다 To Repent.
회당(會堂). See 예배당.
회록(會錄) Minutes; records [의ᄉᆞ록(議事錄)]; minute-book, record-book.
회록검사(檢査)ᄒᆞ다 To examine the minutes or records.
회록교졍(校正)ᄒᆞ다 To amend the minutes.
회록랑독(朗讀)ᄒᆞ다 To read the minutes or records.
회록ᄒᆞ다 To keep minutes; To record minutes [회록긔지(記載)ᄒᆞ다].
젼(前)회록 Minutes of the previous meeting.
회록쳐용ᄒᆞ다 To approve the minutes.
회를쇼집(召集)ᄒᆞ다 To convene a meeting.
회룰졍돈(整頓)ᄒᆞ다 To call to order.
회무(會務) Affairs of an assembly or society.
회ᄉᆞ쳐리(處理) Transaction of business.
회비(會費) Expense of a society.
회셕(會席) Meeting; place for a meeting [회집장소(會集場所)]; seats in a meeting.
회셕졍돈(整頓)ᄒᆞ다 To call to order.
회의(會議). See 회(會).
회의실(室) Room for a meeting.
회일(會日) Date at which a meeting opens.
회원(會員) Member.
회원ᄌᆞ격(資格) Qualification for membership.
회장(會長) Chairman [의장(議長)]; moderator (of session, etc.).
회장셕(席) The Chair (chairman).
회장직(職) Chairmanship.
회장퇴(槌) Gavel [고회].
회흄(會衆) Congregation or assemblage.
회흄의의견(意見) Will of the meeting.
회흄의공허(公許) Consent of the assembly.
회흄문젼(會中文件) Assembly's documents.

(100)

회집(會集). See 집회.
회측(會則). See 회규.
후보자(候補者) Candidate.
후원(後援) Support; backing.
후원회(會) Meeting of supportss.
후원ᄒᆞ다 To support; uphold.
훈계 Advice.
휴가(休暇) Holiday; vacation; furlough; leave of absence.
휴가목ᄉᆞ(牧師) Pastor who has leave of absence.
휴식(休息) Rest; recess. [휴게(休憩)].
휴식시간(時間) Recess time.
휴식ᄒᆞ다 To rest; take a recess.
휴식쳐(處) Rest-place [휴게소(所)].
휴양(休養) Rest; recreation.
휴양소(所) Rest-place.
휴양ᄒᆞ다 To rest; recreate oneself.
휴직(休職) Temporarily resting from office.
휴직목ᄉᆞ(牧師) Temporarily retired pastor.
휴직ᄒᆞ다 To rest temorarily from office.
휴회(休會). See 뎡회.
흠뎡역셩경(欽定譯聖經) Authorized verson.
흠셕(欠席). See 셕.
히결(解決) Settlement [락착(落着)]; solution.
히결ᄒᆞ다 To settle; solve.
히벌(解罰) Removal of suspension.
히벌되다 To be restored from suspension.
히벌ᄒᆞ다 To remove suspension.
히셕(解釋) Explanation; exposition; interpretation; commentary.
히셕ᄒᆞ다 To explain; expound; interpret; comment.
히약(解約) Termination (dissolution) of a contract.
히약ᄒᆞ다 To terminate (dissolve) a contract; free oneself from a contract.
히임(解任) Dismissal.
히임ᄒᆞ다 To dismiss from office.
힝졍(行政) Administration.
흥존(恒存) Permanent. [영구(永久)].
환영(歡迎) Welcome; reception.

(101)

환영

환영회(會) Meeting of welcome.
환영ᄒᆞ다 To welcome ; receive.

부록 (附錄)

회무순셔(會務順序)

1. 교슉(叩囑)(회셕졍돈)
2. 젼회록랑독(前會錄朗讀)
3. 샹비위원의보고(常備委員의報告)
4. 션뎡(혹림시)위원의보고〔選定(或臨時)委員의報告〕
F. 미진ᄉᆞ젼(未盡事件)
6. 신ᄉᆞ젼(新事件)
7. 폐회(閉會)

각종동의(各種動議)

1. 동의(動議)
2. 저청(再請)
3. 긔의(改議)
4. 지긔의(再改議)
5. 디신동의의동의(代身動議의動議)
6. 보고령취ᄒᆞ자ᄂᆞ동의(報告聽取ᄒᆞ자ᄂᆞ動議)
7. 보고슈리혹쳐용ᄒᆞ자ᄂᆞ동의(報告受理或採用ᄒᆞ자ᄂᆞ動議)
8. 위임ᄒᆞ자ᄂᆞ동의(委任ᄒᆞ자ᄂᆞ動議)
9. 유긔연긔ᄒᆞ자ᄂᆞ동의(有期延期ᄒᆞ자ᄂᆞ動議)
10. 무긔연긔ᄒᆞ자ᄂᆞ동의(無期延期ᄒᆞ자ᄂᆞ動議)
11. 존안동의(存案動議)
12. 긔안동의(起案動議)
13. 저론동의(再論動議)
14. 동의의취소동의(動議의取消動議)
15. 토의제한ᄒᆞ자ᄂᆞ동의(討議制限ᄒᆞ자ᄂᆞ動議)

(II)

16. 토의제한을연어ᄒᆞ자ᄂᆞᆫ동의 (討議制限을延期ᄒᆞ자ᄂᆞᆫ動議)
17. 토의ᄭᅳᆺ치자ᄂᆞᆫ동의(討議ᄭᅳᆺ치자ᄂᆞᆫ動議)
18. 의사일정의동의 (議事日程의動議)
19. 의사일정을변ᄀᆡᆼᄒᆞ자ᄂᆞᆫ동의 (議事日程을變更ᄒᆞ자ᄂᆞᆫ動議)
20. 의사일졍에ᄐᆞᆨ별ᄉᆞ건을가입ᄒᆞ자ᄂᆞᆫ동의 (議事日程에特別事件을加入ᄒᆞ자ᄂᆞᆫ動議)
21. 회록에서삭졔ᄒᆞ자ᄂᆞᆫ동의 (會錄에셔削除하자ᄂᆞᆫ動議)
22. 회장의판결을항의ᄒᆞ자ᄂᆞᆫ동의 (會長의判決을抗議ᄒᆞ자ᄂᆞᆫ動議)
23. 규측잠지ᄒᆞ자ᄂᆞᆫ동의 (規則暫止ᄒᆞ자ᄂᆞᆫ動議)
24. 긔립보고ᄒᆞ자ᄂᆞᆫ동의 (젼회위원회에셔뿐) (起立報告ᄒᆞ자ᄂᆞᆫ動議)
25. ᄐᆞᆨ권안의동의 (特權案의動議)
26. 션결문뎨의동의 (先決問題의動議)
27. 아모의안을ᄌᆞ론ᄒᆞ지말자ᄂᆞᆫ동의 (아모議案을再論ᄒᆞ자ᄂᆞᆫ動議)
28. 폐회동의 (閉會動議)
29. 폐회시간동의 (閉會時間動議)

네가지의안(四種議案)

I 원안혹유요안(元案或主要案)
II 보조안(補助案)
III 부슈안(附隨案)
IV ᄐᆞᆨ권안(特權案)

I 원안은무슴문뎨를결뎡키위ᄒᆞ야ᄂᆞ러나ᄂᆞᆫ의안이니아모다른的안이회에ᄂᆞ러나지아니ᄒᆞᆯᄯᆡ에만지ᄒᆡᆼ될수잇스며두원안이동시에진ᄒᆡᆼ될수ᄂᆞᆫ 업슴

(III)

II 보조안은원안에응용되ᄂᆞᆫ것이니원안의션무가되며ᄃᆞ톄ᄐᆞᆨ권안과부슈안에양보ᄒᆞᆷ 보조안은다음과ᄭᆞᆺᄒᆞ야그슌셔대로됨
1. 죤안(存案)
2. 션결문뎨(先決問題)
3. 유긔연긔(有期延期)
4. 위임혹지임(委任或再任)
5. 긔졍(改正)
6. 무긔연긔(無期延期)

III 부슈안은원안과보조안에셔ᄂᆞ러나ᄂᆞ그션무가되며ᄐᆞᆨ권안에양보ᄒᆞ니 다음과ᄭᆞᆺ흠
1. 회장판결에항의(會長判決에抗議)
2. 재론ᄒᆞ지말자ᄂᆞᆫ동의 (再論ᄒᆞ지말자ᄂᆞᆫ動議)
3. 셔류낭독쳥(書類朗讀請)
4. 동의취쇼의인가쳥(動議取消의認可請)
5. 규측잠지ᄒᆞ자ᄂᆞᆫ동의 (規則暫止ᄒᆞ자ᄂᆞᆫ動議)

IV ᄐᆞᆨ권안은원안과보조안과부슈안의션무가되ᄂᆞ니회나ᄆᆞ원의쳔의와ᄐᆞᆨ권에관계되ᄂᆞ것의外에ᄂᆞᆫ토의ᄒᆞ지못ᄒᆞᆷ(ᄒᆞ뢰메三)ᄐᆞᆨ권안을슈용ᄒᆞ리걸교회무를쟝ᄋᆡᄒᆞ거나지톄ᄒᆞ게말것이니ᄐᆞᆨ권안은다음과ᄭᆞᆺᄒᆞ야그슌셔대로됨
1. 폐회시간의결뎡(閉會時間의決定)
2. 폐회(閉會)
3. 쳔리와ᄐᆞᆨ권에관계되ᄂᆞ문뎨 (權利와特權에關係되ᄂᆞᆫ問題)
4. 의사일졍쳥(議事日程請)

(IV)

하긔의안은로의호지못호나긔여의안은 로의홀수잇슴

1. 폐회시간의결뎡 (이의안은다른의안이회에잇 는새에는로의호지못호고아모의안도회에업는 새에는다른원안과맛한가지로토의홀수잇슴)
2. 폐회(閉會)
3. 의소일뎡의동의(議事日程의動議)
4. 회두선후에관되논골때
5. 항의 (아모다른의안이미결노잇슬새에홈)
6. 의안을숙고호고지말자노동의
7. 존안동의(存案動議)
8. 긔안동의(起案動議)
9. 션결문뎨(先決問題)
10. 토의못홀의안의지론

하긔동의는긔의홀수업슴

1. 폐회(閉會)
2. 의소일뎡의동의(議事日程의動議)
3. 부슈안(이상네가지의안메三을보라)
4. 존안(存案)
5. 션결문뎨(先決問題)
6. 지긔의(再改議)
7. 무긔연긔(無期延期)
8. 지론(再論)

하긔의안이결뎡되긔싯지는원안을로의 홀수잇슴

1. 위임(委任)

(V)

2. 무긔연긔(無期延期)
3. 최록삭제(會錄削除)
4. 로의홀수잇는의안의지론

의안중에루표파반수로결뎡되는것이만 흐나하긔의안은三분의二를요구홈

1. 규측뎡지 ⎫ 규측을곱요시호아四분의三을요구
2. 규측뎡지 ⎭ 호논회도잇슴
3. 특별슌셔제뎡(特別順序製定)
4. 모의안의슌셔변킹(某議案의順序變更)
5. 의안을숙고호지말자노동의(議案을熟考호지 말자노動議)
6. 로의제한의연쟝(討論制限의延長)
7. 로의제한혹동결(討論의制限或終結)
8. 션결문뎨(先決問題)

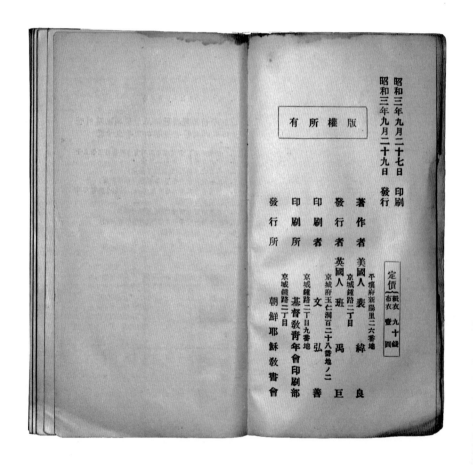

昭和三年九月二十七日　印刷
昭和三年九月二十九日　發行

版權所有

定價　紙衣　九十錢
　　　布衣　壹圓四

著作者　美國人　平壤府新陽里二六番地　裴緯良

發行者　英國人　京城鍾路二丁目　班禹巨

印刷者　京城府玉仁洞百二十八番地ノ二　文弘善

印刷所　京城鍾路二丁目九番地　基督敎靑年會印刷部

發行所　京城鍾路二丁目　朝鮮耶穌敎書會

원문

한국어 사용 초보자를 위한
50가지 도움말

Fifty Helps for the Beginner

in the Use of the Korean Language

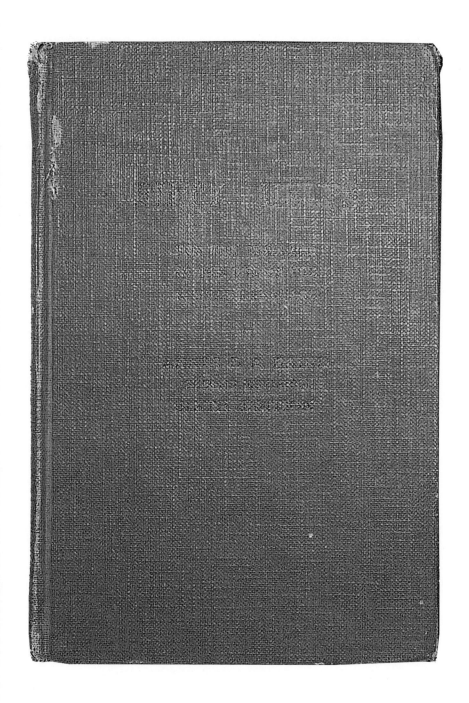

FIFTY · HELPS

FOR THE BEGINNER
IN THE USE OF THE
KOREAN LANGUAGE

BY

ANNIE L. A. BAIRD
SECOND REVISION
SIXTH EDITION

Presented by

Price : Yen 1.50

Moffett 이사

THE CHRISTIAN LITERATURE SOCIETY
OF KOREA

1926

"For thou art * * * sent to a people of a strange speech and of a hard language, * * * to many peoples of a strange speech and of a hard language, whose words thou canst not understand."

Ezek. III. 5, 6.

"A people of a speech that thou canst not comprehend, of a strange tongue that thou canst not understand."

Isa. XXXIII. 19.

FIFTY HELPS

FOR THE BEGINNER
IN THE USE OF THE
KOREAN LANGUAGE

———

This little booklet is not intended for the eye of those who have made considerable progress in the study and use of Korean, but is designed simply to help the beginner to a speedy use of certain common idioms. All that it contains, with the exception, perhaps, of the vocabulary of religious terms, and the prayer and gospel sentences, may be found much more fully and carefully expressed in other works, but not, as we believe, in a form so accessible to beginners.

First of all the student should learn from the following table to recognize at sight the written character, and thus equip himself for the use of Gale's Korean-English dictionary and all other available printed helps.

2   FIFTY HELPS FOR THE BEGINNER

TABLE OF KOREAN CHARACTERS WITH
THEIR EQUIVALENT ENGLISH
SOUNDS.*

VOWELS.

이 ī or ĭ, 아 ä, 어 ŭ or û, 으 eu, 오 ō or ô,
우 oo̅ or o̅o̅, ᄋ ä or almost silent, 애 ă, 에 ā or
ĕ, 외 something like wā with but slight sound of
w, 위 ă.

The character ㅇ in connection with each of
these vowels is omitted whenever the vowel is
preceded by a consonant.

1. 이 =ī in machine, as 비, pī (rain), 깁다
        kīpta, (to mend).
        =ĭ in pin, as 집, chip, (house), 깁다,
        kīpta, (to be deep).

2. 아 =ä in father, as 갓, kät, (hat).

3. 어 =ŭ in tub, as 법, (pŭp), custom.

---

* Taken from an article by Rev. W. M. Baird on ''The
Romanization of Korean Sounds'' in *The Korean Reposi-
tory* for May, 1895.
The system of diacritical marks used is based on
Webster's International Dictionary.

=û in purr, as 벗, pût (friend); 머 오,
mûō (to be far). Both sounds are
found in 건너가오, kûn n kǟō,
(to cross over).

4. 으=French eu, as 그 keu, (that).

5. 오=ō in note, as 솜 sōm, (cotton), 동늬,
tōng-nǎ, (a neighborhood).

=ô in for, as 동산, tông sǎn, (a garden).

6. 우=oō in moon, as 문, moōn, (a door).

=oŏ in woŏl as 풀, p'oŏl, (grass).

7. ᅌ =ä in father, as 물, mäl, (a horse).

=a almost silent, as in closed, unaccent-
ed syllables like the second syllable
of 사룸, säram, (person).

8. 애=ǎ in hat, as 개, kǎ, (a dog).

9. 에=ā in fate, as 제가, chā ga, (he or she
or I).

=ĕ in met, as 가겟소, kägĕsso, (I will
go).

10. 외 =This character has no exact equivalent
in English sounds. It is somewhat
like wā with but slight sound of w,
as 죄, chwā, (fault or sin).

11. 익 =ǎ in hat, as 칙, ch'ǎk, (a book).

4   FIFTY HELPS FOR THE BEGINNER

DIPHTHONGS.

Of true diphthongs there is but one.

12. 의 =French eui. Something like ĭ preceded by a very slight sound of w, as 의원, euĭ wŭn, (a physician).

W as a vowel has no representation except that mentioned under Nos. 10, and 12; and *Y* has no place whatever as a vowel. As consonants they are compounded with other letters as follows :—

VOWELS COMPOUNDED WITH Y.

13. 야 =ä as in father preceded by y, as 양 yäng, (a sheep).

14. 여 =ŭ in tub preceded by y, as 병, pyŭng, (a bottle).

     =û in purr preceded by y, as 면호다, myûn häda, (to escape, avoid).

15. 요 =ō in note with y prefixed, as 욕, yōk, (abuse).

     =ô in for with y prefixed, as in first syllable of 섈쪽호다, byô chōk hädä (to be sharp, pointed).

16. 유 =oo in moon with y prefixed, as 유식 호다, yoo sik häda, (to be learned).

=o͞o in wool, with y prefixed, as 흉년, hyŏong nyŭn, (famine year).

17. 예 =ā in fate, with y prefixed, as 예슌, yāsoon, (sixty).

=ĕ in met with y prefixed, as 예, yĕ, (yes).

VOWELS COMPOUNDED .WITH W.

18. 와 =ä in father with w prefixed, as 실과, sil gwä, (fruit).

19. 왜 =ä̆ in hat with w prefixed, 왜인, wä ïn, (a Japanese).

20. 워 =ŭ in tub with w prefixed, as 원 wŭn, (an official)'.

=û in purr with w prefixed, as 원ᄒ다, wûn häda, (to wish, to desire).

21. 위 =ī in machine with w prefixed, as 위ᄒ 다, wï häda, (to worship). After ㅁ (m), or ㅂ (p), the sound of w is dropped as 뮈워ᄒ다, mï wŭ häda, (to hate,), 븨다 pïda (to be empty).

6   FIFTY HELPS FOR THE BEGINNER

22. 웨 =ā in fate preceded by w, as 웬 wān,
     (what sort of? what manner of?)

23. 위 =ī in machine preceded by somewhat
     slight sound of w, as in 취ᄒᄃᆞ,
     ch'wī häda, (to be drunk). This
     combination seldom occurs except
     after ㅊ (ch') ㅈ (ch), and ㅌ
     (t').

REMARKS ON THE VOWELS.

The sign ㅣ, called 외, is often written alone
as if it were a separate letter. It has no value in
itself, however, its effect being to modify the
sound of the preceding vowel.

A decided umlaut or deflection of vowel sound
caused by the influence of another vowel following either directly or separated by an intervening
consonant is found in Korean.

The disturbing vowel, as is also the case in Old
English, is ī.

ä followed by ī as in the nominative case of 밥
päp, (food) approximates ā as 밥이, päpī.
ŭ followed by ī as in the nominative case of 떡
dŭk, (bread), approximates ā, as 떡이,
dāgī.

ya followed by ï as in the nominative case of
약 yăk, (medicine), approximates ă, as 약
이 yăgï.

yŭ followed by ï as in the nominative case of
병 pyŭng, (bottle), approximates ï as 병
이, pyïngï.

Test with teacher such words as 므 음 이 (밈
이), 형편 (헹편), 경영호다 (계영
호다).

CONSONANTS.

SIMPLE.

ㄱ k, ㅁ m, ㄴ n, ㄹ l or r, ㅂ p, ㅅ s or sh,
ㄷ t, ㅈ ch, ㆁ ng.

ASPIRATED CONSONANTS.

These characters are pronounced as their name
indicates with a sharp outgoing of the breath. In
transliterating, the arbitrary sign ' marks the
aspiration, except in the case of the first character
which is a natural aspirate.

ㅎ =h, as 흙, heulk, (earth).

ㅋ =k', as 코, k'ô, (nose).

ㅍ=p', as 피, p'i, (blood).
ㅌ=t', as 탓, t'at, (fault).
ㅊ=ch', as 촌, ch'on, (village).

REDUPLICATED CONSONANTS OR CONSONANTS WITH 된 시 옷

ㄲ or ㅺ=g, as 꽃, gôt, (flower).
ㅃ or ㅽ=b, as 뼈, byŭ, (bone).
ㅆ=s, or almost z, as 썩다, sûkta (to rot, or decay).
ㄸ or ㅼ=d, as 따리다, därida, (to strike, beat).
ㅉ or ㅾ=j, as 쫓다, jôtta, (to drive away).

The pronunciation of the simple consonants depends upon their position in the word. If at the beginning, or if they occur double in the middle of a word, they are pronounced as follows :—

INITIAL OR DOUBLE MEDIAL CONSONANTS.

ㄱ=k, as 갑시, käpsi, (price), 각각, käk-käk, (each).
ㅁ=m, as 맛, mät (taste), 암만, ämmän, (in whatever way).

ㄴ =n, or l or y, as 내가, năgä, (I). 손님, sôn nim (guest).

When doubled medially with ㄹ both become l, 본릭, pôllä, (originally). Is sometimes y or almost silent, as 니, yi, (tooth).

ㄹ =l or n, or silent, as 릭일, näil, (tomorrow).

When doubled medially with ㄴ is pronounced l, as in the example, 본릭, given above. Often silent before vowels compounded with y, as 룡, yông, (dragon).

ㅂ =p, as 발, päl, (the foot), 입병, ïp pyûng, (disease of the mouth).

ㅅ =s or sometimes almost sh, as 신 sïn, (shoe), 잇소 ïsso (to be).

ㄷ =t, as 돈, ton, (money), 맛당ㅎ다, mät tanghada, (to be necessary).

ㅈ =ch, as 자다, chädä (to sleep).

ㅇ =a silent aid in the formation of vowels, and is called 으힁

10   FIFTY HELPS FOR THE BEGINNER

When the simple consonants are found single in the middle of a word they are pronounced as follows :—

SINGLE MEDIAL CONSONANTS.

ㄱ =g, as 먹었다, mŭgŭttä (ate). Or before the sound of ㅁ or ㄴ it becomes ng, as 췩망흐다, chäng mäng bäda, (to reprove), 녁녁흐오, nŭng nŭk häo (enough).

ㅁ =m, as 아마, ämä, (perhaps). Or before the sound of ㄱ it also becomes ng, as 님금, inggeum, (king).

ㄴ =n, as 안히, änhä, (wife). Or before the sound of ㄱ it may become ng, as 반갑 다, pänggäptä (to be glad).

ㄹ =l, as 울다, ōolta, (to cry). Or between two vowels it becomes r, as 우리, ōorĭ, (our).

ㅂ =p, as 합흐다, häp hädä, (to agree, to suit). Or if between vowels it becomes b, as 보빅, pōbä, (treasure). Before ㄴ it takes the sound of m, as 읍늭, eumnä, (the official town of a district).

ㅅ =s, as 다시, täsĭ, (again).　Or before ㄴ and
ㅁ it becomes n, as 밋 눈, minnan, (believing), 갓모, känmo, (hat-cover).　Before ㅂ it becomes ㅂ as in 깃부다,
kippuda, (happy), and before ㄱ it becomes
ㄱ as in 갓갑다, kakkapta (near).

ㄷ =t, as 업다, ûpta, (to be gone, not to be).
Or between vowels it becomes d, as 서둙,
gädälk, (reason, cause), 흥다, hädä, (to
do).

ㅈ =j, as 미쟝이, mĭjängĭ, (a plasterer).

ㅇ =ng, as 링수, nängsoo, (fresh water).

When found terminating a word the consonants
are pronounced as follows :—

FINAL CONSONANTS.

ㄱ =k, as 벽, pyŭk, (a wall).

ㅁ =m, as 몸, môm, (body).

ㄴ =n, as 산, sän, (a mountain).

ㄹ =l, as 일, ĭl, (work).

ㅂ =p, as 손톱, sôn t'ŏp, (finger-nail).

ㅅ =t, as 밧, pät, (a field).

ㅇ =ng, as 상, säng, (a table).

12   FIFTY HELPS FOR THE BEGINNER

REMARKS ON THE CONSONANTS.

ㄷ and ㅌ become ch and ch' when followed by 이 or the compound letters beginning with y. Initial consonants become hard by reduplication.

The Korean does not make the sounds of k or g, l or r, p or b, t or d, ch or j, or ng as distinctly as we do in English. In his mouth ㄱ often sounds to us like a medium between k and g; medial ㄹ is often as much like d as r; ㅂ is equally p or b; ㄷ a cross between t and d; ㅈ, between ch and j; and ㆁ, ng, in some words is scarcely perceptible.

Of the Korean language sounds, those requiring the most constant practice with a teacher, and those usually last acquired by the foreigner, are the following: Nos. 4, 10 and 12 of the vowels, and the aspirated and the reduplicated consonants.

The very first step is to make a careful study of this table and preserve yourself from falling into serious errors of pronunciation such as pronouncing 죠션, Cho sŭn (Korea), as if it rhymed with amen, 약방, yăk păng (medicine room), with Jack sang, etc.

THE FOLLOWING

are a few things which will be helpful in getting
on a working basis with your teacher. In the first
place, it is not proper to address him as "you" or
speak of him as "he," but by his name, or if he is
not far from your age, as 김셔방 (Kĭm sŭbäng),
or 고셔방 (Kō sŭbäng), or 뎡셔방 (Chŭng
sŭbäng) as the case may be. If he is considera-
bly older, he should be spoken of and addressed
as 션싱 (Sun saing), a word meaning literally,
"born first," but equivalent in use to the word
"teacher." Or, if he has a title, he should be addressed by that, as, 홍쟝로, (Hong Chang No)
or 셔초시, (Sŭ Ch'ō Si).

When he comes in the morning it is polite to
salute him with the query,

평안히줌으셧소?

That is, "Have you slept peacefully?" As you
offer him a chair, bid him,

안지시오.

That is "Please be seated" When he leaves the
house, he may be bidden to "Go in peace," that
is,

평안히가시오.

14 FIFTY HELPS FOR THE BEGINNER

In return he will doubtless bid you to "Remain in peace," that is,

평안히계시오.

The following short list of words and phrases will give you something to begin with.

이, this, (ĭ)　　　　이것, this thing, (ĭ gŭt).

그, that, (keu)　　　그것, that thing, (keu gŭt).

이러케, this way,　그러케, that way,
　(ĭ rŭ k'ē).　　　　(keu rŭ k'ē).

이것무엇이오, What is this thing? (ĭ gŭn
moo ŭ sĭ ō).

이말무엇이오, What is this word? (ĭ mäl
moo ŭ sĭ ō).

지금말이오 It is present talk, or tense, (chĭ keŭm mäl ĭ ō). This and the following phrases may be changed to questions by a rising inflection merely.

젼말이오 It is past talk; or, Is it past talk? (chŭn mäl ĭ ō).

후말이오 It is future talk; or, Is it future talk? (hoo mäl ĭ ō).

The tenses are also expressed as follows:—
현지, Present, 과거, Past, and 미래, Future.

낫즌말이오 It is low talk ; or, Is it low talk?
(nä chan mäl ĭ ō).

가온듸말이오 It is middle talk; or, Is it middle talk ? (kä ōn dă mäl ĭ ō).

놉흔말이오 It is high talk ; or, Is it high talk ?
(nōp heun mäl ĭ ō).

뭇는말이오 It is question talk ; or, Is it question talk ? (moon nän mäl ĭ ō).

똑곳소 They are just alike ; or, Are they just
alike? (dōk käs sō).

흔이흥는말이오 It is a word often used ; or,
Is it a word often used ? (heun ĭ hä nän mäl
ĭ ō).

쓸듸잇소 It is useful ; or, Is it useful ? (seul
tă ĭs sō).

쓸듸업소 It is useless ; or, Is it useless ? (seul
tă ûp sō).

곳흔말무엇이오 What is a similar word?
(kät heun mäl moo ŭ sĭ ō).

모로겟소 I don't know, (mō ro ges so).

알수업소 I don't know, (äl soo ûp so).

16   FIFTY HELPS FOR THE BEGINNER

예 or 녜 Yes, (yĕ).

아니오 No, (ä nĭ ō).

국문 The native written character, (koong moon).

한문 The Chinese written character, (hän moon).

그만흡셰다 Let us stop, (keu män häp sĕ dä).

Several of these phrases, such as the distinctions of tense and of middle talk, are not native but have been invented by foreigners, so that unless the student is so fortunate as to secure one who is experienced, he may find that his first task is to teach his teacher how to teach.

NOUN DECLENSIONS.

Root	사룸	person.
Nominative	사룸이	the person.
Instrumental	사룸으로	by the person.
Genitive	사룸의	of the person.
Dative	사룸의게	to the person.
Accusative	사룸을	the person.
Vocative	사룸아	O person.
Locative	사룸에	to or in the person.

(The Locative case, however, is not used with the names of animate objects).

Ablative {사룸에셔 or 의께셔} .. from the person.

Appositive 사룸은 ...... as for the person.

Learn this by heart and then try to fit these endings to other nouns such as 물, (horse), 갓 (hat), 밧 (field), 나라, (kingdom), 새, (bird), etc. In the process you will learn that there are slight differences made in the form of the ending, depending upon the letter with which the root ends. Notice that the Dative 의게 is not commonly used except with the names of animate objects. With the names of inanimate objects the Locative 에 is preferred, and 에셔 and not 의게셔 is used for the Ablative.

Make up a list of names of common objects and commit them to memory.

PRONOUNS.

Take up now the pronouns 나 (I), 우리, (we), 너, (you), 누가, (who), 제가, (self or myself), 더가, (he, she, or it) and put them through the case endings.

18   FIFTY HELPS FOR THE BEGINNER

나, (I), runs as follows :—

Root .... 나

Nom. ... 내, 내가 .... I.

Instru. .. 날노 .... by me

Gen.... 내 .... my.

Dat. .... 내게 or 내의게 .... to me.

Acc. .... 날, 나를 .... me.

App. .... 나는 .... as for me.

Make out the others according to this paradigm, always securing corrections of your teacher on your work.

For the mode of expressing English relative pronouns see Sec. 43.

For study of personal pronouns see Sec. 49.

Notice that the Korean language is not rich in pronouns and learn to avoid the use of them, especially the first person, except where absolutely necessary to express the thought.

VERBS.

CONJUGATION OF VERBS.

First in order comes the great verb 호다 which plays so important a part in the structure of Korean. 잇다 and 업다 follow, a close second and third.

The copula **일다** is also of great importance:

Let us take up first the form of the verb used to children and known as the

LOW FORM.

훈다, I MAKE, I DO.

Indicative.

Present **훈다** I, you, he, we, they, do or make.

Past .... **훈엿다** I, you, etc. did or made.

Future.. **훈겟다** I, you, etc. will do or make.

Imperative.

훈여라 make or do.

훈자 let us make or do.

Relative Participles.

Present .**훈는** ......making, doing.

Past..... **훈** ....,made, done.

Future.. **훌** ....{to be made or done.
about to be made or done.

Imperfect **훈던** ......{made or was making.
done or was doing.

Perfect.. **훈엿던** ....made, done.

20   **FIFTY HELPS FOR THE BEGINNER**

Verbal Participles.

호여 ..
호야 } making, doing or having
호여셔 }   made or done.

Verbal Nouns.

호기 ....doing, making.

홈 ......deed. action.

———

잇다, I AM, I HAVE. (See Help 45)

Indicative.

Present   잇다...... { I, you, he, etc.
                     { am or have.

Past .... 잇섯다 ... { I, you, he, etc.
                      { was or had.

Future .. 잇겟다 ... { I, you, he, etc., shall
                       {   be or shall have.

Imperative. 잇서라 ... } be or have.
            잇거라 ... }

            잇자 .... let us be or have.

Relative Participles.

Present . 잇는 ...... being or having.

Past.... 잇슨 ...... been or had.

Future .. 잇슬 ...... about to be or have.

Imperfect잇던 ......been or had.

Perfect.. 잇셧던.... been or had.

Verbal Participle.

잇서 ......
잇서셔.... } having been or being.

Verbal Nouns.

잇기 ......being.

잇솜 ......the being.

업다, I AM NOT, I HAVE NOT.

Indicative.

Present... 업다 ....{ I, you, he, etc., have not or am not.

Past...... 업셧다 ....{ I, you, etc. had not or was not.

Future ... 업겟다 ....{ I, you, etc. shall not have or be.

Imperative............. not in use.

Relative Participles.

Present... 업눈 ...... not having or being.

Past...... 업슨 ...... not had or been.

Future ... 업슬 ...... about not to have or be.

Imperfect. 업던 ...... not had or been.

Perfect ... 업셧던 ... not have or been.

22   FIFTY HELPS FOR THE BEGINNER

Verbal Participle.

엽서 ... { not having, not being,
엽서셔 ... { or not having had,
         { or not having been.

Verbal Nouns.

엽기 ...... not being or having.

엽숨 ...... the absence.

MIDDLE FORM.

Next comes the form used among equals or to a grown person of inferior rank, and known as friend talk, or Middle Form.

흥다

Indicative.

Present... 흥오 ...... I, he, etc. make or do.

Past...... 흥엿소 ... { I, you, he, etc. made or did.

Future ... 흥겟소 ... { I, you, he, etc. shall make or do.

Imperative. 흥오 ..... do or make.

잇소

Indicative.

Present... 잇소 ...... I, you, etc. am or have.

Past...... 잇섯소 .... I, you, etc. was or had.

Future.... 잇겟소.... { I, you, etc. shall or will be or have.

Imperative. 잇소 .... be.

업소

Indicative.

Present... 업소 ...... { I, you, etc. am not or have not.

Past...... 업셧소.... { l, you, etc. was not or did not have.

Future ... 업겟소.... { I, you, etc. shall not be or shall not have.

Imperative.............. *not used.*

HIGH FORM.

Next comes the form used toward a superior or between equals when an unusual degree of respect is indicated.

흥다

Indicative.

Present... 흠늬다 .... I, you, etc. make or do.

Past...... 흥엿슴늬다 { I, you, etc. made or did.

Future ... 흥겟슴늬다 { I, you, etc. shall make or do.

Imperative.. 흥시오 .... Please do or make.

흡셰다 .... Let us do or make.

24   FIFTY HELPS FOR THE BEGINNER

잇소

Indicative.

Present... 잇슴늬다 .. I, you, etc. am or have.

Past...... 잇섯슴늬다 I, you, etc was or had.

Future ... 잇겟슴늬다 {I, you, etc. shall be or have.

Imperative. 잇습셰다 .. Let us be.

업소

Indicative.

Present... 업슴늬다 .. {I, you, etc. am not or have not.

Past...... 업섯슴늬다 {I, you, etc. was not or had not.

Future ... 업겟슴늬다 {I, you, etc. shall not be or shall not have.

Imperative.............. *not used.*

Below are the interrogative forms of these three verbs, low, middle and high.

INTERROGATIVE FORM.

Low,

Present... 흥느냐 .... {do I, you, etc. make or do?

Past...... 흥엿느냐 .. {did or have I, you, etc. made or done?

Future ... 호겟느냐 .. { will I, you, etc. make or do ?

The *Middle* Interrogative forms are the same as the Middle Indicative, but spoken with rising inflection. See Page 22.

High,

Present... 홉늬가 .... { do I, you, etc. do or make ?

Past...... 호엿슴늬가 { did or have I, you, etc. made or done.

Future ... 호겟슴늬가 { will I, you, etc. make or do ?

Low,

Present... 잇느냐 .... { have I or am I ? you, etc.

Past...... 잇섯느냐 .. { did I, or was I, you, etc.

Future.... 잇겟느냐 .. will I be or have ?

High,

Present... 잇슴늬가

Past...... 잇섯슴늬가

Future.... 잇겟슴늬가

Low,

Present... 업느냐 ..... have or am I not ? etc.

26　　FIFTY HELPS FOR THE BEGINNER

Past...... 업섯느냐 .. { have I, you, etc. not had or been ?

Future.... 업겟느냐 .. { will I, you, etc. not have or be ?

High,

Present... 업슴닉가

Past...... 업섯슴닉가

Future.... 업겟슴닉가

─────

일다 I AM. (See Help 45).

Indicative.

Low Form,

Present... 이다, or 일다, I, you, he, etc. am.

Past...... 이엿다

Future.... 이겟다

Middle Form,

Present... 이오

Past...... 이엿소

Future.... 이겟소

High Form,

Present... 임닉다, or 이올세다

Past...... 이엿슴닉다

Future.... 이겟슴닉다

Relative Participles.

Present... 인 .... being.

Future.... 일 .... about to be.

Verbal Participle 이라 .... being.

Verbal Nouns .... 이기 .... being.

임 .... the being.

Interrogative.

Low...... 이냐 .... Am I, you, he, etc.?

Middle.... 이오

High ..... 임늬가, or 이오늬가

Negative Indicative.

Low...... 아니다, or 아닐다 I, you, he, etc.
am not.

Middle.... 아 니오

High ..... 아님늬다

Negative Interrogative.

Low...... 아니냐.... Am I, you, he, etc. not ?

Middle.... 아니오

High ..... 아님늬가, or 아니오늬가

일다, (이오) is the copula used with the predicate noun. Some forms, such as the Imperative,
are missing, and even some of the existing forms
are little used.

ACTIVE VERBS.

Verbs in Korean are divided into two classes, active and adjectival. Under the first head come all words known as verbs in English except the copula *to be*. Commit to memory the following list of active verbs. They are arranged in sets for aid in memorizing and are all conjugated in the main according to the models given above.

For subject of adjectival verbs see Page 33.

LIST OF ACTIVE VERBS.

Make, do	흥다
Go	가다
Come.....................	오다
Walk....................	거러가다
Run......................	다라나다
Stand	서다
Crawl	긔여가다
Fly......................	놀아가다
Swim.....................	헤염치다
Mount, or Ride........	트다
Sleep....................	자다

Dream...................... 꿈꿰다

Wake .... 세다

Rise....................... 니러나다

Sit .... 안다

See .... 보다

Hear .... 듯다

Taste..................... 맛보다

Smell..................... 맛하보다

Touch .... 문져보다

Talk....................... 말ᄒ다

Eat .... 먹다

Drink .... 마시다

Tell .... 고ᄒ다

Think .... 싱각ᄒ다

Wonder at............... 이상히녁이다

Laugh.................... 웃다

Cry .... 울다

Shout..................... 소릭지르다

Whisper .... 숙은숙은ᄒ다

30   FIFTY HELPS FOR THE BEGINNER

Warn .... 경계ᄒ다
Exhort .... 권면ᄒ다

Chase .... 쏫차내다
Drive .... 몰아가다
Lead .... 인도ᄒ다
Follow .... ᄯ라가다

Push .... 밀다
Pull .... 잡아다리다

To be damaged...... 샹ᄒ다
Kill .... 죽이다
To be born .... 낫다
To live .... 사다
Marry .... 혼인ᄒ다
Die....................... 죽다
Bury..................... 쟝ᄉᄒ다

Come out.............. 나오다
  „   in .... 드러오다

Go out .... 나가다
Go in.................... 드러가다

Go up .... 올나가다
Go down............... 느려가다

Buy .... 사다
Sell .... 팔다

Sew .... 바느질ᄒ다
Wash .... 쌀뇌ᄒ다
Iron .... 다림질ᄒ다

Inquire................. 무러보다
Answer................. 디답ᄒ다

Get........................ 엇다
Ask for................. 구ᄒ다
Borrow................. 빌다
Steal .... 도적질ᄒ다
Earn .... 벌다

Give .... 주다
Receive............... 밧다

Try .... ᄒ여보다
Fail .... 못ᄒ다

32   FIFTY HELPS FOR THE BEGINNER

To feel with the hand	어르문지다
Strike	싸리다
Forget	니져ㅂ리다
Remember	긔억ㅎ다
Throw away	내여ㅂ리다
Lose	일허ㅂ리다
Find or seek for....	찻다
Conquer	이긔다
Be beaten	지다
To be dry.........	ㅁ르다
To rot	썩다
To shut	닷다
To open	열다
Grow	자라다
Bloom	피다
Fade or wither	스러지다
Ripen	닉다
Know	안다(알다)
Not know	모르다

Perceive .... 씨둧다
Guess .... 짐작ᄒᆞ다

Bring .... 가져오다
Take .... 가져가다
Send .... 보내다

Await .... 기ᄃᆞ리다
Prepare for........ 예비ᄒᆞ다
Welcome .... ᄃᆡ졉ᄒᆞ다

ADJECTIVAL VERBS.

An Adjectival Verb is the equivalent of what is expressed in English by the copula (is) with Predicate Adjectives. They resemble verbs in form, but are adjectival in idea. For example, 됴타 means "It is good," and is conjugated as follows :

Indicative.

Present 됴타; I, he, she, etc. am good.
Past 됴핫다, I, you, he, etc. was good.
Future 됴켓다, I, you, he, etc. shall be good.

34   FIFTY HELPS FOR THE BEGINNER

Verbal Participle.

　　　　　됴하 good.

Relative Participles.

Present
Past   }**됴흔** good.

Future   **됴흘** good.

Another example of Adjectival Verbs is **넉녁흥 다**, which means "It is enough." Note that **흥다** used with Adjectival Verbs is not the same as **흔다** meaning "to make, or do," but is the copula meaning "is." Its conjugation differs from that of **흔다** in a number of forms. Compare pages 19, 23, 24, and 25 with the following :—

Indicative Present.

　　Low......**넉녁흥다** .... It is enough.

　　Middle ...**넉녁흥오**

　　High .....**넉녁흠늬다**, or **흥올세다**, or **흥외다**

Interrogative Present.

　　Low......**넉녁흥냐** .... Is it enough ?

　　Middle....**넉녁흥오**

　　High......**넉녁흠늬가**, or **흥오니가**

Imperative .... *not in use.*

Relative Participles.

Present
Past } 녁녁훈   .... Sufficient.

Future.... 녁녁홀   .... Sufficient.

These adjectival verbs can be run through all the changes of low, middle and high talk, interrogative, etc. It will be good practice to select some from the list given below and conjugate them, getting corrections from your teacher as you work, and noting carefully the slight but important differences between certain forms of the endings of the two kinds of verbs, active and adjectival.

ADJECTIVAL VERBS IN COMMON USE.

Little	쟉다
Big	크다
Flat	넙쟉ᄒ다
Round	둥그럽다
Thin	얇다
Thick	두겁다
Long	길다

36　　　　FIFTY HELPS FOR THE BEGINNER

Broad .... 넙다
Narrow .... 좁다

Tall .... 키크다
Short .... 짧다

Pretty .... 묘ᄒ다
Ugly .... 흉ᄒ다

Sweet .... 둘다
Sour .... 싀다
Bitter .... 쓰다
Sharp .... 밉다

Hot .... 덥다
Cold .... 차다
Lukewarm .... 미지근ᄒ다

Sick .... 압흐다
Well .... 셩ᄒ다

Dull, (as a knife) .... 무지다
Sharp .... 날카롭다

Blunt	둔ᄒ다
Pointed	샢족ᄒ다
Full	ᄀ득ᄒ다
Empty	뷔다
Bright	빗최다
Dark	어둡다
Black	겁다
White	희다
Old	늙다
Young	졂다
Old	묵다
New	새롭다
Beautiful	아름답다
Hateful	뮙다
False	거짓되다
True	춤되다
Fierce	사오납다
Gentle	슌ᄒ다

38   FIFTY HELPS FOR THE BEGINNER

Right	올타
Wrong	그르다
Good	착ᄒᆞ다
Bad	악ᄒᆞ다
Ignorant	무식ᄒᆞ다
Learned	유식ᄒᆞ다
Wise	지혜롭다
Foolish	어리셕다
Early	일다
Late	늣다
Near	갓갑다
Far	멀다
High	놉다
Low	늣다
Sorry	셥셥ᄒᆞ다
Glad	반갑다
Grateful	감샤ᄒᆞ다
Cheap	헐ᄒᆞ다
Dear	빗사다

Few	젹다
Many	만타
Easy	쉽다
Difficult	어렵다
Peaceful	평안ᄒᆞ다
Agitated	답답ᄒᆞ다
Clean	졍ᄒᆞ다
Dirty	더럽다
Weak	약ᄒᆞ다
Strong	강ᄒᆞ다
Deep	깁다
Shallow	엿다
Useful	유익ᄒᆞ다
Useless	무익ᄒᆞ다
Busy	분주ᄒᆞ다
Idle	한가ᄒᆞ다
Slow	ᄯᅳ다
Fast	날내다

40   FIFTY HELPS FOR THE BEGINNER

Heavy .... 무겁다
Light .... 가볍얍다
Soft .... 부드럽다
Hard .... 둔둔흐다
Deficient....................... 부쪽흐다
Enough .... 녀녀흐다

ADVERBS.

ADVERBS FORMED FROM ADJECTIVAL VERBS.

These adverbs can be formed in most cases by adding the syllable 게 to the root of the verb. Thus :—

작게 .... Little.
크게 ...... Greatly.
묘흐게...... Prettily.
      Etc.

Many adjectival verbs may take an adverbial form in 히. Thus :—

슌히 ...... Gently.
온견히...... Entirely.
갓가히...... Near.
      Etc.

LIST OF OTHER ADVERBS.

Some Adverbs in constant use are :—

엇지—엇지ᄒ여 } How.
엇더케 .... }

이러케 ...... Thus, this way.

그러케 ...... That way.

얼는)
어셔 (
속이 (...... Quickly, at once.
밧비)

몃)
얼마 } ...... How much? How many.

얼마나 ...... About how much?

여러 ...... Seyeral.

더러 ...... Some.

미우, 대단히 Much, very

그만 ...... Enough.

만)
분 } ...... Only.

잘 ...... Well.

42   FIFTY HELPS FOR THE BEGINNER

다
모도 } ..... All.

너무 .... Too much, too.

더 .... More.

덜 .... Less.

쏘흔
쏘 } .... And, again, still more.

도 .... Also, too.

더옥 .... So much the more.

조곰 .... A little.

아마 .... Perhaps.

혹 .... Possibly.

웨 .... Why.

어디 .... Where. 어데

언졔 .... When.

우연이 .... Unexpectedly.

홈씨
흔가지로 } ... Together, all at once.
흔껍에

처럼 .... Like.

굿치 .... Like, the same as.

IN THE KOREAN LANGUAGE.   43

별노
거반 } .... Almost altogether, nearly.

부러
일부러 } ...... On purpose, purposely.
짐짓

불가불 .... Of necessity.
미샹불 .... Probably.

스스로
즈연이 } ...... Naturally, of itself.
절노

추추 .... Little by little.
아까 .... Just now, a moment ago.

아직 .... As yet.
어느때 .... When? What time?

임의
발셔 } .... Already.

일샹
흥샹 } .... Always.
늘

이때 .... This time.
그때
뎌때 } .... That time.

44   FIFTY HELPS FOR THE BEGINNER

잇다가	Presently, in a moment.
오래	Long.
요ᄉᆞ이	These days.
각금 자조 }	Often.
즉시 곳 }	Immediately.
못ᄎᆞᆷ내 ᄆᆞ지막 }	Finally.
미리	In advance.
몬져	At first.
나죵에	At last.
시방 지금 }	Now.
쉬이	Soon.
다시	Again, once more.
도로	Back.
잠ᄭᅡᆫ	For a moment.
다음에	After.
이리 여긔 }	Here.
거긔 뎌긔 }	There, yonder.

POSTPOSITIONS.

The following is a list of postpositions, so called because they follow the noun instead of preceding it as in English.

밋헤	...... Under.
우혜	...... Over, or on top of.
뒤혜	...... Behind.
압헤	...... In front of.
녑헤	...... At the side of.
아래에	...... Below.
석지	...... To, until.
부터	...... From, beginning with.
즁에 가온티	.... In the middle of, between.
안으로	...... Into.
안헤 속에	...... Inside.
업시	...... Without.
인ᄒ여	...... On account of.
위ᄒ여	...... For the sake of.

46   FIFTY HELPS FOR THE BEGINNER

외에
밧긔 } ...... Outside.

셰리 ...... Between, as 우 리 셰 리
(between us).

건너 ...... Across.

디신 ...... Instead of.

후에 ...... After, as 이후에, (after
this).

젼에 ...... Before, as 이 젼에, (before
this).

동안에...... During.

만에 ...... After.

대로 ...... According to, as 모 음 대로,
(just as you please).

드려
더러 } ...... To, as to speak to a person.

Commit these words perfectly to memory.

With these preliminaries let us begin the process of language building.

1. 홀수잇소

This sentence is composed of 홀, the future relative participle of 혼다, modifying 수, a noun meaning "means," together with the verb 잇다. See Pages 19 and 20. This is, literally, "Doing means are," and is equivalent to our English expression, "It can be done." The negative form is

홀수업소   It cannot be done.

Take these two forms and run them through all the variations of 지금말, 젼말, 후말 and of 늣존말, 가온딕말, 놉흔말, (see page 15) also through the 뭇는말. Your teacher will suggest correct forms and pronunciation.

Thus you will have :—

Low talk,

Present... 홀수잇다
            홀수업다

Past...... 홀수잇셧다
            홀수업셧다

Future.... 홀수잇겟다
            홀수업겟다

48   FIFTY HELPS FOR THE BEGINNER

Middle talk,

  Present... 홀수잇소
             홀수업소
  Past...... 홀수잇섯소
             홀수업섯소
  Future.... 홀수잇겟소
             홀수업겟소

High talk,

  Present... 홀수잇슴늬다
             홀수업슴늬다
  Past...... 홀수잇섯슴늬다
             홀수업섯슴늬다
  Future.... 홀수잇겟슴늬다
             홀수업겟슴늬다

And the interrogative forms, low, middle and high, past, present and future. Thus :—

Low talk,

  Present... 홀수잇느냐
             홀수업느냐
  Past...... 홀수잇섯느냐
             홀수업섯느냐

Future.... 홀수잇겟ᄂ냐
홀수업겟ᄂ냐

Middle talk,

Present... 홀수잇소
홀수업소

Past...... 홀수잇섯소
홀수업섯소

Future.... 홀수잇겟소
홀수업겟소

High talk,

Present... 홀수잇슴늬가
홀수업슴늬가

Past...... 홀수잇섯슴늬가
홀수업섯슴늬가

Future.... 홀수잇겟슴늬가
홀수업겟슴늬가

Continue this process with any other verb of action, as 가다, 보다, 먹다, etc. Thus, 갈수잇소, I can go. 볼수업소, I can not see. 먹을수업소, I can not eat, etc, etc.

50   FIFTY HELPS FOR THE BEGINNER

The student will readily see that instead of but two new forms, he has acquired a number only limited by his knowledge of verbs of action, and this he will find to be the case in every exercise herein presented.

Since pronouns are seldom expressed in Korean, and since the plural number is used only when it is impossible to express the desired meaning without it, these phrases may convey the idea of any or all persons, genders, and numbers. As, 갈수 엽소, I, you, he, she, they, we, or it, cannot go. 올수잇소, I, you, he, she, they, we, or it, can come, etc. Koreans usually rely upon the context to give definiteness, and the result is not so vague as it seems at first thought.

Notice the invariable construction of Korean sentences. First, the subject, if expressed, preceded by its modifiers, if there are any. Then the object, preceded by its modifiers, if any, and lastly the verb.

For example :—

이젼에보지못흔사룸이나를잘디졉흥엿소.

"A person whom I never saw before welcomed me well." Literally, "This before not seen person me well has welcomed."

With the help of your teacher, the dictionary, other text-books, and any other available source of information, as servants, visitors or friends, make up ten short sentences containing expressions such as these,

칙볼수업소
I can not see, (or read) the book.

죠션밥먹을수업소
He cannot eat Korean food. *rice*.

릭일갈수업ᄂ냐
Can you not go to-morrow ?

Etc., Etc.

Go slowly, and put what you learn to immediate use. More, much more, depends upon this than upon hours spent toiling over a text book.

2. 홀수밧긔업소

Literally, "Doing means beside are not," and is equivalent to our idiom, "Nothing else can be done."

Instead of 홀 in this expression take 갈 and you have,

52   FIFTY HELPS FOR THE BEGINNER

갈수밧긔업소

I cannot but go, or you, he, she, they, or it, as the case may be, cannot but go.

Or, substitute 볼, and you have,

볼수밧긔업소

I, you, he, etc., cannot but look or see.　Take the future participles of any or all verbs that you can get hold of, and run this expression through the present, past and future tenses, low, middle and high talk, and interrogative, as before.

Make up ten short sentences containing this expression.　As : —

집에갈수밧긔업소

I, he, she, etc., cannot but go to the house.

날이더울수밧긔업소

The day cannot but be warm.

Etc., Etc.

---

3. **ᄒᆞ여라**

Make, or do.

보아라

Look, or see.

가거라

Go.

This is the low imperative form to be used to children and coolies. When you wish to include yourself, the form becomes,

ᄒᆞ자

Let us do, or make.

보자

Let us see.

가자

Let us go.

Etc.

A higher form for directing servants is **ᄒᆞ게**, or higher still, **ᄒᆞ오**. For example :—

아기잘보게

Watch the baby well.

돈가져오

Bring the money.

In intercourse with Christians of the serving class it is much better to use the middle, or, as it is often called, the friend talk.

In giving directions to your teacher or any equal, use **ᄒᆞ시오**

Thus :—

그러케ᄒᆞ시오

Please do so.

54   FIFTY HELPS FOR THE BEGINNER

사룸보내시오
Please send a man.

일쪽오시오
Please come early.

In including yourself in the proposition, say

그러캐홉셰다
Let us do so.

사룸보냅셰다
Let us send a man.

공부홉셰다
Let us study.

Make sentences as before.

———

4. **홋지마라**
Do not do.

Take this **지마라** and add it to the root of the verb **가오** and you have :—

가지마라
Do not go.

Or add it to the root of the verb to see :—

보지마라
Do not look.

Put this through the middle and high forms
with the help of your teacher, and make up other
sentences, such as :—

오래잇지마오

Do not stay long.

거즛말밋지마시오

Do not believe false talk.

---

5. 호지못호오

I, he, she or it, cannot do or make.

호지아니호오

I, he, she or it, do (does) not do or make.

The former is used to express inability. The
later expresses either simple negation or unwill-
ingness.

지못호오 and 지아니호오, like No 4,
may be added to the root of any verb, thus :—

먹지못호오

I, you, he, it, cannot eat.

먹지아니호오

I, you, he, it, do (does) not eat.

됴치못호오 or 됴치아니호오

It is not good.

56　　　FIFTY HELPS FOR THE BEGINNER

지안소 is a common contraction of 지아니
호오, and 치안소 of 치아니호오, as :—

멀지안소
It is not far.

깁지안소
It is not deep.

됴치안소
It is not good.
Etc.

The student will find it advantageous to accustom himself to learn by sound rather than by sight, and with this in view it will be well to avoid at first too much writing out of exercises. Committing them and reciting them aloud as rapidly as possible will be much better.

Take frequent reviews, and vary the routine of study herein suggested in any way that you may find profitable. Remember these are only suggestions for study. But do not omit the construction of original sentences with each form. You cannot have better practice than this. The short vocabulary of religious terms on p. 92 and the other lists of words herein presented will be found useful for this purpose. Use the words and terms which you learn from day to day.

6. 홀므 음잇소
Doing mind is.

홀므 음업소
Doing mind is not.

These are equivalent in our English idiom to "I have a mind to do (thus or so)" "I have no mind to do (thus or so)."

Applications of this useful form will speedily suggest themselves.

졀에올나갈므 음잇소
I have a mind to go up to the (Buddhist) temple.

ᄒ여볼므 음업소
I have no mind to try.

동싱도아줄므 음업ᄂ냐
Have you no mind to help your younger brother?

---

7. ᄒ고시브오
I, you, we, etc., wish to do.

ᄒ기실소
I, you, we, etc., do not wish to do.

58   FIFTY HELPS FOR THE BEGINNER

Applications :—

집구경호고시브오
We wish to see your house.

머리싹기슬타
He does not want to cut his hair.

쟝에가고시브냐
Do you want to go to the fair ?

----

8.   호기쉽소
Doing is easy.

호기어렵소
Doing is hard.

Idiomatically, "It is easy to do," "It is hard to do."

잘못호기쉽다
Wrong doing is easy.

약먹기어렵소
Eating medicine is difficult, or as we would say, "It is hard to take medicine."

Get your teacher to suggest allied forms such as,

보기됴소
It is good to look at.

보기뮙소
It is hideous to look at.

듯기됴소 .

It is good to hear.

        Etc.

Run these through the various tenses with the negative forms, thus :—

ᄒᆞ기쉽지안소......It is not easy to do.

ᄒᆞ기어렵지안소..It is not hard to do.

보기됴치안소......It is not good to see.

보기뮙지안소......It is not hideous to see.

듯기됴치안소......It is not good to hear.

———

9.   ᄒᆞ면됴겟소

    If you do (thus or so), it will be good.

This is convenient to use in expressing a wish, or in giving directions, and is a relief from the constant use of the imperative forms. Being equivalent to our conditional *if*, it opens up a wide range of expression.

오면됴켓소

If he comes it will be well.

교군부르면곳가겟소

If you will call the chair coolies, I will go at
    once.

60   FIFTY HELPS FOR THE BEGINNER

일ᄒᆞ면삭주겟소
If he does the work I will give him the wages.

부모ᄶᅦ효도ᄒᆞ면안됴켓소
If he reverences his parents, is it not well?

---

10. ᄒᆞ거든
If or when.

This form is given in connection with ᄒᆞ면, since they both convey the idea of our *if*, but there is a very important difference in their use. ᄒᆞ면 is of wider application and may be followed by a clause denoting either a result of the condition stated, a choice resting with the person acting, or a command; whereas, ᄒᆞ거든 is never followed by a clause denoting a result, but always a choice resting with the actor or by a command.

칩거든문닷겟소
If it is cold I will shut the door, (that is, the speaker chooses to do so).

방덥거든불굿치오
If the room is warm cease making a fire.

This difference in the use of 면 and 거든 is not easy for foreigners, but that it is a very real one may be easily verified by proposing to your teacher such a sentence as

첩거든못견듸겟소

or, 방덥거든파리드러오겟소

or any other sentence in which 거든 is followed by a result. It must always be followed by a choice or a command.

---

11. 호여야쓰겟소

If only you will do (thus or so), it will do ;
    or, very often, You must do (thus or so).
This is also a pleasant way of expressing a wish or a necessity, or of giving an order.

먹을것잇서야먹겟소

If only there is something to eat, I will eat it.

귀신만위호여야집이편안호겟소

If you will but worship the spirits the house
    will be peaceful.

돈잇서야호겟다

I must have the money to do it.

62   FIFTY HELPS FOR THE BEGINNER

12. 호게호오

To make to do, or, to let to do.

바느질호게호오

Have her do the sewing.

어젹긔다호게호엿슴늬다

I had it all done yesterday.

목수드러오게호오

Let the carpenter come in.

---

13. 호랴고호오, or as it is often spelled,
    호려고호오

To intend to do (thus or so).

편지쓰랴고호오

I am intending to write a letter.

싀골언졔가랴고홈늬가

When do you intend going to the country ?
    An equivalent phrase is,

호고져호오, or as it is often spelled,
    호고쟈호오

---

14. 호러가오

To go to do (thus or so).

호러오오

To come to do (thus or so).

용식 이제집셰간이사ᄒᆞ러갓소

Yong Siki has gone to move his household goods.

마부ᄆᆞᆯ보러왓소

The hostler has come to see the horse.

ᄃᆞᆰ사러갓소

He has gone to buy a chicken.

This 러 form is used with verbs of motion to express purpose.

———

15. ᄒᆞ오마ᄂᆞᆫ

I do or make, but,—

나ᄂᆞᆫ공부ᄒᆞ오마ᄂᆞᆫ비호기어렵소

As for myself I do study, but learning is difficult.

괴롭소마ᄂᆞᆫ링수좀주시오

It is troublesome, but please give me a drink.

마ᄂᆞᆫ may be added to any tense as,

ᄒᆞ엿소마ᄂᆞᆫ

It did, but,—

가겟다마ᄂᆞᆫ

I will go, but,—

64　　FIFTY HELPS FOR THE BEGINNER

The similiarity of this idiom to our own may lead the student into a perpetual use of it, which is un-Korean. Often where we would say, "So and so but,"—the Korean will prefer the following terms :—

----

16. 호여도

Although, I, he or she, etc., do (thus or so).

나는공부부즈런히호여도비호기어렵소

As for myself, although I do study dilligently learning is difficult.

약만히써도안낫소

Although I take much medicine I am no better.

가도관게치안소

Although you go it is no matter, that is, Go if you like.

The past tense is

호엿서도 or 호엿슬지라도 Although I did.

갓서도 or 갓슬지라도　Although I went.

먹엇서도 or 먹엇슬지라도 Although I ate.

Etc., Etc.

Future tense,

홀지라도 .....Although I will do.

갈지라도 .....Although I will go.

먹울지라도.....Although I will eat.

Etc., Etc.

These forms are used indiscriminately for "according to fact" and "contrary to fact" ideas. Thus :—

오날갈지라도오래잇지안켓소

Although I am going today, I shall not be long.

오날갈지라도맛날수업소

Even if I should go today, I couldn't meet him.

Make a study of similar, though perhaps slightly varying terms, as, 훈되, 훈나, 훈거니와, 훈려니와, etc.

By this time the student should be able to make up sentences of considerable length by combining the forms already learned. Try it with twenty-five sentences or so. Construct them yourself and submit them to your teacher for correction.

Thus :—

답장훈랴고훈엿서도니져브렷소

Although I intended to answer (the letter), I forgot it.

66　　FIFTY HELPS FOR THE BEGINNER

풍년되엿소마눈셔풍이이처름불면
곡식이샹ᄒ기쉽겟소

An abundant year has become, but if the
west wind blows like this spoiling of the
crops will be easy.

Etc., Etc.

_____

17. ᄒ니
ᄒ니싸

These two forms are exceedingly common, and
convey the idea of, *as, since, because.* The former
is the weaker of the two, and sometimes means no
more than *and.*

셩경보니춤말이오
I read the Bible and it is true.

도젹질ᄒ니싸옥에가도겟다
Because he steals they will put him in jail.

The past and future tenses are formed as one
would expect.

ᄒ엿스니　　　　　ᄒ겟스니
ᄒ엿스니싸　　　　ᄒ겟스니싸

IN THE KOREAN LANGUAGE. 67

무당발셔왓스니굿ᄒᆞᆫ소릭곳시작
ᄒᆞ겟소

Since the exorcist has already come, the noise
of the devil worship will begin directly.

릭일은더헐ᄒᆞ겟스니ᄱᅡ오ᄂᆞᆯ안삿소

Since they will be cheaper to-morrow I did
not buy to-day.

Your teacher will furnish you with similar
forms, as, ᄒᆞ니ᄭᅡᆫ드로 and also ᄒᆞᆫ고로, ᄒᆞ
ᄂᆞᆫ고로, ᄒᆞᆫᄯᅥ문에, ᄒᆞᄂᆞᆫᄯᅥ문에, which
are a degree stronger in meaning.

---

18. ᄒᆞᆯ듯ᄒᆞ오
     I, you, etc. will probably do (thus or so).
     집힝이가져올듯ᄒᆞ다
     He will probably bring the cane.
     날이치우면못갈듯ᄒᆞ뇌다
     If the day is cold he probably cannot go.
     A form used in precisely the same way is,
     ᄒᆞᆯ가보오
     As, 비올가보오
     It will probably rain.

68   FIFTY HELPS FOR THE BEGINNER

The past tense is managed by,

ㅎ엿슬듯ㅎ오

ㅎ엿슬가보오

As, 샹급발셔밧엇슬듯ㅎ다

He has probably already received the reward.

제리웃사룸다도아주엇슬가보오

His neighbors all probably helped him.

———

19. ㅎㄹ번ㅎ엿소

I, he, etc., was on the point of doing.

너머질번ㅎ엿소

I was on the point of falling, or, I nearly fell.

죽을번ㅎ엿소

He was on the pointing of dying.

———

20. ㅎㄹ만ㅎ오

It is worth doing.

척볼만흠늬가

Is the book worth reading?

구경ㅎㄹ만흠늬다

The sight is worth seeing.

A similar expression, but conveying more nearly the idea of our English ending—*able*, is,

흡죽호오

As, 오늘둙알삼죽호오

Eggs will be purchasable to-day.

김치닉으면먹음죽홀겟소

The "kimchi" (pickles) when ripe will be edible.

21. 호논톄호오

I, he, etc., am pretending to do.

그ᄋ희우논톄혼다

That child is pretending to cry.

Past tense,

이녀편네국문모로논톄호엿소

This woman pretended not to know kook-moon.

Future tense,

모로논사롬들이아논톄호겟소

Those who don't know will pretend to know.

22. 흘싸녕려호오 often abreviated to 흘가호오

I fear this or that is happening or will happen.

힘만허비홀사념려ᄒᄋ

I fear he will only waste his strength.

아니올사념려ᄒᄋ

I fear he will not come.

The contrasting expression, to hope that this or that will happen, is :—

홀사ᄇ라오

As, 더집어룬도라올사ᄇ라오

I hope the man of that house will come back.

The form naturally expresses the future idea. The past tense is expressed as follows :—

보리잘되엿슬사ᄇ랏소

I hoped that the barley had turned out well.

편지아니왓스니사제남편죽엇ᄂ가 념려ᄒ겟소

Since no letter has come, she will fear that her husband has died.

Notice in these sentences that all tenses of hoping and fearing as well as all tenses of the thing hoped or feared, are expressed.

Similar forms are 홀사무셥소, 홀사겨졍 잇소, 홀사기ᄃ리오, and other verbs of hoping, expecting and fearing.

23. ㅎᄂ지

This is used to express our *whether*, and very often equals *whether or not*, by taking on 아니 ㅎᄂ지, or 못ㅎᄂ지

잘ㅎᄂ지잘못ㅎᄂ지모로겟소
Whether he is doing well or badly, I do not know.

가ᄂ지안가ᄂ지알수업소
I don't know whether he is going or not.

ᄂ지 added to the root of the past tense ㅎ엿, gives ㅎ엿ᄂ지, the past form:

혼인ㅎ엿ᄂ지알수업소
Whether he is married I do not know.

우리집아바지잘줌으셧ᄂ지가보아
라
Go and see whether our father slept well.

ᄒᆯᄂ지 or, as it is often spelled, ᄒᆯ너지 and ᄒᆯ지 give the future by natural formation.

난리날너지안날너지누가알겟소
Who knows whether or not war will arise ?

72   FIFTY HELPS FOR THE BEGINNER

잘될지잘못될지보아야알겟소

Whether it will turn out well or not we must
see to know.

The student will notice that these forms are always followed by a clause denoting either knowledge or ignorance. This fact established, he will
be prepared not to confound them either with the
following expression, or with No. 30 which is
similar in form only.

---

24. 흥던지

Is also equivalent to our *whether*, but instead of
being followed by a clause denoting that you do or
do not know, it is invariably (with one exception
which need not now be referred to) followed by
the idea of being of consequence or of no consequence.

흥던지아너흥던지내게샹관업소

Whether he does or not, it is no matter to
me.

살던지죽던지졔ㅅ아너흥겟소

Whether I live or die, I will not sacrifice (to
ancestors).

25. 홀때

While or when doing.

감긔들때에바룸부는듸에가지마라

When you have a cold (literally, when a cold enters) do not go where the wind is blowing.

밥먹을때마다긔도흡늬다

He prays every time he eats.

홀졔 and **홀겨에** are synonymous expressions, and used almost as frequently.

26. 흥기젼에

Before doing.

시작흥기젼에싱각잘흐오

Before beginning consider well.

숑스흥기젼에죄잇는지업는지즈셰히알거시오

Before accusing one must know certainly whether or not there is fault.

27. 흥후에

After doing.

심부림흥후에또오너라

After you have done the errand come again.

74   FIFTY HELPS FOR THE BEGINNER

말솜알아드른후에쏘무러보지아니 훙엿소

After he understood the talk he made no more inquiries.

---

28. 훙눈줄아오

I think or know (thus or so).

훙눈줄모로오

I do not think or know (thus or so).

As, **부인이손님오눈줄아오**

The lady knows that guests are coming.

더방에잇눈줄아오

I think it is in that room.

The past form is :

흔줄알앗소
흔줄몰낫소

As, **집쥬인이발셔간줄몰낫소**

I did not know that the master of the house had already gone.

여섯살먹은줄알앗소

I thought he had eaten six New Year's cakes. (that is, was six years old.)

The future tenses are expressed by

홀줄아오

홀줄모로오. As :—

오늘비올줄알앗소

I thought a boat would come to-day.

이처럼오래기드릴줄몰낫소

I did not know that you would wait this
long.

The future form is capable of conveying another
and very different meaning : to wit, to know how
to do thus or so.

미쟝이담곳칠줄아오

The mason knows how to mend the wall.

농ㅅ일홀줄모로겟소

He does not know how to do farm work.

---

29. 호도록

Conveys the idea of *until, up to the point* or
time of, the more.

곤호도록일호엿소

He worked until he was tired.

우리어머니죽도록알앗소

Mother was sick unto death.

76   FIFTY HELPS FOR THE BEGINNER

사름만도록됴소

The more persons the better.

울도록자란ᄒᆞ엿다

They played until they cried.

The idea of 'until' is also expressed by the use of 석지 with the verbal noun. Thus, instead of 죽도독힘쓰소, the Korean is just as likely to say, 죽기석지힘쓰소. That is, He worked himself to death. For 흘스록 see Section 5 of the Additional Helps.

----

30. 혼지

Sometimes used to express time since.

아기난지아홉돌되엿소

The baby was born nine months ago.

본지오래오

It has been long since I saw you.

혼지오 is used to express wonder, fear, admiration, etc., as, "How strange," "How beautiful."

엇지큰지오

How big !

갓이엇지됴흔지오

What a good taste !

And if the Korean wishes to be more explicit he drops the 오 and adds,

말홀수업소

It is inexpressible.

---

31. 와 and 과

These are used as connectives, in joining two or more subjects or objects of the same verb.

셕이와질승이쟝에가셔감과비와둙 사왓소

Sāgi and Chil-seungi, having gone to the fair, came back, having bought persimmons, pears and a chicken.

The difference between 와 and 과, as the student will see by a look at the sentence given above, is merely euphonic, 와 being used after words ending in a vowel, and 과 after words ending in a consonant,

78   FIFTY HELPS FOR THE BEGINNER

32. 호고

호고 is also a very common connective used in the same way as 와 and 과 above, as

사람호고즘싱이만히죽엇소
Many persons and animals died.

고

Do not confuse the above form, 호고 with the verbal connective 고, when used with the root of 호다. This connective means "and," and may be used with any verb, as :—

호나흔칙잘보고호나흔잘못본다
One reads the book well, and one reads it badly.

군스비로도가고륙로로도갓소
The soldiers went by boat and by land.

33. 호여, 호야, 호여셔

These forms are used for joining unequal parts of a sentence, as :—

하느님의뜻을슌종호야십계명을잘 직히오
Obeying the will of God, he keeps the Ten Commandments well.

집을쩌나먼곳에갓소

Having left home he went to a distant place.

Note well that in each of these sentences the
two verbs have the same subject, and this is always the case where the participle is derived from
an active verb, except in occasional instances
where the verb, though active in form, may be
strongly adjectival in meaning. Generally speaking, the clause immediately following an active
participle must have the same subject as the
participle.

Where the participle is derived from an adjectival verb, however, the subject of the following
clause may or may not be the same as the participle. For instance :—

쏫이아롬다와쌀ㅁ 음난다

The flower being beautiful, I feel like plucking it (literally, plucking mind arises).

Or :—

쏫이아롬다와사롬의ㅁ 음을즐겁게 호오

The flower being beautiful, it makes the
mind of man glad.

80   FIFTY HELPS FOR THE BEGINNER

34. ᄒᆞᄂᆞᄃᆡ

A form very much used in narrative, spoken or written, and indicating in print a pause longer than a comma and not so long as a period. It may be said to be about equivalent to a semi-colon. In speech it may be translated by "and" or "but," or simply by a pause, as :—

지금잔치ᄒᆞᄂᆞᄃᆡ여러가지됴흔음식을예비ᄒᆞ엿소

They are having a feast now, and have prepared several kinds of nice food.

셥셥ᄒᆞᆫ일나ᄂᆞᄃᆡ웨웃소

A sorrowful affair has occurred; why do you laugh?

The past and future tenses are formed as one would expect :—

셰례를발셔힝ᄒᆞ엿ᄂᆞᄃᆡ더듸왓소

The baptismal ceremony has already been performed; you have come late.

닉일쓰겟ᄂᆞᄃᆡ아직아니삿소

I will use it tomorrow, but have not yet bought it.

35. 홀더라

An ending used in speaking to another person of something which the speaker knows to be a fact, but which the hearer has not seen or known.

미국학교에셔는소리조급도업시공부홀더라

In American schools they study without making the least noise.

The polite form for the same expression is 홉데다, as :—

영국물들이대단히큽데다

English horses are very large.

Ques. 목스어듸계신지알겟소

Do you know where the pastor is ?

Ans. 츌입홉데다

He has gone for a walk.

The interrogative forms, high and low, are also used in enquiring of another about something of which I am ignorant, but which he has seen or known. Thus, to a child :—

아바지어듸가시더냐

Where has your father gone ?

82   FIFTY HELPS FOR THE BEGINNER

촌에갑데다
He has gone to a village.

회당에잇습데가
Is it in the church?

잇습데다
It is.

---

36. 흐더니

A past imperfect connective, corresponding to No. 35 and used like it to convey the idea of something seen or known by the speaker but not by the listener, translated by "and."

양씨만밋고든니더니이제는남편도
예수를밋소

> Only Yang Ssi believed and attended (church), and now her husband too trusts in Jesus.

Notice that these forms, Nos. 35 and 36 cannot be used in the first person in active verbs although they may be so used with adjectival verbs. For example, 어져게곤흐더니오날관계지안소

---

37. 흐엿더니

This is a past perfect connective and has the same force as No. 36 except that it can be used with all persons. For instance,

눈물을흘너고긔도ᄒ엿더니하ᄂᆞ님씌
셔도르셧소

I (or he) wept and prayed and God heard. It is
very commonly used when the speaker wishes to
convey the idea that a change has taken place, and
is translated by "but," as :—

이젼에일만히ᄒ엿더니지금은늙어
셔못ᄒᆞᆸ니다

> Formerly I worked a great deal, but now,
> being old, I cannot.

38. ᄒᆞ면셔

A connective used between verbs having the
same subject, to indicate simultaneous action,
as :—

길가면셔칙보앗소

> As he was going along the road he read a
> book.

하ᄂᆞ님을공경ᄒᆞ면셔부모의게도효
도ᄒᆞᆯ거시오

> While we reverence God we must also be
> filial to our parents.

84   FIFTY HELPS FOR THE BEGINNER

39. 호다가

A connective indicating interrupted action, as :—

길가다가호랑이맛낫소
As he was going along the road he met a tiger.

하느님을밋다가불힝히죄에빠젓소
He believed God but, unfortunately, he fell into sin.

The past form, 호엿다가, indicates completed action. The difference between 호다가 and 호엿다가 is illustrated by the following sentences :—

셔울가다가도로왓소
I went part of the way to Seoul and came back.

셔울갓다가도로왓소
I went to Seoul and came back.

———————

40. 홀뿐더러 or 홀뿐만아너오
Not only that but—

고싱홀뿐더러죽기서지호엿소·

Or, 고성흘뿐만아니오죽기 지 호엿소
He not only suffered but died. (Literally,
up to death did).

비만흘뿐더러바룸도부럿소
Or, 비만흘뿐만아니라바룸도부럿소
There was not only much rain, but the wind
blew.

---

41. *The Idea of Duty or Obligation* conveyed
by the English word *ought* is expressed by the use
of the future participle. For example:—

술먹고노름을 호 거슨어진사룸이흘
일아니오
Drinking and gambling are not work that an
upright man ought to do.

볼일만아셔못왓소
There being much work to see to, I could
not come.

것, meaning thing, is used almost interchange-
ably with 일 after the participle.

---

42. *Indirect Discourse* is expressed by adding
any mode or tense desired of the verb 고 다 to
the root form of the remark quoted.

86   FIFTY HELPS FOR THE BEGINNER

호라고호여라
Tell him to do, (thus or so).

말호라고호여라
Tell him to speak.

나무사라고호시오
Please tell him to buy the wood.

학당에가라고호겟소
I will tell him to go to the school.

교군왓다고홈늬다
He says the chair coolies have come.

새벽에써나겟다고호엿소
They said they would leave at day-break.

And so on through all the modes, ranks and tenses.

A variation is furnished by

혼단말드럿소
I heard he was doing, (thus and so).

압흐단말드럿소
I heard he was sick.

쟝가갓단말드럿소
I heard you were married.

43. *Relative clauses* are expressed by means of the past, present and future participles. Thus:—

일ᄒᆞᄂᆞᆫ사람 이돈달나홈ᄂᆡ다

The man who is doing the work is asking for money.

새로지은집문허졋소

The house which was newly built has tumbled down.

오늘흘일별노업소

There is no special work which ought to be done to-day.

---

44. *The verb* HAVE, so indispensable in English, is not found in Korean. The idea is expressed by 잇ᄉ with or without 게 or 의게. Thus, where we would say, "I have a book," the Korean says simply, 칙잇소, or, if he wishes to be more explicit, 내게칙잇소

---

45. *The purpose answered by the one word* IS in our language, requires two in Korean :— 잇소 to express mere existence, 이오 expressing nature or condition.

88   FIFTY HELPS FOR THE BEGINNER

착호사롬잇소

There is (or exists) an upright man.

착호사롬이오

He is an upright man.

To distinguish between the use of these two words in all their possible forms constitutes one of the difficulties of the spoken Korean.

---

46. *Degrees of comparison* are expressed by 더, more, and 덜, less.

염병더무셥소

Typhus fever is more dreadful.

이밥덜더럽소

This rice is less dirty.

The superlative degree may be expressed by 데일.

그산데일놉소

That mountain is highest, or literally, first high;

or, very often, by the use of 즁에.

산즁에놉소

Among the mountains it is high.

Comparison between objects may be expressed by 보담 or 보다

이그릇보담그것크다

Compared with this vessel that one is large.

---

47. *To give assent* in proper Korean fashion is quite an art, since there is no one word like our *yes* that can be used under all circumstances. 예 approaches yes, but is used properly only between equals or by an inferior to a superior. Such words as 그럿소, 올소, etc., have their place, but a way often preferred by the Korean is to assent by repeating the verb.

Ques. 그사룸왓소
Has the man come ?

Ans. 왓소
He has come.

Remark. 곡식잘되엿소
The crops have turned out well.

Assent. 잘되엿소
They have turned out well.

---

48. *Our much used* THANK YOU has no exact equivalent in Korean. If he wishes to express appreciation of a kindness rendered, a Korean says,

90   FIFTY HELPS FOR THE BEGINNER

됴소, or 잘ㅎ엿소. or it may be 고맙소.
The latter word approaches *thank you* in use, but
has more nearly the sense of *I am grateful.* For
instance one Korean says to another, "I was sick
yesterday but am much better to-day." To which
his friend responds, "고맙소."

In asking a favor of another the idea of *please*
may be conveyed by the use of 주오, the verb
to give or *grant.*

문여러주시오
Please open the door.

아기안아주어라
Please take the baby.

This form is much used in prayer, as will be
seen by referring to the prayer sentences on a
subsequent page.

----

49. Although *personal pronouns*, as such, are
in little favor among Koreans, yet substitutes,
especially for the second person, are common and
useful. 로형 meaning elder brother, if used between men, and elder sister, if used between women; 당신, 딕, 딕늬, 공 and other words
which your teacher can suggest, will furnish a
profitable morning's study.

A safe and always appropriate mode of address is simply to use the name or title of the person spoken to. In the case of women, who have no names of their own, it is necessary to address them as descendant of so and so, or as wife or mother of so and so. Thus, **고씨** descendant of Ko ; **김셔방딕**, wife (literally, house) of Mr. Kim ; **달셔이모친**, mother of **달셔이**. Lower forms for these latter expressions are **김셔방집, 달셔이어머니**. In addressing an audience **여러분들이** answers a useful purpose.

---

50. *To offer an apology* in acceptable fashion is not accomplished as the foreigner is apt to think, by a literal rendering of our "I am sorry." If a Korean wishes to express regret for some omission or commission, he says simply, **잘못ᄒ엿소,** that is, "I have not done well," or **용셔히주시오** Please forgive me. Or if he wishes to use a more elevated turn of expression he may say, **허물마시오**, that is, "Avoid," or, "overlook the fault."

92　　　FIFTY HELPS FOR THE BEGINNER

LIST OF RELIGIOUS TERMS.

Angel, 텬亽

Angry, to be, 노ᄒ오

Apostle, 亽도

Baptism, 셰례

Baptize, 셰례주오

Baptized, to be, 셰례밧소

Believe, to, 밋소

Believer, 예수밋ᄂ사름, 교우, 교인, 신쟈, 신도

Bible, 셩경

Bless, to, 복주오

Blessed, to be, 복밧소

Blessing, 복

Bow, to, 절ᄒ오

Born again, to be, 거듭나오

Buddha, Image of, 부쳐

Buddhism, 불도

Church building, 회당, 례비당

Commit, to, as sin, 범ᄒ오, 짓소

Confess, to, 조복ᄒ오

Confucius, 공즈, 부즈
Confucianism, 공밍도, 유도
Congregation, 교회
Cross, The, 십즈가
Crucify, to, 못박아죽이오
Crucified, to be, 못박혀도라가셧소
Demon, 귀신
Destroy, to, 멸망식히오
Destroyed, to be, 멸망호오
Destruction, 멸망홈
Devil, 마귀
Disciple, 뎨즈, 문도
Disobey, (a rule or law), 어긔오
Doctrine, 교, 도, 도리
Escape, to, as destruction, 면호오, 피호오
Eternal, 영원훈
Eternal life, 영성
Faith, 밋음, 신앙
Fall into, to, as into hell, 싸지오
Forgive, to, 샤호오, 용셔호오, 면호오
God, 하느님, used by Protestant mission-
aries. 텬쥬, used by Roman Catholics.

94   FIFTY HELPS FOR THE BEGINNER

Gospel,   복음
Grace,   은혜
Heaven,   하놀, 텬당
Heavenly Father,   하놀에게신아바지
Hell,   디옥
Holy Spirit,   셩신
Jesus Christ,   예수그리스도
Joy,   즐거워홈
Judgment,   심판, 재판
Kneel, to,   무릅꿀다
Kneel, to, face to the ground as Koreans do ;
            업디오
Live forever, to,   영원히사오
Lord,   쥬
Lord's Supper,   셩찬
Love, to,   스랑호오
Magic or sorcery, to practise,   굿호다
Martyr,   슌교자
Mencius,   밍즈
Obey,   슌죵호오
Pastor,   목스

Persecute, to,　핍박ᄒᆞ오
Persecuted, to be,　핍박밧소, 해밧소
Pity, to,　불샹히녁이오
Pitiable, to be,　불샹ᄒᆞ오
Pray, to,　긔도ᄒᆞ오, 비오; to Buddha, 념불ᄒᆞ오
Prayer,　긔도, 비는말
Preach, to,　강도ᄒᆞ오, 젼도ᄒᆞ오
Preacher,　젼도ᄒᆞ는사ᄅᆞᆷ
Punish, to,　형벌ᄒᆞ오
Punished, to be,　형벌밧소
Punishment,　형벌
Religion,　종교
Repay, to,　갑흐오
Repent, to,　회기ᄒᆞ오
Resurrection,　다시살아나신것; 부활
Sabbath,　안식일; 쥬일; 례비날
Sacrifice, to, as to ancestors,　졔ᄉᆞᄒᆞ오
Salvation,　구원홈
Satan,　마귀
Save, to,　구원ᄒᆞ오

96   FIFTY HELPS FOR THE BEGINNER

Saviour,   구원호신쥬

Sing, to,   찬미호오

Sin,   죄

Sin, to,   죄범호오, 죄짓소

Sinner,   죄인; 죄잇눈사룸

Son of God,   하ᄂ님의아들

Soul,   령혼

Spirit,   신

Suffer,   고셩호오; 욕보오

Trust, to,   밋소; 의지호오

Worship, or reverence, to,   공경호오; 위
호오

SHORT SENTENCES USEFUL IN

PRESENTING THE GOSPEL.

셰샹사룸즁에죄업눈사룸어딕잇소
Among all mankind where is there one without
    sin?

하ᄂ님띠셔셰샹사룸 다죄에 빠져죽게된
거슬불샹히녁이셧소
God pitied the sin-striken and lost condition of man.

죄 만히 잇셧스되우리를 스랑ㅎ셧소
Although our sins were many He loved us.

예수는 하ᄂ님의외아들 이오
As for Jesus, He is God's only son.

하ᄂ님꾀셔그외아들을셰상에보낫셧소
God sent His son to earth.

우리죄를속하러오셧소
He came to atone for our sins.

셰샹사름의게해를밧앗소
He suffered at the hands of men.

우리죄를디신ㅎ야그몸게악훈형벌밧앗
소
On account of our sins He received bitter punishment in His own body.

십즈가에못박혀죽으셧소
He died nailed to a cross.

엇지ㅎ여야그은혜를갑겟소
How can we repay such kindness?

예수말슴대로ㅎ여야쓰겟소
We must do according to the word of Jesus.

우리다죄잇는줄을셔듯고회기ㅎ야죄를
ᄇ려야쓰겟소
We must realize our sinfulness, and having repented forsake it.

98   FIFTY HELPS FOR THE BEGINNER

예수를밋으면텬당에가겟소

If we believe in Jesus we will go to Heaven.

밋지아니ᄒ면디옥에ᄲᅡ질수밧긔업소

If we do not believe in Him there is nothing for
    us but to fall into hell.

이말은사롬의말이아니오

As for these words, they are not the words of man.

하ᄂ님의말슴이오

They are the words of God.

It will be good practice for the student to take
these sentences and join them together by the
proper connectives, as has been done in the following prayer sentences.

PRAYER SENTENCES.

하ᄂᆯ에게신우리아바지

Our Father which art in Heaven,

하ᄂ님압혜범흔죄를샤ᄒ여주옵시고

Forgive the sins that we have committed against
    Thee, and,

죄를지을ᄆ 옴다시먹지말게ᄒ여주옵쇼
   서

grant that we may have no more mind to sin,

저의들이약ㅎ고미련ㅎ줄아오니
We know that we are weak and foolish, and,

도아주시고ㄱ르쳐주시기를비옵뇌다
we pray that Thou wilt help and teach us.

잠시라도써나지마옵시고
Leave us not for a moment,

하늘에갈길노인도ㅎ여주옵시기를비옵뇌다
but lead us, we pray Thee, along the path to Heaven.

남의죄진거슬용셔ㅎ여주게ㅎ옵시고
Help us to forgive the sins of others, and,

다른사름을우리몸과ㄱㅊ치스랑ㅎ게ㅎ여주옵쇼셔
grant that we may love others as ourselves.

예수모르고안밋는사름을불샹히녁이시고
Have pity upon those who know not and trust not Jesus, and,

셩경말숨듯고써듯게ㅎ여주옵시기를비옵뇌다
grant that they may hear and understand the words of the Bible.

100　　　FIFTY HELPS FOR THE BEGINNER

제몸에잇는죄를셔 ᄃ라알고
Realizing their sinfulness, and,

예수ᄭ와셔ᄌ복ᄒ여
coming and confessing to Jesus,

죄샤홈을엇게ᄒ여주옵시기를비옵고
do Thou grant that they may receive forgiveness
　　for their sins, and,

ᄯᅩ새사롬되게ᄒ여주옵시기를비옵ᄂ다
also, make them to become new persons, we pray
　　Thee.

죠션관쟝브터빅셩ᄭ지예수밋기를비옵
　　고
From the official class to the common people may
　　Koreans become believers, and

하ᄂ님밧긔아모위홀것업는줄알게ᄒ여
　　주옵시고
make them to know that beside Thee there is no
　　God, and,

하ᄂ님만공경ᄒ게ᄒ여주옵시기를비옵
　　ᄂ다
grant that they may worship only Thee.

예수일홈을의지ᄒ야비옵ᄂ다　아멘
Trusting in Jesus' Name we pray.　Amen.

ADDITIONAL HELPS.

1. 으로ᄒ여곰

우리로ᄒ여곰범죄치안케ᄒ옵쇼셔
Cause us not to sin.

바로 로ᄒ여곰이스라엘빅셩을노아 보내재ᄒ셧
소
He caused Pharaoh to set free and send away
the Israelites.

뎌희들노ᄒ여곰됴혼사람이되게ᄒ소셔
Cause us to become good people.

2. 으로말매암아

우리가예수로말미암아구원을엇엇소
We have obtained salvation through Jesus.

하ᄂ님ᄭᅦ셔그의아들노말미암아우리를구속ᄒ
셧소
God has saved us through His Son.

3. 으로더브러

긔도ᄒ는것은하ᄂ님으로더브러교통ᄒ는것이
오
Praying is having fellowship with God.

그사람요로로더브러농사ᄒ엿소
He farmed in partnership with that man.

102   FIFTY HELPS FOR THE BEGINNER

4. 겸ᄒᆞ야

농ᄉᆞ와쟝ᄉᆞ를겸ᄒᆞ여셔홈너다
I am engaged in farming and business both.

쟝날파쥬일이겸ᄒᆞ째에조심ᄒᆞᄫᆞ죄짓지마시오
When the Lord's Day and market day come
on the same day, be careful not to sin.

문동병파폐병이겸힛슴니다
He had leprosy and consumption both.

5. 홀ᄉᆞ록

성각홀ᄉᆞ록우셥쇼
The more I think of it, the funnier it is.

볼ᄉᆞ록자미잇쇼
It gets more interesting the further I read.

그사람돈줄ᄉᆞ록더달나고ᄒᆞ오
The more money I give him the more he asks.

6. ᄒᆞ자, or ᄒᆞ자마자

집을짓자마자팔앗쇼
He had no sooner built the house than he sold
it.

담을쌋자마자헐으러젓소
He had no sooner built the wall than it fell
down.

7. 인호야 and 위호야 contrasted.

죄로인호야형벌을밧앗쇼
He received punishment on account of sin.

예수씌셔죄인을위호야죽으셧쇼
Jesus died on behalf of sinners.

8. 호둣호오

사람을파리죽이둣횟쇼
They killed people off like flies.

열심이불붓둣니러낫쇼
Enthusiasm spread (arose) like fire.

9. 홀ᄯ름

사실을말홀ᄯ름이오
All you have to do is to state the facts.

순사는죄인을잡을ᄯ름이오
All the policeman does is to arrest criminals.
(not try them).

10. 홀것굿소

비올것굿호셔일호러안갓소
It looked like rain, so I did not go to work.

그사람이일잘홀것굿소
He looks as though he would do the work
well.

104   FIFTY HELPS FOR THE BEGINNER

될껏곳 지안소
It does not seem as though it would work.

11. 흥여지다 or 흥여가다

그사름이늙어감너다
He's getting old.

날이츳츳치워집너다
The days are gradually getting colder.

12. 흘지언뎡

조식이업슬지언뎡말듯지안은오히를두저마시
오
Have no children at all, rather than disobedient ones.

13. 흥기에

그고양이는쥐잡기에적습너다
That cat is too small for catching rats.

하ᄂ님셔셔보시기에합당치안소
In the sight of God it is not right.

가겟다흥기에돈주엇소
As he said he was going, I gave him the
money.

손님이오겟기에방을예비히두엇소
As a guest is coming, I made ready the room.

14. 되흥야

그일에되흥여셔메라고말습흥심데가
What did he say concerning that matter?

그겻되희셔말홀겻업쇼
I have nothing to say about it.

15. 흥나마나흥오

It makes no difference whether it is done or not.

잇스나업스나흥오
It's all the same with or without it.

16. 말고라도

됴흔겻말고라도잇는되로가져오시오
Even if there are no good ones, bring whatever there are.

17. 의게잇다, or 의게달녓다

흥고아니흥는겻이내게잇다
Whether to do it or not is for me to decide.

급데흥고락데흥는겻이여러분게잇쇼
Whether you pass or fail depends on you.

18. 흥여버릇

일즉니러나버릇힛쇼
He had the habit of rising early.

106   FIFTY HELPS FOR THE BEGINNER

먹어버릇을못ᄒᆞ엿스니가그럿치

It was because he was not in the habit of
(accustomed to) eating it.

19. ᄒᆞ엿다말앗다ᄒᆞ는사람이오

He is the kind that does it for a while and
then stops.

열엇다닷앗다ᄒᆞ음ᄂᆞ다

It opens and shuts.

ᄲᅧ웟다ᄭᅵᆷ앗다ᄒᆞ는책이오

It's a loose-leaf note-book.

20. ᄒᆞ는ᄃᆡ로

그사룸ᄒᆞ는ᄃᆡ로ᄒᆞ라

Do it the way he is doing it.

되는ᄃᆡ로가져오시오

(1) Bring it the way it is.

or (2) Bring it whenever it is done.

좀에이는ᄃᆡ로큰길노가시오

Go by the big road even though it is a little
round about.

어려오신ᄃᆡ로속히오시오

(1) Do come soon, though it will be difficult
for you.

or (2) Do come quickly, though it will be difficult for you.

A FEW THINGS TO BE AVOIDED.

It is not best to spend too much time at first in trying to get at the bottom of every expression. The better way is to take the words and expressions as you learn them and use them without question. Etymological distinctions can be looked up later.

The habit of using such words as 마는, 썌무 니, 흥샹, 혹, 모양, etc., to excess, should be avoided. These words have their place but not to the extent that they are used by foreigners.

The 소 endings should not be exclusively used any longer than you can help. Notice that 지오, a somewhat higher form, can be used in place of 소 in all but interrogative forms, and furnishes a pleasing variety to the listener.

Sometimes new comers imagine that low talk is low or degrading to the recipient in our sense of the word, and thus fall into the error of refusing to use it. It is entirely acceptable in its place, and should be used without hesitation.

Do not neglect any opportunity to exercise yourself in the use of high and low forms, the latter always to children, and, in theory, to all servants.

As a matter of practice, however, friend-talk should be used to men and women servants. This

108   FIFTY HELPS FOR THE BEGINNER

is especially true in country districts, where class distinctions are much less sharply drawn than in Seoul, but it is applicable in all cases where the desire is to emphasize the relation of friend rather than that of servant and served.

Aged men and women among your acquaintances will afford valuable occasion for the use of the highest forms. You will lose nothing by it in the estimation of Koreans, even if the person's actual rank is not high.

Avoid the use of half-talk until you have had considerable practice of the proper forms. It can be used after you know just how, when and where to use it.

Get rid of your first poor makeshifts just as soon as you have learned something better. Weed out errors of construction and pronunciation as fast as you can.

Do not allow the Koreans whom you talk with habitually to continue to use to you the imperfect talk which you are at present obliged to use to them. Insist that they shall talk slowly, and simply, but in good, idiomatic Korean.

Avoid the sad mistake of talking English to your teacher, and do not interlard your own speech with interjections such as, "Well," "Oh," "Ah," "Yes," etc.

Beware of the faults of other foreigners. A good many of us are mispronouncing words yet, simply because we took them from a faulty transliteration, or just as we heard them from a foreigner, instead of having the pronunciation verified by a native.

Do not hesitate to go to older missionaries for assistance. They are more anxious than you can know, that you shall make a good start and have a better chance at the language than they had themselves.

Learn as many Chinese characters as you can, but at any rate, learn their names, as 사룸-인, ᄆ옴-심, 아들-ᄌ, etc. This will enable you to recognize the meaning of Chinese derivatives when you hear or see them. For instance, if you know that the Chinese equivalent of 사룸 is 인, and of ᄆ옴 is 심, it requires no great mental agility to grasp the fact that 인심 probably means "man's mind," or "disposition."

Do not be satisfied with what is sometimes euphemistically styled a "good working knowledge" of the language. Remember that a knowledge which falls short of being able to say easily and well all that you want to say, is not a "good working knowledge" of the language.

110   FIFTY HELPS FOR THE BEGINNER

Avoid the mistake of thinking that you can gratify all your literary and social tastes and learn Korean too. You may do so, and attain to a "pigeon" use of the language, but you will never talk Korean as the Koreans do, without some sacrifice. It is the greatest of undertakings, but with pains, prayer, perseverance, and right methods of study, every one has the right to expect to accomplish it. Drudge faithfully through the first three years, and at the end of that time, the promised land, tho yet far distant, will be in view, and study will be a pleasure and acquisition a delight.

Read the church paper in the vernacular regularly, and thus keep informed at first hand as to what your people are thinking and doing.

IT MAY NOT BE OUT OF PLACE in a booklet intended for the help of newcomers, to mention a few points which most of us are naturally a little slow to apprehend. Koreans, as a people, are much more attentive to all the niceties of etiquette than the Western nations from which we come, and unless we wish to make a very unfavorable impression, we must cultivate a similar politeness of manner.

For instance, never fail to salute your teacher, or other Koreans of similar rank, when you find yourself in their presence, not in a hurried fashion, and perhaps half turning away as you speak, but standing properly facing them, and with due deliberateness.

Always acknowledge all politely proffered salutations from high or low.

Do not, as a rule, salute children or servants first, but expect and return their salutations.

In meeting and talking with Koreans, pay especial attention to the aged among them, whether man or woman, rising when they enter and take their departure, and addressing them in the best language.

When in a mixed company of foreigners and Koreans, be careful not to devote yourself to the former to the exclusion of the latter, but try to carry on the conversation mostly in Korean.

We should take care not to offend the best social customs of the people. Whatever may be the reason, it is often unfortunately true that foreigners are tempted to greater freedom of behavior than in their own home countries, whereas much more carefulness should be observed.

When foreign men and women meet on the street, dignified reserve should be the rule, and on all occasions where Koreans are onlookers, ladies and gentlemen should be careful not to indulge in

112   FIFTY HELPS FOR THE BEGINNER

what would otherwise, perhaps, be only harmless familiarity.

Ladies should bear in mind that the liberty which they have always been accustomed to exercise is not known to the better classes of Korean women, and should take pains not tou nnecessarily compromise themselves, as, for instance, by appearing in public in company with their teachers or Korean male acquaintances other than a servant. This is especially objectionable if the teacher is a young man. Other things being equal, single ladies should select an elderly, rather than a young man, for teacher.

They should also be slow to attempt joking or pleasantry with Korean men, remembering that nothing in the experience of a native gentleman, previous to his connection with foreigners, can enable him to understand a modest woman making herself innocently free with any man except her father, brother, or husband.

That women can itinerate in Korea has been abundantly proved, but it should be done with as little publicity as possible, and with due precautions against misunderstandings. For a woman itinerator, for instance, to attempt to propagate the gospel by singing and addressing a crowd of promiscuous idlers, is worse than futile. Singing by women missionaries before a heathen audience, under any circumstances whatever, is not to be recommended.

A man missionary, in necessary dealings with native women, should be quick to notice that they are much more at ease in his presence if he keeps at a good distance, and does not subject them to too close a scrutiny, however kind and friendly.

In dealing with Koreans a great deal of annoyance may be saved by observing the fact that no people ever prized their own self esteem more highly. No loss is so serious to a Korean as to "lose face" before others. If then, a grave rebuke must be administered, do so in private, and if it becomes desirable to convey a hint that such and such conduct is not acceptable it is often advisable to do so through the medium of a friendly third party or in some other round-about way. If you are to get on happily, and carry out your purposes, it will often be necessary to drop your Anglo-Saxon abruptness.

Learn early in dealing with Koreans to efface as much as possible all traces of impatience or irritation from the face as well as words and bearing. Mildness and firmness, in equal parts, compounded with love, and administered constantly and regularly, will usually enable the missionary to carry

114   FIFTY HELPS FOR THE BEGINNER

any reasonable point. The necessity for these words may not be apparent to a newcomer, but he will, without doubt, if he stays long in Korea, often find himself hindered and thwarted in plans and purposes by circumstances almost unbearably irritating. If at such times he gives vent to his natual feelings in a burst of angry impatience, he will undo much earnest and prayerful effort, for, and this is a point well worth considering, what truthfulness and honesty are to the Anglo-Saxon, patience, forbearance and courteous bearing are to the Korean. A down-right lie on the part of a native Christian is not more shocking to us, than a display of ill-temper on our part is to them. In this connection it is suggestive to notice that while the Old and New Testaments by no means underestimate the importance of truth and uprightness, yet at least as much stress is laid upon brotherly love, meekness, patience, self-control and kindred virtues which perhaps are not so fashionable nowadays in the push and stress of Western life.

Many more suggestions might be made in detail, but enough has been said to enable the thoughtful reader to draw his own conclusions as to the nature of things that are better done or left undone in Korea.

The contents of this little volume are not offered to the reader in the spirit of one who "has already attained," but merely as one who, like himself, "follows after."

INDEX.

— 116 —

— 117 —

大正十五年八月二十五日四版發行
大正十五年八月二十二日四版印刷

定價金壹圓五十錢

著作兼發行人　美國夫人　安　愛理
朝鮮平壤新陽里

印刷人　郭　寅　燮
京城府樓下洞百三十二番地

印刷所　中央基督教青年會印刷部
京城府鍾路二丁目九番地

發行所　朝鮮耶穌教書會
朝鮮京城鐘路

┃ 저자

윌리엄 마틴 베어드(William Martyn Baird, 裵緯良, 1862~1931)

윌리엄 마틴 베어드는 숭실대학교를 설립한 미국의 장로교 선교사였다. 1862년 6월 인디애나에서 태어났다. 선교활동을 위해 애니 애덤스와 결혼한 지 두 달도 되지 않은 1891년에 한국에 도착했다. 개신교 선교사로서 평양 숭실학당을 설립하는 것을 시작으로 교육사업과 선교에 큰 공헌을 했다. 1931년에 세상을 떠났다.

애니 베어드(Annie L. Baird, 1864~1916)

애니 베어드는 웨스턴여자신학교를 졸업한 후 윌리엄 베어드(William Baird)와 함께 선교활동을 위해 한국에 왔다. 애니 베어드는 선교사 부인으로서의 역할뿐만 아니라 평양 숭실에서 생물학을 가르친 교육자이자 과학교과서를 번역한 번역가, 다수의 소설, 에세이를 남긴 저술가로도 활발한 활동을 벌였다. 주로 생물학에 큰 관심을 가졌는데, 실제 평양 숭실의 교과서로 사용된 『식물도설』, 『동물학』, 『싱리학초권』을 번역한 것이 대표적이다.

┃ 번역·해제

윤영실

연세대학교 영문학과를 졸업하고 서울대학교 국문과에서 석박사를 마쳤다. University of Toronto에서 Postdoctoral Researcher, 교토대학교 인문과학연구소에서 외국인공동연구원으로 재직하고, 인하대학교 한국학연구소와 연세대학교 근대한국학연구소에서 연구교수로 재직했다. 저서로는 『육당 최남선과 식민지의 민족사상』(고대 아연출판부, 2018)이 있고, 역서로는 『다시 에드워드 사이드를 위하여』, 『역사의 요동』(공역) 등이 있다. 현재 숭실대학교 한국기독교문화연구원 HK교수로 재직 중이다.